1975

THE ORIENTAL CERAMIC SOCIETY OF HONG KONG

1

COMMITTEE 1974–75

President	Dr Philip Mao Wen-chee
Vice-President	Mr B.S. McElney
Hon. Secretary	Mr Duncan Macintosh
Hon. Chinese Secretary	Mr K. Liu
Hon. Treasurer	Miss C.M. Goldney
Hon. Editor	Mr R. Jones-Parry
Committee Member	Professor B. Lofts
Committee Member	Mr P. Matthews
Committee Member	Mr Edwin Wong

EDITORS OF THE BULLETIN
(For Issue 1)

Mr R. Jones-Parry
Mr D.M. Joyce
Mr M. Smithies

The *Bulletin* is the official annual publication of the Oriental Ceramic Society of Hong Kong. While it is intended that the *Bulletin* should serve to put on permanent record a selection of the addresses presented in the annual pro-gramme of the Society, other contributions and suggestions for forth-coming issues will be welcomed.

CONTENTS

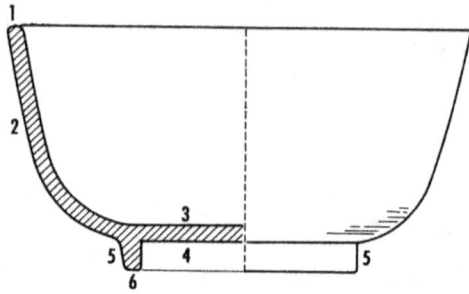

Figure 1
Parts of a bowl   1. Lip and lip rim.   2. Body.
3. Bottom of inside base.
4. Base.   5. Foot.   6. Foot rim.

Figure 2
Bowl shapes   1. T'ang.   2. Sung.   3. Ming

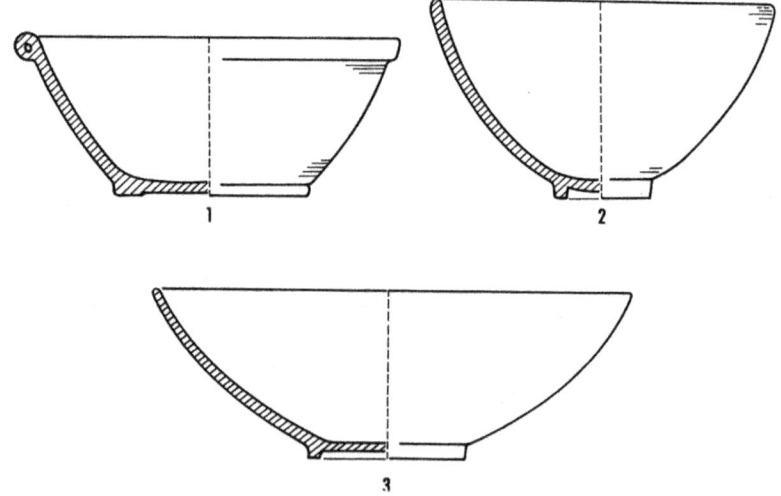

The Teapots of I Hsing

SOAME JENYNS

'For steeping tea leaves there is nothing better than a fine sand pot, and·further what is better for this purpose than those of Yang hsien, as all the world knows,' wrote Li Yu. He was referring to the small red stone-ware teapots, which are a specialized product of the village of I Hsing (sometimes romanized Yi Hsing) of which the old name was Yang Hsien. These teapots have always kept, and still retain, a particular niche in the affection of Chinese scholars, who may care nothing for the beauty of other Chinese ceramics. But besides catering for the tastes of the scholar, I Hsing has also catered for the ordinary Chinese citizen; and when you go to the humblest Chinese restaurant to-day, if your tea is not brought to you in a porcelain teapot, it usually arrives in a modern I Hsing teapot. Most of these teapots are deep brown or light red in colour, but they are also made from chocolate, purple-brown, greyish or yellowish white clays; they are sometimes speckled with quartz to give the celebrated 'pear skin' effect.

Their bodies, usually unglazed, but sometimes showing a natural gloss formed in the kiln, are of a substance sufficiently hard to be polished, if necessary, on the lapidary's wheel, until the purple specimens may take on the appearance of porphyry. The Chinese scholar never ill-treated these teapots in this unbecoming manner, but it is a common occurrence to find I Hsing teapots made for the general market and even for general use at court, or exported to Thailand or Annam, polished in this way.

The best of these teapots are without any decoration whatsoever, relying on their finely chiselled or moulded forms and simple but sophisticated shapes for their effect. Others have had engraved designs or inscriptions cut on them with a steel or bamboo knife; usually a line of poetry or an antique saying, in which great attention has been attached to the calligraphy.

'These sandstone creations of I Hsing are just the thing for boiling tea, for they avoid the bad smell of brass or tin and the heavy expense of gold or silver, and, being good at holding the fragrance of the leaf, are suitable for practical use....' says Li Ching K'ang.

'Scholars of successive ages,' he continues, 'have either composed inscriptions for these pots or have written their signatures or carved flowers and plants on them or chiselled out seal impressions...This handwriting is no mass production but is of outstanding interest and expression. Although the famous porcelain pieces of Ching-te Chen fetch higher prices by a thousand times they are just the handiwork of an artisan and rarely have a scholarly inscription to show us, and so lack cultural interest.'

'Latterly the West has become passionately devoted to our arts, our painting, our porcelain and our bronzes in which our national genius is enshrined; and high prices are spent in search of them. And we sigh deeply to think that our fine and beautiful works are almost exhausted. Unhappily, although they have not yet turned serious attention to the sandpots of Yang Hsien, gentlemen from Japan have hauled these off in their nets. And none who is devoted to the Country's national culture can fail to be keenly distressed.'

Fortunately for him there is still little interest shown in I Hsing teapots in either European or American ceramic circles. European and American books on Chinese ceramics allow a bare page or less to these kilns, in a chapter shared with the wares of Kwangtung, Fukien and other provincial factories while they are seldom collected on either continent.

Yet this ware has been the special favourite of the Chinese scholar for over four centuries, and for a hundred years is said to have been sought after by the members of the tea-clubs of Japan. The Chinese scholar despised the silver teapot, and although the pewter teapots of I Hsing were fashionable in some circles, he did not tolerate them unless they had a lining of I Hsing pottery. But in England it is the silver teapot which still presides over the drawingroom tea table, while the good honest brown earthenware teapot is banished to the kitchen.

The reason for this neglect is not far to seek. I Hsing lacks glamour. It cannot compete with the glossy painted beauties of Ching-te Chen. Its proper function is to adorn the scholar's writing desk. Through the excellence of its material, the skill of its construction, and the artistry of its design it must arouse the scholarly interest. Chinese pottery of the Ming and Ch'ing dyn-asties, as opposed to porcelain, has never commanded much interest in China. But to this rule the I Hsing wares provide the exception.

ORIGINS

I Hsing is a district of the Ch'ang Chou prefecture in the province of Kiangsu, or, to be more precise, in that part of Kiangsu which lies south of the Kiangnan river and not far west of Shanghai. The name I Hsing is familiar to all Chinese today; but many writers of the sixteenth, seventeenth and eighteenth centuries prefer the older name Yang Hsien; while the more antiquarian-minded call it by its feudal name, Ching Ch'i or Ching Nan.

The legendary story goes that when in the early years of the Cheng Te period an official, Wu Shih, commonly known as Wu I-shan, an I Hsing man who took his doctorate in the year 1514, was on one of his visits to the Chin Sha, a monastery situated a mile or two outside the borders of the I Hsing district, his servant Kung Ch'un spent his spare time watching one of the monks making a coarse pottery from the local clay. Intrigued, Kung Ch'un tried his hand at this work and soon discovered that the clay was worthy of greater things, and in particular, seeing that this was a noted tea-producing country, for the making of teapots. From these small beginnings sprang the craft which was to make I Hsing famous.

The immediate popularity of I Hsing teapots was the result of a revolution in tea-making during the Ming period. In the past the tea leaf had been moulded into bricks, sometimes treated with salt or other preservatives, or pressed into round slabs known as 'dragon rounds', which might be kept for years before using, and when required for the table had to be soaked before they could be consumed. But under the Ming the new idea of infusion by pouring boiling water on the green or dried leaves, as is universally done to-day, first became fashionable; and the 'dragon rounds' were abandoned.

This new process required small teapots, preferably 'one-man' pots, enabling each member of the company to add water according to individual taste. Here was something which I Hsing was in a position to supply to perfection; and thanks to the consistent skill of its craftsmen, I Hsing grasped the possibilities of the new fashion and has continued to monopolize the market up to the present day.

It was a new idea to have a teapot so small that every guest could be provided with a teapot to himself with a spout fashioned not to obstruct the tea leaves. For as one Chinese author remarks, 'One drinks tea for pleasure and one feels justly irritated if the beverage declines to come out of the pot!' It was on account of their qualities that the I Hsing teapots became so popular with the European tea tasters in the latter part of the seventeenth century.

CHINESE SOURCES

The English student of I Hsing pottery will find himself ill-served for guides in his own language to this subject. In fact, if we leave out (on the grounds that it is available to a limited circle only) Mr Geoffrey Hedley's monograph printed in the proceedings of the Oriental Ceramic Society for the year 1937, he has nothing to turn to except Captain Brinkley's account in Vol. IX of his *Japan and China*, published in 1907, an English translation of a Japanese work, the *Yang Hsien ming t'ao lu,* which suffers seriously from a system of romanization calculated to daunt the most enthusiastic, and includes no Chinese characters.

For this state of affairs we cannot blame any lack of Chinese sources; for I Hsing, a comparative late-comer onto the ceramic stage, is well documented in its native country, not to mention Japan. Unfortunately, with the exception of Brinkley's brief extract, none of this material has ever been translated into English, or, so far as this author can ascertain, into any Western language, except for some passages in Hedley's article.

Yet these I Hsing teapots were honoured as early as the middle of the seventeenth century by a special book to themselves—the *Yang Hsien Ming hu hsi* (the story of the teapots of Yang Hsien) extracts from which appear in the *T'ao Lu.*

'Under the Ming, Chou Pai-kao wrote *Yang Hsien ming hu hsi* (Catalogue of I Hsing teapots) and Chou Chia-Chou the *Yang Hsien ming hu t'u p'u* (Illustrated treatise on I Hsing teapots). While under the Ch'ing, Ch'i-t'ang compiled the *Yang Hsien ming t'ao shuo*

(Talks on famous pottery from I Hsing) and during the reign of Ch'ien Lung and Wu Ch'a-k'ê wrote the *Yang Hsien ming t'ao lu* (Account of famous pottery from I Hsing) while during the Chia (Ch'ing)/Tao (Kuang) periods Chu Shih-mei produced his *Hu shih* (History of pots). Other accounts may be found scattered throughout the literature of the two dynasties; but unfortunately in all cases the remarks are lacking in detail and in method.[1]

HISTORY

The history of I Hsing teapots is usually described by the Chinese in the following manner. The pots were invented in the early years of Cheng Te (1506–21). They flourished throughout the days of Wan Li (1573–1619), T'ien Ch'i (1621–7) and Ch'ien Lung (1736–95) and declined under the reigns of Hsien Feng (1851–61) and Kuang Hsü (1874–1908).

Between the time when their founder Kung Ch'un was active in the Cheng Te period and the reign of Wan Li, there is a blank covering the reigns of Chia Ching (1522–66) and Lung Ch'ing (1567–72), during the whole of which not a single potter's name is recorded in a list which is otherwise exceptionally full. Some Chinese commentators explain this away by suggesting that these years threw up no craftsman of sufficient distinction to warrant having his name recorded on I Hsing's roll of fame. This may well be so but we are left in doubt.

If this is the true picture, then the five so-called 'co-founders' comfortably take their place as revivalists of a second start, breathing new life in the middle period of Wan Li into a tottering enterprise. But it seems to this author not impossible that the story which surrounds the invention of the I Hsing teapot in the Cheng Te period is a myth and that they did not actually make their appearance till the reign of Wan Li. Li Ching-k'ang however records twelve Wan Li teapot makers whose existence depends on three late Ming texts of doubtful reliability.

The particular type of small teapot which was to make I Hsing famous did not appear immediately. The credit for introducing something handier than the large porcelain and pottery vessels hitherto in vogue is given to one of 'the five', Li Mao-lin, who is believed not to have lived in the Wan Li period.

This reduction in size was by no means universally acclaimed. It was popular in Swatow, Fuchow and Ch'ao Chou in the south and southeast; but Kiangsi, Chekiang, and other northerly provinces clung to their traditional ways. Moreover, a fierce battle had first to be fought in Kiangsu with a rival, and one who was for some time firmly in possession of the field; for not everyone believed that stoneware teapots were the ideal. K'o Tan-ch'iu, author of *Tea Things Classified* said 'In my opinion silver and tin (teapots) are best; porcelain and stone second best. The fact is vessels used for boiling water are easily broken and hard to keep.'

'Of tinpots, those of Chao Liang-pi are good. They are suitable for use in the winter months,' says Wu Mei-ting in the *Yang Hsien ming hu hsi* rather condescendingly. 'We learn that today the tin vessels of Kuan of Wu and Huang of Chia Ho fetch higher prices, but they are small and their construction is common-place. Gold and silver do not come in for comment.'

Porcelain was ruled out at the period for everyday use among the scholar class, partly because it was too costly and partly because it was fragile. It was thus left to pewter and tin to fight it out with the red sand-clay of I Hsing.

ASSOCIATION WITH THE CULT OF TEA DRINKING

The appearance of the I Hsing teapot is without question connected with the elaborate cult of tea drinking which came in with the Ming dynasty. By the seventh year of Hung Wu (1374), a fixed quota of tea was required from all the tea-growing districts of China, of which Ching Nan, where I Hsing was situated, ranked the highest. Each year this tribute was hurried to Peking and the first share went to the officials of the Imperial court. Books appeared like Ko Chui-su's *Record of Tea Things*, and *Tea Records of the Ming* by Wang Hsiang-chên, which laid down four rules for making tea. The first was choosing the water. Hill streams were best and then rivers; well water came last. Unless the water is good the flavour of the tea is lost. The second was the choice of container. Copper provided rancid tea and iron a harsh brew; earthenware was best, if it was kept clean. 'When true tea is served, to be sipped as soon as boiled...the force of the boiling water and the fragrance of the tea leaf must be allowed to coalesce under the influence of heaven and earth.' Other rules (not unknown to European tea makers) were: to make sure the water is boiling before you pour it onto the leaves; not to let the tea stand but drink it at once; and to warm the pot before putting in the leaves, and also the cup before pouring out the infusion.

'Those who drink tea assuage their thirst,' wrote the Taoist Kao Tsan-sheng, 'digest their food, get rid of phlegm, reduce sleep, assist the waterworks, clear the sight, benefit thought, get rid of worry and disperse bile. People cannot do without tea for a single day.' He lays down the names of the 'sixteen sorts of tea things' and the 'seven things for storing tea.' The first included such articles as a bamboo scraper to clean the pot, a ladle to measure the water, copper fire irons for piling up the fire, a fan to raise the fire; a bamboo tray to put the cups on, and a duster to clean the cups. All this is very reminiscent of the Japanese *Cha-no-yu* which must have originally derived its tenets from such volumes.

There were fashions in tea cups as well as teapots. For tasting tea some people preferred white porcelain cups to Chien ware tea bowls. But for teapots Wen Chen-hêng says, in his *Chang Wu chih*, 'Sand [i.e. earthenware] is the best material.' Of the I Hsing teapots he writes: 'Kung ch'un is the most prized, but his shapes are not elegant; moreover he made no small pots. Shih Ta-pin's pieces on the other hand were too small. Those which take a half pint of water and are formed on clear antique lines should be chosen as particularly suitable for pouring out tea.... The Hsüen Te period had tapered legged tea cups of fine material and elegant shape, and thick substance which make it difficult for them to cool off. These may be ranked with the best among tea cups for one can test the colour of the tea. The Chia Ching period had cups with "tea", "soup", "fruit" and "wine" inscribed on them, followed by "for altar use by the golden signet at the sacrifice of propitiation". These too are fine pieces. Others such as white Ting ware are collected as curios and are not suitable for daily use.' There seems to have been a serious difference of opinion about the use of pewter teapots.

'For steeping tea,' says the *Yang ming hu t'u lu*, 'sand pots are not the only things used. The ancients used gold, silver and porcelain. Today some use jade. The fact is that gold and silver however valuable, lack elegance and taste. As for tin, it is a case of cheap and nasty. Some of our fathers used it, but today none take to it.'

All the same, the pewter teapots of Chu Chien of the Tao Kuang period were favoured by many tea drinkers. One even hears of a pewter teapot with decoration in relief by Chen Ming Yüan covered in black lacquer and inlaid with mother of pearl, of which the design was 'notably elegant and archaic'. Fashion in teapots was never stationary. At one time, for instance, Peking dealers and connoisseurs were fascinated by the *Chu lu chien* (the full wheel pearl or goose egg), and nothing else would do. 'They [the connoisseurs] strive eagerly and with mouths watering to compete with one another to buy, and will not grudge a hundred or two gold ounces for them; nor will they stop until they have got one remarking "unless one has a full wheel pearl one is scarcely qualified to discuss tea things." So it is that the slippery dealers use their opportunity to make profit. Most ugly of all is to see collectors owning a pretty long list of fine creations, who delight in preserving the dirt and stains upon them. They unroll their sleeves and finger them, but fear lest they will rub off the dirt saying it is the old colouring.' All these characteristics are reflected in the behaviour of the tea ceremony adepts of Japan.

It is to the literary figures such as poets and painters, connoisseurs of books and rubbings, amateur carvers of bamboo brush pots and inkstones, that one must turn for information on I Hsing teapots. But there were also great officials, and administrators, rich merchants, and even princes of the royal blood, who inscribed and collected them.

AGE

'Yang Hsien sand pots first made their appearance in the reign of Cheng Te of the Ming dynasty. Gentlemen admired their elegant simplicity and praised their composition' wrote Li Ching K'ang.

'The date at which the sand pots of Yang Hsien started—i.e., at the time of the priest of the Chin Sha monastery in the Cheng Te period—is not so long ago' Li continues, 'and the facts should not be hard to verify. Yet neither the accounts of the Ming nor of the

Ch'ing period mention surviving pieces by his hand. There are only two reasons for this. Firstly, this priest certainly did not make many pieces; consequently the number that have survived are very few and difficult to find. Secondly, such pieces as were made had no inscriptions or 'chop' on them with the result that future generations who came across surviving examples, being unable to trace the authorship, were also unable to identify the piece itself. Probably the reason why later generations took Kung Ch'un for the originator was that he was the first to sign his creations.' Since this priest's work has never been identified and is never likely to be, it is with the teapots of Kung Ch'un that the tradition first comes to life. The fashion does not seem to have established itself immediately, for as mentioned above, we hear of no I Hsing teapots datable to the reigns of Chia Ching (1522–66) and Lung Ch'ing (1567–72). No Chinese text strives to explain this deficiency. But by the time of Wan Li (1572–1620) the I Hsing teapot seems to have established itself in the affections of the Chinese and by the time of Chia Ch'ing (1796–1821) and Tao Kuang (1821–50) when most Chinese ceramics had sadly deteriorated, I Hsing continued to provide charming pieces and the tradition is still alive today.

The difficulty of dating I Hsing teapots is almost insuperable. Even when they are signed and dated one cannot accept the information at its face value, as the work of all the famous potters has been continually copied. But although signature and date cannot be relied upon, workmanship, material, shape and size can all help in their evaluation. For example, the second most famous teapot maker Shih Ta p'in, whom Li gave as a Wan Li man, but whose exact dates are unknown, was the son of Shih P'êng who is supposed to have lived in the same period. Hedley says he flourished 'between 1620 and 1640' but goes on to discuss pieces by him dated 1597 and 1604. This presumably is a misprint for 'between 1597 and 1640' We are told how he imitated Kung Ch'un and was celebrated for his skill in combining coloured clays. Hedley also tells us that Chao Wên-chin especially excelled in imitating Shih's pieces in the form of square bricks, and that Shih's disciple Li Chung-fang became so skilful that his master often put his name on his pupil's pieces, and that 'a great many handed down to us are the work of Li Chung-fang'. Ch'ên Huang-fu apparently

9

'excelled in imitating the works of Kung Ch'ün and Shih Ta-p'in', while Ch'en Hsin-ch'ing not only imitated Shih Ta-p'in but also the work of his pupil Li Chung-fang. Four other disciples of Shih are mentioned, all of them no doubt imitated his works. So that a Westerner despairs of separating the genuine examples from the counterfeit.

Li Ching K'ang tells us 'that among the Ming and early Ch'ing teapots the purple ones had hard bones, and were sleek and shining, while the red ones were warm and translucent and the white and yellow ones strong and firm. By the time of Yung Cheng (1723–36) and Ch'ien Lung (1736–96) the sleekness and translucence had fallen off among the purple pots, and the red ones were soft and not well knit, but the yellow and white ones were as good as those of the early Ch'ing. By the time of Chia Ch'ing (1796–1821) and Tao Kuang (1821–50) the purple and yellow ones were very inferior to those that came before them, but the red ones made during this period were scarcely inferior to those of the Ch'ien Lung and Yung Cheng periods. While the purple teapots made under the reign of Hsien Fêng (1851–61), T'ung Chih (1862–73), Kuang Hsü (1874–1908) and Hsüan T'ung (1909–12) were equal to those made in the reign of Chia Ch'ing and Tao Kuang, but the bones of the red ones were dry and their countenance bleak.'

All this is very interesting but too vague to provide vital considerations for purposes of dating. Nor is it feasible to date I Hsing teapots on grounds of size, although the inclination has been for them to grow progressively smaller. We can trace certain export types back to the 1670's, from the mounts added to them in Europe and from the copies of them made by European potters in the late seventeenth and eighteenth centuries.

The lip of the spout and the rim of the lid of the more ordinary I Hsing teapots were often mounted in metal, sometimes gold, but usually brass in their own country. One cannot think that a Chinese scholar would have approved of these embellishments. Indeed, some I Hsing teapots were apparently made for the general public in the first instance and then supplied with metal handles and spouts. It is usually not difficult to detect whether a teapot was originally made for metal mounts, or whether these are repairs added in Europe where silver and silver gilt mounts, unknown in

China, were supplied. The metal put round the mouth of the spout is simply a measure of precaution against breakage, for this is the most delicate part of the whole pot and the most liable to chip. Any additions of this kind in the eyes of the connoisseur are defects.

A pot which provides two holes to be fitted with a metal or basketwork handle is called a *Juan erh t'i liang* (soft ear raised handle) pot. Often the 'soft' handle was made of wire covered with string, a precaution against heat. Sometimes, for the sake of durability, the owner fitted on a hard bronze handle. A pot made with a clay handle was called *Ying erh t'i liang* (hard ear raised handle). Many I Hsing pots were polished on the wheel till the surface shone. This process was called *Ch'u Shiu* (to give out water). Such teapots were defective in the eyes of Chinese scholars. It may not be that in every instance the polishing on the wheel was done in China but it probably was.

INTRODUCTION INTO EUROPE AND JAPAN

The first I Hsing teapots to reach Europe were brought by the Portuguese, but the bulk of them to reach the continent came through the hands of the Dutch in the latter part of the seventeenth century.

When tea drinking became an institution in Europe in the last half of the seventeenth century, the East India Companies set themselves to supply the necessary apparatus; among these imports were the I Hsing teapots. They must have been the first teapots to reach England and they are the ancestors of the teapot we use today. Indeed, their shapes are often reflected in the English silver teapots of Queen Anne made by the Huguenot silversmiths. They became so popular in Europe that they were widely copied in England, Holland and Germany.

They were highly treasured in Holland where they sometimes appear in still-life paintings of the period, along with Ming blue and white porcelain and where, because they were so precious, they were often mounted; small gilt finials, surmounted in some instances by figures, were supplied to the handles and, in some cases, to the lids and connected to the spout by little gilt chains, so that the latter were less likely to fall and break. The lip of the spout was also mounted in gilt bronze, lest it should chip. The names of the workmen who undertook this mounting and the exact date at which they worked are unknown to us. But most of them were Dutch working in the closing years of the seventeenth and early years of the eighteenth century.

When an I Hsing teapot, found in Europe, boasts of a silver spout or handle (which is also not an uncommon occurrence among both Chinese and Japanese porcelain teapots imported at the end of the seventeenth century) it means almost invariably that the original parts of the teapot had been broken and lost, and that its remains had been repaired in Europe. European silver repairs to such damaged pieces invariably date to the late seventeenth or early eighteenth century, when such pieces were highly valued, and not to the nineteenth century.

I Hsing teapots appear in old English registers under the name of 'the genuine old Indian teapots'. From the earliest days of their importation they were known in Italy, Spain and Portugal by the Portuguese name of 'Buccaro' which seems to have become a regular Latin term for any unglazed red pottery, whether it came from South America, China, or from Etruscan tombs. These imported teapots are usually unsigned and decorated in relief. Among the patterns which are not uncommon is the 'vine and squirrel' motif and the plum blossom sprays in relief, and there are many others. They do not usually boast of inscriptions which would have been meaningless in Europe, but there are many exceptions to this. They were sometimes gilded or lacquered in Europe after arrival, practices the Chinese scholar would have abhorred. They were not, of course, of the quality of the Chinese scholars' teapots, but of far more ordinary types made for the local market and perhaps in some instances designed for export to Europe.

We know very little either about the I Hsing teapots made for the Japanese market, where they were certainly at one time very popular with the Japanese tea-masters, but this was probably not before the nineteenth century, nor do we know much about the Japanese imitations. Hedley reproduces two teapots, which he says were made by otherwise unknown Chinese potters for the Japanese market but it is probable both of them are Japanese imitations. Excellent imitations were made at the Taruta kilns (chiefly small red brown pieces in the Hui Ming-ch'en tradition) and others according to Hobson from the Taruta Bonko kilns and at Kyoto. Little interest seems to be taken in I Hsing teapots since the collapse of the Chinese form of tea ceremony and it is virtually impossible to find in Japan interesting or documented pots.

CLAY

The clays from which the I Hsing teapots were made are reputed to have come from small deposits in caves to the south east of I Hsing. A soft yellow clay, sticky but suitable for the construction of stoneware, and a red clay, which when it is baked turns purple, are the most important of these. Black liver (clay), cold pear colour, pine flower colour and bean green light brown clays, all came, we are told, from Li Shan. White clay was said to come from the Tuan Hill. For the selection, sieving, pounding and mixing up of these clays, each potter had his own recipes, which he would not transmit to others. Hedley quotes a passage from the *T'ao Lu* describing the colours of numerous clays and the colours they become when baked. Chinese sources on the subject of the clay and glazes make difficult reading. It is evident, however, that the potters were continuously seeking for and finding new sources of clay, as the old ones became exhausted, and, as they were not uniform, the bodies of the teapots varied. Li Ching K'ang discusses the consequent change in the quality of the teapot clays through the Ming and Ch'ing dynasties, but his conclusions are too imprecise to make it possible to use them in practice for purposes of dating.

SHAPE

From the Chinese point of view, the spout and handle of the I Hsing teapot are irrelevant to the general design. This does not mean that their shape or their relation to one another need not be carefully determined; but it does mean that they must be as unobtrusive as possible so as not to catch the eye and distract attention from the body of the vessel.

It is the profile of the teapot that counts. To this profile the lid, with its knob, contributes an essential element; but being detachable and indeed, regularly detached, it is particularly liable to loss.

No doubt for this reason, and also in the hope of adding to the difficulties of the forger, a chop additional to that on the body of the pot is not infrequently found on the inside of the lip of the lid. The loss of a lid is a serious matter, for replacement, however honest, demands great skill by the restorer.

Both spout and handle owing to their exposed position are particularly liable to damage and disaster; and one frequently finds, as already mentioned, metal spouts, doing duty for a clay original. On the other hand, handles made of material other than clay may well be originals preferred as non-conductors of heat; as, for example, the tin-coated guitar-shaped pot with a handle of sandalwood attributed to the unidentified Tan Yüan T'ang, or Chu Chien's tin-coated pot with handle, spout, and knob of jade. It is doubtless for this reason that the bridge handle, a normal feature of the *chu* or hot water jug, is sometimes adopted on teapots.

There seems to have been some differences of opinion among the critics as to the proper shape of the spout; some hold that on functional grounds it should never be bent lest tea-leaves clog the angles, while others allowed one bend, in the interests of appearances, but not more than one.

To turn to the variations of shape of surviving or recorded teapots, the first thing one notices is the high proportion that may be regarded simply as what may be called teapot shape, which does not call for an elaborate description. Among these the finest specimens of all are found, when the potter is not distracted by the need to introduce some novel and extraneous form. But perhaps for this very reason they include also the most hackneyed of reproductions, the sort that Li Ching-k'ang dismisses with the words: 'in shape these sandpots repeat themselves again and again, the general run being comparable to official forms—a thousand all alike. They do not merit further attention.' Leaving these aside we come to the named shapes, all of which were represented, sometimes more than once, in the plates intended to illustrate Li's *Illustrated Enquiry*. They include the straw hat, sometimes known as the monk's cap, the flattened flower basket, the inverted peck, the steelyard weight, the wellhead, the bell, the round pearl, the melon, the water-chestnut and the sea pear.

In addition there is the square, comprising vessels built on a square base, including the Han square, the square bamboo (all right angles like a square box), the octagon, the tight-waisted pots with a girdle round the middle and the bridge-handle with a fixed or detachable handle forming an arch across the pot lid. It must not be supposed that this list is exhaustive.

All the above are broadly variations on the same theme, namely a straightforward article for infusing tea with appropriately designed decoration. But there is also a wide variety of far-fetched extravagances; fanciful representations of flowers, trees, fabulous animals, musical instruments and so on, the leading exponent of which was the distinguished potter Hsü Yu ch'üan of the Wan Li period, who was closely imitated under the Emperor Ch'ung Cheng by Shen Tsü-chi. Here the distinctive mark of this type is not their subtlety, and the pot is largely used as a convenient object on which to exercise virtuosity. Among these, according to Li, will be found examples of 'originality, exuberance, showy display, and extravagance'; but for sheer 'vile bad taste beyond relief or remedy', we must wait till the middle of the Ch'ing period for the unidentified products of Ta Hêng who, by tradition, is responsible for a teapot with a dragon's head knob—a dragon's head which not only waggles itself but also waggles its tongue.

Here again Li Ch'ing-k'ang comments authoritatively: 'Although in regard to shape both antique simplicity and sophisticated elegance have their adherents, in the end the best are those which do not take the past for their master, but achieve an antique simplicity in their own right. Next come those which reproduce the antique and catch its divine flavour. After them come those which have a high reputation for skill. Then those whose strangeness gives them a peculiar interest. And finally those whose virtuosity places them among the vulgar.'

'I Hsing teapots may have many shapes', says the *Ming hu t'u lu*. 'They can be round, square, angular, flat, level, lofty, low, big or small, egglike.... On examination of their quality some will be found to be warm and genial like old gentlemen, some brave as heroes, some stylish as men of letters, beautiful as pretty girls, lovely as children, small as pygmies, simple and slow like old men, jaunty and fanciful as fairies, austere as philosophers, others are unworldly like Buddhist priests. Connoisseurs and collectors must love them in their hearts before one can discuss with them such delights.'

'Pear shaped, flattened, globular or boldly faceted they recall,' says Honey 'the incomparable silver teapots of Queen Anne'. In another passage he calls them 'the most nearly perfect teapots ever made'. He is referring of course to those in the scholars' taste which 'stand out with their glossy appearance, simple old shape and cultured air', and not to the run of the mill teapot made for the proletariat, or to those eccentric forms, which were mere displays of virtuosity.

CONSTRUCTION

I Hsing teapots were made with coiled clay, hand-kneaded, or with the body spun on the wheel or from clay pressed in a mould. In reference to the last method, Li says, 'since everything is done mechanically, all is slippery and sleek, precise and exact; and there are absolutely no joints or pores. In the case of elegantly modelled pots, any finger marks made at the time of kneading the clay, or knife marks made when the body is on the wheel, are rubbed off with the utmost care by means of a water-brush which completely removes all blemishes and produces a perfectly brilliant and sleek surface. It is only when passing through the kiln flames that the earth material experiences the force of the heat and automatically starts to melt. Moreover there is a certain amount of contraction, so that with hand-kneaded pieces the grainlike wrinkles still persist and are quite easily distinguished.'

DECORATION

I Hsing teapots can be decorated in seven different ways:

1. with engraved designs or inscriptions cut when the body is still soft—usually the inscriptions are of a poetic nature;
2. with stamped diaper, key fret or other familiar patterns to form a background;
3. with low reliefs, usually formed in a mould, stamped out or stuck on;
4. with ornamental addition in high relief, which has been applied; like the teapots with feet and lids in the form of nuts or small fruit;

5. with openwork, applied often in panels with an inner lining: pierced floral work, with no background, is usually left *à jour*;

6. with coloured glazes or enamels or gilding;

7. with etched or painted designs in a light buff slip, sometimes in relief.

'I Hsing pots with glaze started during the declining years of the Ming dynasty', says Li Ch'ing-k'ang, 'flowers and birds in powdered colours flourished under Ch'ien Lung.'

'From my limited observations,' says Li, 'first class teapots are those which preserve their natural colour; the middle sort are those which mingle the colour pigment with the body clay; the lowest are those which have enamels applied after the pot has been made so as to make it look nice from the outside.' He then proceeds to demolish the popular notion that the enamelling of I Hsing pots was unknown before the time of Ch'ien Lung, calling to his aid three authorities. The first is the familiar statement made by the *T'ao Shuo* that 'in the Ming period Ou of I Hsing made pots reproducing the grain of Ko ware and the colour, in great variety, of Kuan and Chün.' The second recalls that the potter Ch'en Chung-mu transferred to I Hsing from Ching-te Chen in Ming times and brought with him the 'know-how' of Ching-te Chen polychromes. And the third is a quotation from the section entitled *Ling li pu ju ch'ih* (Cleverness is not as good as folly) taken from the *Liang p'an ch'iu yü an sui pi* (Jottings from the retreat from autumn rain) by Liang Shao-jen (1884). He says 'I once saw...a pot of Yang Hsien sand.... On the side was a composition consisting of a green water-chestnut (*ling*), a red lichee branch (*li*), and a pale yellow 'as-you-will' (*jü i*) sceptre; on the base was a coiled chimera (*ch'ih*).... Below were carved the two ideograms Ta-pin.' On which Li observes: 'In the light of this statement, if Ta-pin made pots decorated with red, green, and yellow enamels there can be no question that the colouring of I Hsing pots did not date back to the Ming period.' Incidentally, the relevance of the four objects depicted are an elaborate example of the Chinese practice of playing with homophones; for *ling li* can mean 'cleverness'; *ju-i* 'not so good as'; and *ch'ih*, 'folly'.

Enamelled I Hsing of the Ming period must be exceptional. It is not uncommon, however, to meet Ming I Hsing wares covered

with monochrome glazes in imitation of Kuan Ko, Chün wares of
the Sung period, but these are outside the scope of this paper.

It is not generally known that another and today apparently rare
type of I Hsing teapot exists covered with purple, yellow, and
green lead glazes in the so-called Kochi style. This author has only
seen two of these teapots, and both are in the possession of Mr
W.W. Winkworth. As one of them has a spout and handle supplied
in Europe in the eighteenth century, after the originals had been
broken, it would appear they are likely to have been imported in
the late seventeenth or early eighteenth century by the Dutch.

When gilding appears on an I Hsing teapot it is in my experience
always an export piece and in every instance it would seem it has
been added in Europe soon after importation.

'A later type of ornament,' writes Hobson, 'consists of opaque
coloured enamels in painted designs on a ground colour completely hiding the surface of the work. The colour is always of
the *famille rose* variety including an opaque pink and I do not know
of any example which suggests an earlier date than Ch'ien Lung
(1738–85). Most indeed appear to be nineteenth century.' Enamels
usually include white and a soft blue. Chinese sources say this
style became fashionable about 1763.

When decorated with incised designs, instead of inscriptions,
flower or bamboo are the commonest motifs. 'Sand pots display
a suitable surface for carving flowers and plants, bamboos and
rocks, but not for scenes of life and landscape,' says Li.

INSCRIPTIONS

The I Hsing clay lends itself to the stroke of the knife, and stencil,
and the Chinese script can be recorded upon its surface to perfection. Quotations from the classics may provide a flavour which
only the Chinese themselves can fully appreciate. Such inscriptions
were valued more for their form than for their content. Their
importance springs from being examples of calligraphy, rather
than of literature. The Westerner who can see their beauty and
admire their spacing and general composition need not distress
himself too much if their literal meaning eludes him. Indeed, many
of them express ideas no more profound than the sentiments to
be found on a Christmas card.

The Chinese scholar believed that inscriptions should be apposite. 'Vaguely quoted poems of the past without connection with the pot or tea are out of place;' says one writer, 'better no inscription at all'. These inscriptions might be in the true character, the running hand, the grass hand or in the curly or square script.

Such inscriptions are at the best of times—when written in plain current copy-book script—not easy for the Western student of Chinese to decipher. When the carver elects to use the 'curly', the cursive, the semi-cursive, or the grassy script he enters a rarified atmosphere in which few, if any, Western sinologues can stand on their own feet; and none but native Chinese scholars of distinction can move freely.

Inscriptions fall into two separate categories according to the purpose they are designed to serve. The one is purely for record. This consists simply of the name of the ware or that of the potter or his studio and perhaps the date when the pot was made. Like the hallmark on English silver it forms no part in the decoration of the piece; and so it is no surprise to find it as a rule written on the pot-base where it is invisible.

The commonest inscription of this type takes the form of the name of the potter: for example, *Shih Ta-pin*. Not infrequently one comes across, after the name of the potter, the words *chien chih* (Made under the supervision of), or more rarely *tu chih* (made to the order of)—a form particularly used in cases where the gentleman patron has designed or selected the pot. Sometimes the date is added, usually in cyclical terms—*Wan Li ping shên nien Shih Ta-pin chih* (Made by Shih Ta-pin in the *ping shên* year of Wan Li) (1586). Sometimes there is a greater precision—'Made by Hsü Yu-ch'üan in the second moon of winter of the wu wu year,' which, knowing Hsü's date, we can deduce is 1618; or 'Made by Chung-fang for Yeh K'an on the 15th day of the 9th moon on an autumn day of the wu wu year of Wan Li', which is the same year.

These are elementary forms frequently repeated with slight variations and do not present insuperable difficulties.

The other form of inscription, the purely decorative, naturally demands a space on the face of the pot where it can be conspicuously displayed. According to Li prior to the reign of Ch'ien Lung (that is to say during the first two hundred odd years of the I Hsing potteries) not a single vessel has an inscription on its face. But the base may be embellished with such words as 'For my friend so-and-so' or 'When the pot boils there is a pleasant fragrance' or similar propitious sentiments. Then, about the middle of the eighteenth century, a striking change occurs, perhaps under the influence of the distinguished amateur Ch'ên Man-shêng and his equally distinguished craftsman-collaborator, Yang P'eng-nien, who for the first time inscribed ideograms on the pot's face.

The new fashion won wide acceptance during the next century. Li Ching K'ang's investigations show that out of thirty-two vessels dating between Ch'ien/Chia and Tao Kuang no less than twenty-two bear these inscriptions. Thereafter a second change occurs, for seven out of the next eight (bringing us to the twentieth century) are devoid of any decoration.

The I Hsing teapots exported to the West may have designs in relief, either formed in the mould or stuck on, but they are not usually engraved with designs or poems. They may have stamped designs or patterns like key fret usually forming the background or borders. Openwork designs, usually prunus or bamboo over an inner lining, are not uncommon, nor are pieces moulded in the form of a section of a bamboo. Enamelled pieces were rarely exported until the nineteenth century. Fantastic teapots in the form of a finger citron, or stuck all over with models of nuts and fruit with handles in the form of water chestnuts were made either for export, or for the more vulgar home markets. But there is little doubt that many teapots originally made for the indigenous market were exported and it is not possible to say that any group was made only for export.

SIGNATURES

In early days (that is, during the late Ming and early Ch'ing period) the potter's name was occasionally cut on the pot. The famous tree-bark pot of the founder is a notable case in point. It has a chop *Kung Ch'un* in curly script beneath the handle. But it was the quality of the vessel and not the name of the maker that counted. An exhaustive enquiry into the early authorities undertaken by Li Ching-k'ang shows that Shih Ta-p'in usually signed his creations and rarely sealed them; and an examination of extant pieces suggests that while the signed pieces are finely executed, the seal pieces are coarse and primitive (and are possibly imitations). This is clearly a useful aid to collectors; but as the enquiry was directed solely to Shih Ta-p'in, it is unsafe to apply this conclusion to other potters. In the light of the prevalent belief, originating with Chou Pai-kao, that some of the pots which were signed by Shih were actually made by his pupil Li Chung-fang, one is still unsure which were genuine 'Shih's' and which were 'school of Shih'.

After K'ang Hsi it became the fashion for a man of culture to carve the signature, or the name of the potter, on his pot. Under Ch'ien Lung and Tao Kuang, this practice was carried a step further and the names of both potter and patron or the carver of the inscription (if any) commonly appear together. This practice has been abused in modern times for people no longer consider whether the pot is good or bad but only whether it is signed.

I HSING POTTERS AND THEIR PATRONS

The attitude of I Hsing towards its potters differs widely from that of Ching-te Chen (or for that matter from the Sung and T'ang kilns). Ching-te Chen potters did not sign their works, and with rare exceptions their names have not been handed down to posterity. I Hsing on the other hand has from the very beginning kept an ample record of its potters. In the *Yang Hsien sha ku t'u k'ao* (Illustrated enquiry into the sand pots of Yang Hsien), Li has produced a list of no less than fifty-four professional potters complete with their period, and in many cases, place of birth, with a further forty-six whose names appear either in the literature of the subject or on extant vessels but whose identity has still to be established; together with fifty-six distinguished amateurs more or less intimately connected with the I Hsing industry. The relations of the potters with their employers at Ching-te Chen were hardly those of free and independent craftsmen. They were not recruited, nor paid by the Palace, at least before the Ch'ing dynasty; but were detailed on a rota from a number of districts surrounding the factory who were bound to furnish the Palace with its pottery needs by way of tribute. In these circumstances the signing of works by individuals was not to be expected. In the course of time private establishments sprang up round the official factory, at first no doubt to handle the Imperial rejects, and later private kilns appeared turning out pots for the general public, and from time to time standing in for the official kilns when the latter were closed down for reasons of retrenchment. But the habit of anonymity clung; and in any event the vessels, whether official or unofficial, were produced by a team, each piece even before the painters were called in, passing through up to twenty hands. Who then was to sign the finished article?

In I Hsing different conditions ruled. It is true there was an official bureau (one authority speaks of its 'reconstruction' under the Ch'ing, which suggests that it was established under the Ming) but this seems to have been merely a sort of tax office receiving the Imperial tribute in kind, such as the pots incised 'offered as tribute'. We learn from John Ferguson (*Survey of Chinese Art*, Shanghai 1939), that 'some of the best specimens of this ware (I Hsing) were made in the *Tsao Pan ch'u* in the reign of Ch'ien Lung.'

This Palace office had many departments and superintended everything from the production of the Imperial furniture to the quality of the Imperial lavatory paper. The mark of some of its departments, can be found both on lacquer and porcelain, with references such as 'made for the Imperial kitchen'. This would suggest that there existed a group of I Hsing potters at this period working to Imperial order inside the Palace.

The potteries were otherwise wholly unofficial, established by private speculators for the purpose of producing 'merchant goods' for all and sundry. We do not know what precisely was the form of the original arrangement; but to judge from the frequent repetition of clan names and from several examples of son succeeding father and younger brother taking over from his elder, some kilns would appear to have been something in the nature of a family business; a sort of co-operative venture to which business men contributed the finance and the potters the skill. In such conditions the status of the potter, even though he may not actually have been a partner, was one of considerable dignity; and it is easy to see how the practice of signing selected vessels by the craftsmen grew up. But the circumstance which above all else assured the success of the venture was the wholehearted support of that most important section of the public—the litterateurs and the dilettantes. Apart from ministering to the civilized pleasure of tea-drinking, the I Hsing teapot possessed two qualities precisely calculated to attract the cultured or the would-be cultured. The first was its homely material of simple honest clay. And the second was the firm yet pliant surface yielding gently to the knife, whether steel or bamboo, until the baking irrevocably fixed the subtle strokes. It was the perfect medium in which to preserve the written word.

In such an atmosphere the craftsman, however deep the gulf between him and the artist or man of letters, was assured of sympathetic consideration; and the practice of signing his work by the potter would be accepted as proper, and indeed welcomed by the collector as a valuable aid to identification. In practice, the decorations were often carved and the signatures written on behalf of the craftsman by a man of letters.

The amateurs might be thought to occupy much the same position as our patrons of the arts. But in fact their relationship to the craftsman is not quite the same. Some, for example, would not just purchase their pots off the craftsman's shelf but would design the pots themselves for the craftsman to construct; many undertook their own carving on pots made by the professional; some cut the signature or carved the 'chop' on behalf of the potter; and some built private kilns (and supplied the clay) for the expert to work at. I Hsing teapots appealed to a scholar class many of whom were totally uninterested in the general field of Chinese ceramics.

ED. NOTE. *The above is the text of an address given to the Society on 18 March 1974.*

NOTES

[1] Li Ching-k'ang *Yang Hsien sha hu t'u k'ao* (1957); this book, upon which this paper is built, is the most recent and is probably the best volume devoted to the subject, as it incorporates all the previous information available. It is divided into two volumes of which only the first was ever published. The text of the first volume is sub-divided into ten chapters, which in turn are divided into further sub-headings.

The first three chapters of the first volume deal with the traditional origin of the I Hsing teapot, and its struggle to establish itself against its tin or tin-coated rivals. Chapter Six is devoted to the different clays and sources of supply. Chapters Seven and Eight are concerned with the construction of the pots themselves, their glazes, decoration, the temperature of the kiln and the use of moulds, followed by Chapter Nine which is devoted to signatures and seals together with a record of inscriptions and poems inscribed on these teapots and a section given over to problems awaiting research. The last chapter is an anthology devoted to tea-making, together with a tea talk by Chang ku-ch'u on the origin of tea, tea-making and tea infusion and the usefulness of I Hsing teapots for this purpose.

By far the most interesting sections are Chapters Four and Five containing the biographies of the potter craftsmen who made these teapots. Li divides them into (a) the potter craftsmen, and (b) the fine gentlemen who ordered the teapots or who made them as amateur pottery.

The second volume, which was never printed, would have consisted of one hundred and nine woodcut illustrations, supplemented by seal impressions and inscriptions, all taken from pieces in the collection of Li Ching-k'ang and Chang Ku-ch'u.

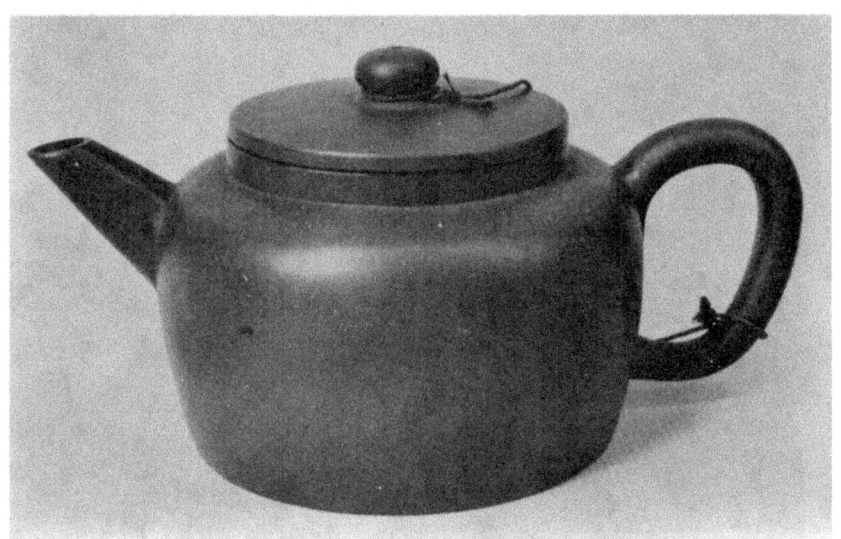

Plate 1: Potter: Shaw Hsiang-yu, Wan Li, h: 7.5 cm.

Plate 2: Potter: Chen Hsin-ching, Wan Li, h: 11 cm.

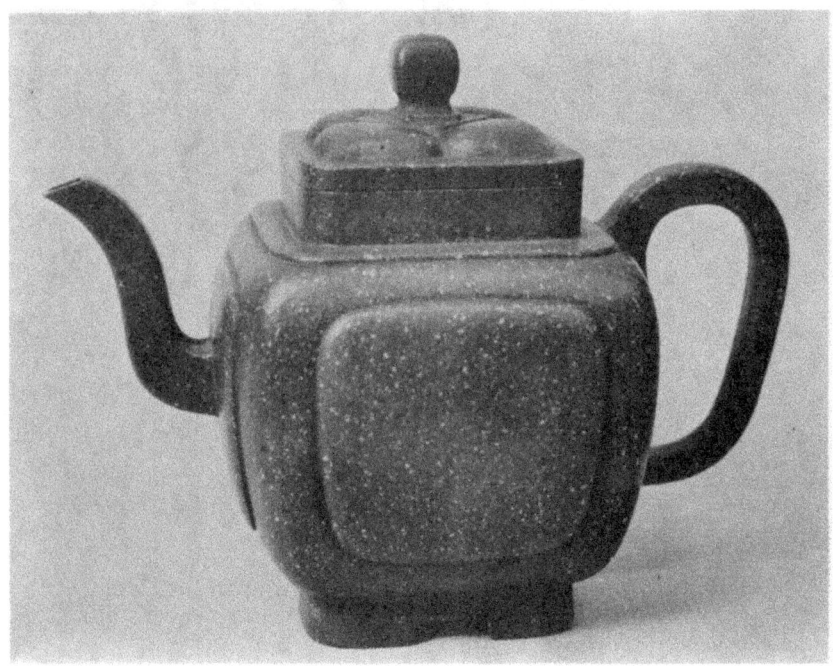

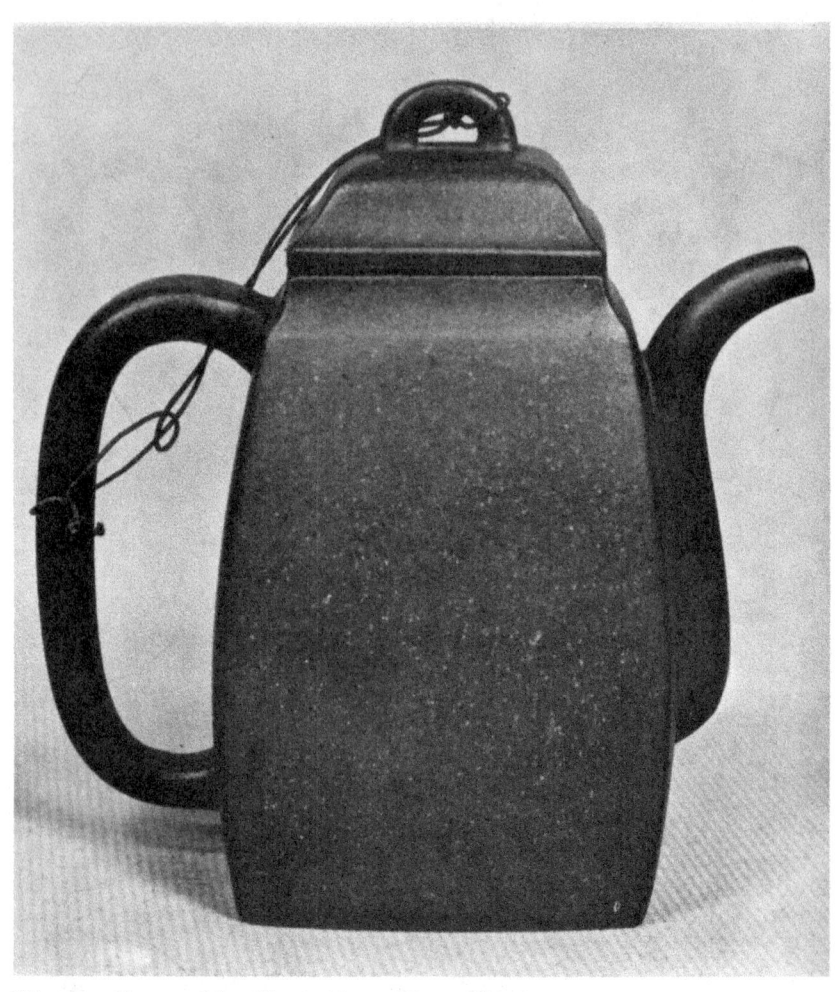

Plate 3 : Potter : Hua Fung-chiang, K'ang Hsi, h: 11.5 cm.

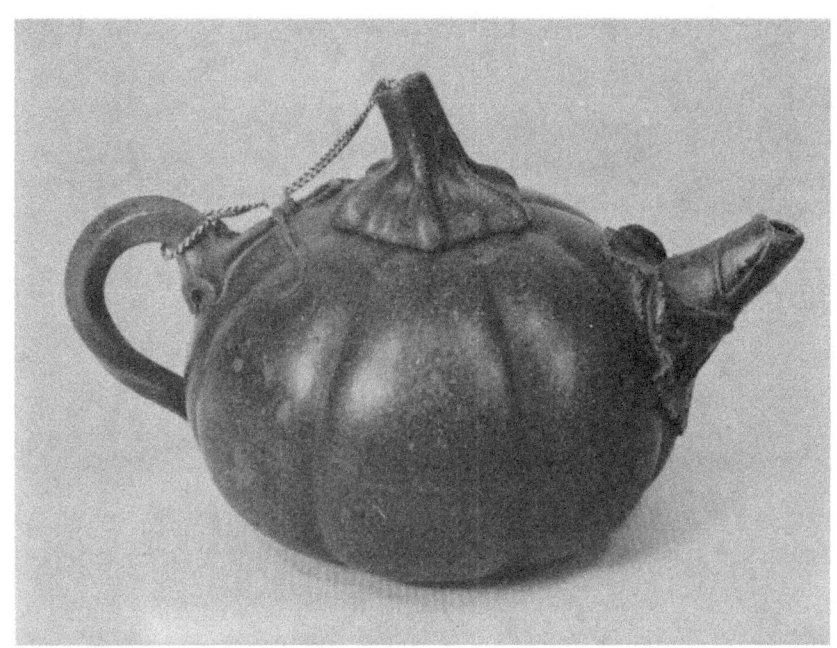

Plate 4: Potter: Chen Tzu-hsi, Ch'ung Cheng, h: 8 cm.

Plate 5: Potter: Chen Ming-yuan, K'ang Hsi, h: 8 cm.

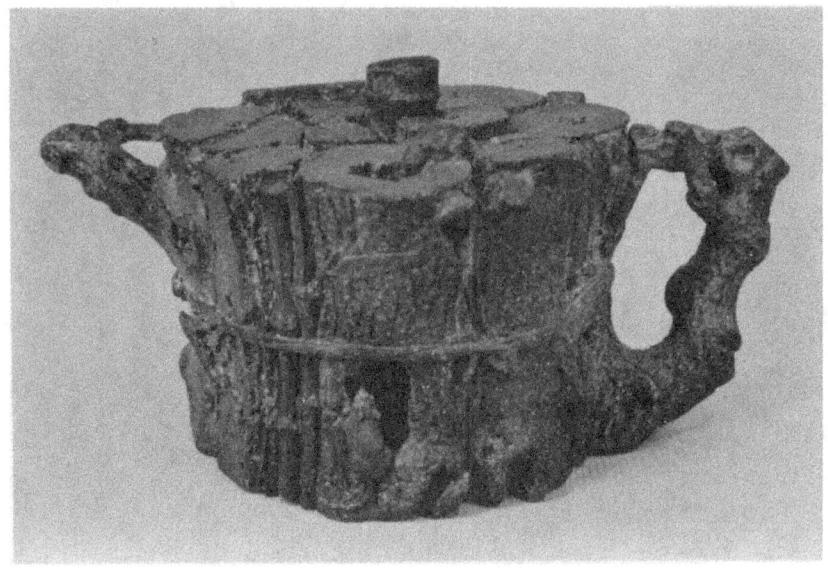

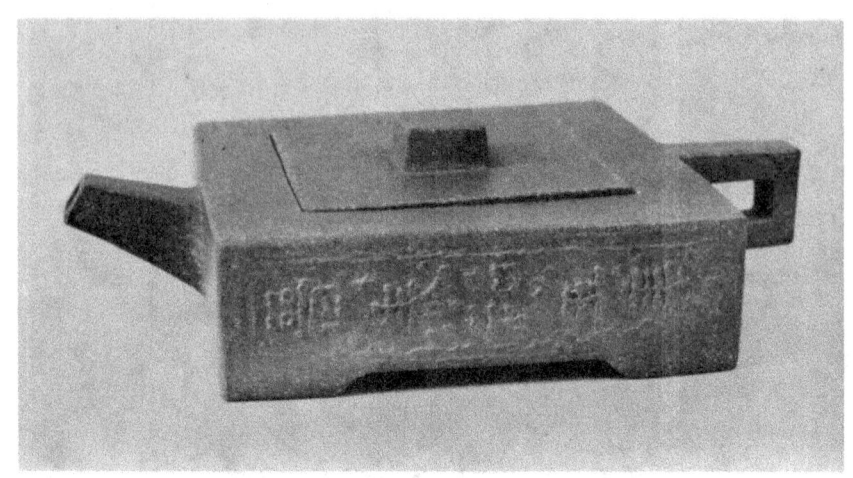

Plate 6 : Potter: Yang Peng Nien, Chia Ch'ing, h: 4.5 cm.

Plate 7 : Kung Ch'un type (reproduction), h: 13 cm.

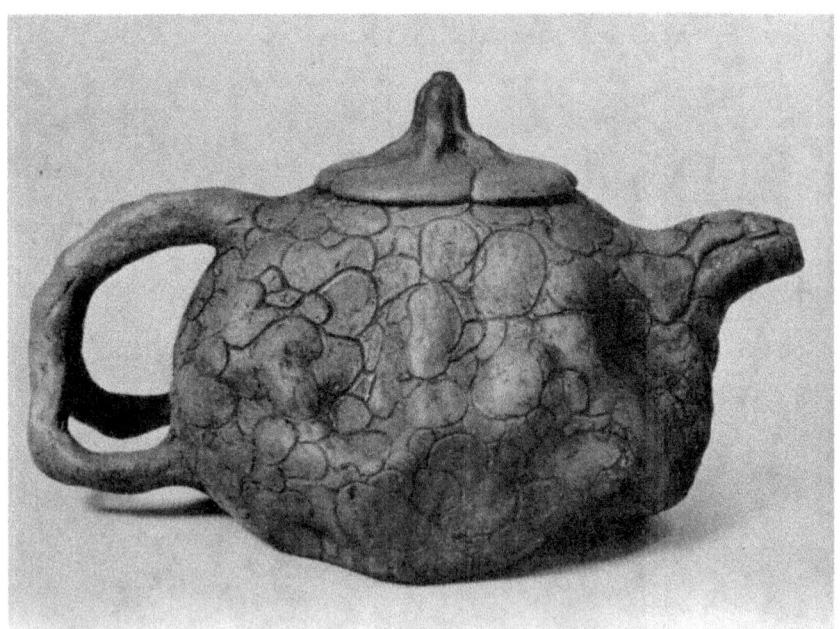

宜興茶壺（簡譯）

宜興茶壺成爲中國文人的寵物，足足有四個多世紀了。一般中國人也喜歡宜興茶壺，而日本的茶道俱樂部在近百年來都一直在蒐羅宜興茶壺。

宜興茶壺多數呈深褐或淺紅色，也有用棕色、紫褐、淺灰或淺黃的黏土製造。一般最佳的宜興茶壺往往毫無圖案，以做工精巧、形狀優美、結構簡單而雅緻者均屬之。有些茶壺雕有圖案，刻有詩句或格言。這種以鋼刀或竹刀刻成的文字，很講究書法。

宜興屬江蘇常州縣離上海西面不遠之處。現代中國人熟悉宜興之名，但十六、十七和十八世紀的許多作家，均稱之爲揚縣。

相傳明正德初年，一宜興官吏，名爲吳仕偕僕龔春遊覽城外數里之金沙寺。龔春得閒無事，靜觀一和尙用黏土捏製粗陶器。他覺得很有趣，於是捏了一下，發覺黏土用途甚大。鑒於宜興乃產茶之地，他認爲黏土適於製茶壺。此後茶壺製造工藝蓬勃發展，宜興因而名傳遐邇。

宜興茶壺之著名，是明代泡茶技術革新的結果。從前，茶葉多製成茶磚，有時加鹽或別種防腐劑，以便保存；或製成圓形茶餅，可藏數年，用時先將茶餅浸濕。但在明代，以開水泡茶之法開始流行，直至現代仍沿用此法。後來，茶餅就被淘汰了。

用新法泡茶時，小茶壺就用得着，最好用「單人茶壺」，按個人嗜好增減水量，就可以泡出濃淡適中的茶。幸虧陶匠保持一貫的工藝水平，宜興茶壺才能推陳出新，壟斷市場，直至今天。由於宜興茶壺具有許多優點，故十七世紀末葉的歐洲嗜茶者，都普遍採用。

歷　　史

關於宜興茶壺的歷史，中國人通常說：發明於明正德（1506—1521）初年，大量生產於萬曆（1573—1619）、天啟（1621—27）和清乾隆（1736—1795）期間，而衰落於清咸豐（1851—1861）和光緒（1874—1908）統治時期。

在正德和萬曆之間有一段時期，即嘉靖（1522—66）至隆慶（1567—72）這段時期被遺漏了。在上述期間，沒有一個陶匠的姓名被錄入名册，而這本名册却充滿了其他時期的陶匠姓名。有些中國人解釋道，因爲那段時期的陶匠，技術並不高超，所以無資格被錄入宜興名人史册。不過，本文作者認爲，宜興茶壺發明於正德年間這個傳說可能是虛構的，它出現於萬曆年間並非不可能。

宜興茶壺傳入歐洲和日本

葡萄牙人首先將宜興茶壺帶到歐洲，到十七世紀末葉，荷蘭人才採購大批輸往該地區。

十七世紀末葉，當歐洲盛行喝茶時，東印度公司開始供應茶具，其中有宜興茶壺。這是傳入英國的第一批茶壺，也是現代西方茶壺的祖先。事實上，宜興茶壺的形狀，可以從安妮皇后的英國製銀茶壺反映出來。由於宜興茶壺馳名歐洲，英國、荷蘭和德國的陶匠都紛紛仿製。

在歐洲出現的宜興茶壺，如果鑲有銀壺嘴或銀壺耳，則必定是原來部分損壞或遺失後在歐洲修補的。歐洲人用銀修補損壞的部份，始於十七世紀末葉或十八世紀初葉，而不是十九世紀，因爲在前述那段時期，即係損壞的茶壺亦受人們十分愛戴。

形　　狀

從中國人的觀點看，宜興茶壺的咀和耳與全面設計無關。這並非表示壺咀和壺耳或咀和耳之間的關係無須仔細規劃；但意味着咀和耳須盡可能做得平凡一點，以免喧賓奪主地轉移人們對壺身的注意力。

最重要的就是茶壺的輪廓。有蒂的壺蓋是構成輪廓的要素；但由於蓋可以揭開而且經常被揭開，很容易失去。正因爲如此，而且爲了增加仿製者的麻煩，除壺身加上圖章外，壺蓋邊緣也有同樣的標誌。

關於壺咀的特有形狀是怎樣的，眞是意見紛紜；有人認爲基於功能上的理由，壺咀不應做得彎彎曲曲，免得茶壺阻塞彎曲部

分，但有人說，爲了顧及外表的美觀，彎曲處不得超過一個。

說到茶壺形狀的變化，人們注意到的第一點就是所謂壺形的鮮明比例。此外，宜興茶壺有許多形狀：圓的、方的、有角的、偏的、平的、高的、矮的、大的、小的、卵形的等等。

宜興陶匠和獎勵者

宜興對陶匠的態度與景德鎮不同。景德鎮陶匠沒有把自己的姓名簽在他們所製的陶器上面；除極少數人外，他們的姓名都永遠湮沒無聞。另一方面，宜興始終都保存着該地陶匠的完整記錄。

宜興受到各種條件的支配。過去，宜興有一個官方機構，似乎是專替皇帝收取貢品的稅務局。貢品中的茶壺，都刻有「進貢品」字樣。除作爲貢品的陶器外，其餘都是供老百姓用的商品。

文人和附庸風雅者這羣社會上最重要的階層，保証了陶器行業的成功。宜興茶壺除有助於喝茶這種高尚賞受外，還具有兩個特點，足以吸引一般知識分子。第一個特點是，茶壺以當地純黏土作材料製造。第二個特點是，陶胚表面硬中帶軟，用鋼刀或竹刀刻字不成問題；入窰烘乾後，字形永遠不變。這是保存字跡的最佳媒介。

在這種情況下，無論陶匠與畫家與文人之間的鴻溝是多麼深，總難免得到同情的敬意；陶匠在他所製的陶器上簽名這種做法，被認爲適當。事實上，收藏家因陶器上的署名有助於鑑別眞僞而表示歡迎。其實，陶器上的圖案和簽名，通常是由文人代陶匠加上去的。

Collecting Chinese Ceramics: A Personal Approach

P.W.C. MAO

In January 1921 the Oriental Ceramic Society was founded in London. Our own Society was formed in March this year, and we are not even one year old. In the short space of our existence we have had at least three lectures by well-known specialists in this field, some rather esoteric and narrow in subject-matter for an organization as young as ours. Indeed, we are still in our swaddling clothes and it is highly unlikely that some of us have not suffered from indigestion on this diet. Sir Alan Barlow, a former president of the Oriental Ceramic Society, quoting Duveen said that 'the raison d'être of the collector is to provide a livelihood for the dealer and profitable sport for the faker.' But please do not be disheartened; in my opinion there is no such thing as a real expert. The field is too wide and the ramifications so extensive that we are learning all the time. There are still a lot of unsolved problems and every day new discoveries are being made in China and elsewhere. There must be a beginning for everyone. To start on a good foundation is to allow you to learn and expand on your own faculties later on.

The story of Chinese ceramics goes back more than 3,000 years, and it is intimately related to China's geography, cultural development and economics, and relations with other countries. You should therefore have a good idea of this to begin with, especially the sequence of the dynasties (see list appended), and changes of taste in various periods. To help you I would suggest that excellent book by Professor C.P. Fitzgerald *China: A Short Cultural History*. A knowledge of Chinese, especially calligraphy, would be useful but not essential. You will remember that most dealers in 'Cat Street', render Chinese names in Cantonese while books and periodicals render them in Mandarin or *kuo yu*, the national dialect; but if you know the characters for them you will not be lost. There are many books on Chinese pottery and porcelain but two that are particularly worthwhile are Sir Harry Garner's *Oriental Blue and White* and John Pope's book on the Ardebil Shrine collection.

33

Bulletins and museum catalogues are useful, as are magazines such as *Oriental Art,* the *Wen Wu* (文物) monthly published in Peking, and the *Transactions of the Oriental Ceramic Society* (T.O.C.S.).

Accurate and standard nomenclature is a *sine qua non,* whether referring to the shape of a piece, the use, the material, the glaze and colouring matter, or the various parts of the item in question. For instance with reference to a bowl (fig. 1), it will have a lip, a body, it may have a foot and a foot rim, outside and inside surfaces, an inner bottom and an outside base, or outside bottom. The lip may be inverted or outward sloping, or everted, or turned over. The body may be a straight slope or have a curve, or a combination of the two, or angulated. The foot may be small or big in proportion to the body, splayed or vertical, and the foot rim may be wide or narrow, square-cut or wedge-shaped in cross-section, or rounded. An ewer will have, in addition to the above, spout, neck, shoulder, and sometimes a handle. To save time in description certain proper names must be learned for specific articles, e.g., *kuan* (罐), *yu hu chun* (玉壺春), *cha t'ou* (渣斗), *mei p'ing* or plum blossom jar (梅瓶) (really a wine jar), brush pot, brush washer, rouleau vase, stem cups, and so on.

Let us now go to 'Cat Street'. We see a piece on display which we like. The first thing not to do is to take it in your hands. Look at it and quickly run through in your mind an exercise on the following lines.

1. Identify the shape or name of the piece.
2. Is it pottery, stoneware or porcelain? Is it celadon?
3. Note the finish of the ware, glazed or unglazed, the colour of the body, the nature of the glaze, and the use of the slip.
4. Note any enamel decoration and type, whether over the glaze or under the glaze, and the colours.
5. Note drawing or decoration, painted, incised, excised, moulded, or combined, or slip decoration, or appliqués.
6. Is there any crackle?
7. Look for any cracks or chipped areas or mended areas.
8. When at last you take the piece in your hands, take it firmly and support it, being sure to avoid holding it by the handles, thin areas, or mended areas. Note the weight and feel the finish of glaze and body. By flicking the article with a fingernail you will hear

either a clear tinkle, or a cracked or dull sound.

9. Look for any marks. Reign marks did not come into common use until Hsüan Te (1426–35) in early Ming. Note the name, the number of characters, the position of the characters, the type and how the mark has been made. The subject of reign marks is so extensive it calls for further treatment in another talk.

We are now in a position to discuss some of the important points already mentioned.

Form is very important in the study of Chinese ceramics of the various periods, shape and usage being important factors. Generally, T'ang forms tend to be vigorous, strong and alive with abrupt changes in contour, Sung forms are elegant and languid, with gracious curves, while the porcelain of the Ming period is characterized by solidity and dependability. The usual T'ang bowl has a rolled, everted lip rim with a hollow cross-section, a low profile with a fairly straight sloped side, and a relatively wide foot with a broad foot rim (fig. 2.1). Frequently the lip is doubled by a vertical downward projection of the edge. The typical Sung bowl is conical in shape with curved sides, small foot, and a narrow foot rim, graceful but easy to tip over (fig. 2.2). The Ming bowl looks like the horizontal lower section of a circle on a fairly wide foot in profile (fig. 2.3), or squat with the upper part of the bowl with straight sides and the lower part curving in rather horizontally on top of a wide foot, the foot rim cut square or slightly wedge-shaped (fig. 1). It should be remembered that certain forms can only date from after a certain period or within a definite period, such as the mei p'ing, which is found from Sung onwards, or the cha t'ou, 'scrapbowl', found from T'ang to Ming, and possibly deriving its shape from a foreign design. Most of the awkward vase forms, such as the double or triple vases, or vases with revolving sections, belong to the Ch'ing period.

The distinctive features of porcelain are that it is hard, nonporous, that it gives a ringing tone when tapped with the nail, and that it cannot be scratched with the point of a steel knife. These features are the result of a plastic mixture of kaolin and petuntse, or little white bricks, fired to a temperature of 1300°C, and then gradually cooled. Pottery is low-fired clay or clay with sand, and stoneware a similar composition fired to a higher temperature but not to 1300°C. Both pottery and stoneware if unglazed will absorb water, and both can be scratched with the point of a knife. Bone china is not porcelain, being much softer, as it is fired at a much lower temperature, utilizing the lime in the bone as a flux.

The earliest pottery in China, Yang Shao (仰韶) or Painted Pottery Culture, goes back about 6,000 years and came from Honan, Kansu and Shensi, about the middle reaches of the Yellow River. This pottery is reddish grey-brown or grey, the basins or jars being painted with simple geometric designs or drawings in black, red or white. Sometimes these wares carry simplified drawings of fish, insects or human faces. Contemporary with such wares or slightly later and found even more extensively towards the east was the Lungshan (龍山) or Black Pottery Culture, distinguished by the presence of thin, well-potted, wheel-made pottery burnished black and the presence of tripods. The commonly used ware was, however, grey pottery. Within this so-called 'nuclear' area the earliest civilizations of China were to develop. Within this area are the regions where North China pottery and porcelain were produced in later times. Towards the coast and south of the Yangtse River we have the Geometrical Pattern (幾何紋) Pottery, to which the term Lungshanoid has also been given as the wares have some features quite akin to the Lungshan type although dating from a somewhat later period. This would also encompass the whole coastline down to the area of Hong Kong. The earliest celadons were produced in the region of North-east Chekiang and the adjoining part of present-day Kiangsu. Later writers were to speak of Northern White and Southern Celadon (strictly speaking not correct), the dividing line being the Yangtse River.

One of the requirements of the Western definition of porcelain is whiteness; the Chinese regard all high-fired kaolin ware as porcelain irrespective of colour. With this in mind we can say that celadon or *ching tzu* (青瓷), a better term, was the first type of porcelain in the world. The body of celadon ware can be grey, putty-like, homogenous, buff, or greyish-black in colour, sometimes even whitish, not infrequently uneven and gritty. But the glaze is always a greyish-green to a bluish-green or olive colour. The major class of porcelain other than celadons is the white porcelain group, dominated in the last six to seven hundred years by the products of Ching-te Chen (景德鎮) in Kiangsi province.

The glaze, the transparent final smooth covering of the article, can be a low-fired lead glaze, or a high-fired felspathic glaze which is usual and hence fired at one and the same time as the body of the ware. Before covering the ware with the glaze, it is customary to smooth the body with a slip, commonly white and fine, made from a special glaze mixture, which after covering with the usual glaze and fired gives the article its fine finish. Slips are also used to decorate the ware, like the beading on Yüan wares, or function as white linear designs projecting somewhat from the surface on a darker coloured background. Slips are also used to lute separate pieces of an article into one before firing, this feature being sometimes seen on bigger pieces of the Ming dynasty wares as a palpable ridge or slight depression lying horizontally, say, on the body of a *mei p'ing* or *kuan*.

Early glazes tended to have a greenish or yellowish tinge to the transparency, with some being more opaque. The glaze was then too viscous to be well-controlled and in many of the earlier pieces, even down to the Tang, one can see a coagulation or clumping of the glaze in darker thick spots along its line of flow while drying. This, of course, is the reason for the 'tear drops' on Sung Ting ware, much regarded as a sign of authenticity.

The earliest glazed ware found in China is dated to the Shang period. The ware must have been fired to about 1200°C to get such a glaze. As celadons were the earliest type of porcelain, and as they are still being manufactured, the variety and scope is tremendous. The earliest were probably made in Chekiang and Kiangsu, but celadons have been made below the Great Wall, in Szechuan in the west, and Kwangtung in the south, and in most of the other provinces (Fukien, Kiangsi, Anwhei, Hunan, Shansi, Shensi, Hopei, Honan and so on), in many cases as early as late Han. Among the varieties we must mention are famous ones such as the Yüeh (越), the Lung Ch'üan (龍泉), the Ko (哥), the Southern Kuan (南宋官), and the Changsha wares (長沙), among the southern celadons, and the Yao Chou (耀州), Li Shui (麗水), Ju (汝), Chün (鈞), and Northern Kuan (北宋官) among the northern wares. The term Northern Celadon is commonly used to denote the Yao Chou and Li Shui type of celadon in the West; As Lung

Ch'üan celadon became the best known amongst Chinese a bad habit has grown up, especially with dealers, to call all celadons resembling it as Lung Ch'üan, and to call the Northern Celadon Northern Lung Ch'üan.

The earliest white porcelain as far as we know dates from just before T'ang, in the Sui dynasty. Well-known later types include the Hsing (邢), Tz'u Chou (磁州), Ting (定) and Liao (遼) made in the North, and from the South mainly Ching-te Chen wares, and others from Chi Chou (吉州) in Kiangsi, and Te Hua (德化) and Chuan Chou (泉州) in Fukien province. *Blanc de Chine* is Te Hua ware, and also called white 'Fukien ware' among dealers.

Colours in pottery and porcelain may be due to materials in or on the body, or materials added under the glaze, or on top of the glaze, usually in the form of enamels or coloured glass, or present in the glaze itself. Taking the last first, the common type is the black to brown 'Temmoku' (天目) glazes due to ferric iron in the glaze. Among famous types of the Sung dynasty are the Honan Black, the Kiangsi Black from Chi Chou, and the Fukien Black or Chien Black as opposed to the Fukien White, or *blanc de Chine*. This black finish is also seen on much of the present-day kitchen-ware in the market and is still being made in Honan. Ferrous iron gives a range from bluish-green to green, as seen on the celadon wares. Cobalt is commonly used underglaze, giving a rich blue colour to the decoration when fired with the body and glaze at the same time. It is generally thought that cobalt glazes were in common use in China by the Yüan dynasty, perhaps employing foreign cobalt. This cobalt gave a strong colour but was often difficult to control, causing the 'heaped and piled effect' seen on early Ming pieces. Later, Chinese cobalt was used which gave a less intense blue. According to Garner, Chinese cobalt contained manganese as an impurity, while foreign cobalt appears to have been manganese-free. Chinese sources state that the flow of foreign cobalt was cut off after the middle of the fifteenth century, and the blue of this period is generally weaker. About the second quarter of the sixteenth century foreign cobalt was again available; it was this cobalt that gave the famous dark, rich Mohammedan Blue of Chia Ching and Wan Li, and the slight touch of purple in the blue of the Transitional period. The K'ang Hsi blue of the Ch'ing dynasty is a true deep blue, even in colour, and vivid, technically of the highest order, and providing a strong contrast to the background of a now perfect white porcelain. The cobalt was now totally of Chinese origin, pure and refined and of the very best quality.

Underglaze copper red first came into fashion also during the Yüan dynasty and early Ming, but being difficult to handle was not fully exploited until early Ch'ing, during the reign of K'ang Hsi. There was the even Sacrificial Red and the brighter Fresh Red, including the Sang de Boeuf and the Peach Bloom. Coral Red and Sealing-wax Red were other varieties. The red could be applied either underglaze or in the glaze. All of the above wares were high-fired, body, glaze and colour matter being fired simultaneously.

Enamels are really coloured glass, the colours of which will change at high firing temperatures. This limits the methods by which they can be applied. They can be used on low-fired wares with lead glazes. They can be put on the body of an unglazed high-fired ware, already fired, then covered with a lead glaze and fired a second time at a lower temperature. Coloured enamels can also be applied on the surface of a glazed high-fired ware already fired, and fired at a lower temperature a second or more times. If multi-coloured the Chinese call the first type *san ts'ai* (三彩), literally 'three colours', even if there are more or less than three. The third class of ware is called *wu ts'ai* (五彩), 'five colours', irrespective of the number of colours used. We generally expect, however, a blue, a red (which is an iron red paint-like colour), a green, or greens of different shades, a yellow, and sometimes an aubergine, and white. The first type we see in the T'ang *san ts'ai* tomb ware, and later Sung and Liao, pillows and dishes, made in Honan and Hopei. But enamel colours came into general use during early Ming. The *fa hua* (法花) ware of Ming is a form of *san ts'ai* where the colours were prevented from running into each other by raised ridges of clay formed into designs as exemplified by the garden barrel seats, the *mei p'ings* and *kuans*. The *tou ts'ai*(鬥彩), 'contrasting colours', which was first made during the Ch'eng Hua period of Ming, is one variety of overglaze enamels where the outlines of the designs were in underglaze cobalt blue, and the colours of the designs were filled in, in overglaze enamels. *Famille verte* is a general term used by Westerners referring to multi-coloured enamel ware in which there was a predominance of green colours. These glassy enamels were also called Hard Enamels. In K'ang Hsi's time the underglaze cobalt blue was replaced by an overglaze blue enamel. These were all transparent enamels; in late K'ang Hsi, a new variety of soft or opaque enamel came into being. A white powder derived from tin was added to the glassy colours to obtain various shades of the same colour. At the same time a new rose colour derived from gold was added, and henceforth the term *famille rose* was applied by foreigners to this new multi-coloured decoration. Ku Yüeh Hsüan (古月軒), 'fine enamel', made for imperial use was perhaps the ultimate in Ch'ing porcelain.

Many new types of wares were produced in the period between Yung Cheng and Ch'ien Lung, new forms and colours such as the Tea Dust glaze, the Robin's Egg glaze, and Ch'ien Lung's porcelain copies of bronze, lacquer and wood. Books and books could be written on motifs and designs. Suffice to say that each and every period had its special tastes and preferences, accordingly reflected in the decorations and finishes of the articles including porcelain, silver, jade, lacquer, sculpture and painting.

Examine as many pieces as you can, visit the museums, read up as much as possible, ask questions, and discuss with others. Be assured that there are many lesser, to my mind, ways of disposing of your superfluous time. With diligence and care you will pass many hours of relaxed enjoyment, and en route acquire some knowledge of the achievements of a great culture and a great civilization. Ladies and gentlemen, may I wish you happy hunting.

NOTE: *The above is the text of an address given to the Society on 13 September 1974.*

漫談對於收藏中國古瓷（簡譯）

作者：毛文奇醫生

中國陶瓷器有三千多年歷史，它與中國地理、文化發展、經濟和該國與別國關係有密切的連繫。為了便於敍述，某些陶瓷器的特有名稱必須熟悉，例如罐、玉壺春、渣斗、梅瓶、筆筒、筆洗、寶子尊、高足鉢等。

讓我們到香港嚤囉街參觀一下。比如我們很喜歡陳列品中的一件古董。那麼讓我們仔細觀察，而注意下述各點：

（一）鑑定古董的形狀及其名稱。（二）鑑定它是否屬於陶胎、石胎或瓷胎；白瓷或青瓷。（三）注意器物表面是否上了釉，它本身的顏色，釉的性質。（四）注意有無上彩，彩是在釉層面上還是在釉層底下，它的顏色如何。（五）注意圖案或裝飾是什麼方法加上去的，它是手繪的、雕刻的、朔造的、併成的還是嵌鑲的？（六）聽聽有無破裂聲。（七）找出裂縫、崩缺或修補之所在。（八）取古董觀摩時，要拿得緊，用另一手托住，切勿執古董的耳、薄的或修補過的部份。注意古董的重量，摸一下釉層及胚身。用指輕彈表面，可以聽到清脆的玎玲聲或啞音。（九）注意標記和欵識。明初宣德時期（1426－35），年號才普遍使用。留意年號名稱、字數、字的位置以及加標誌的方法。年號這個主題是很廣泛的。

現在逐一叙述上述各要點。

研究中國各朝代瓷器時，須十分注意其形狀。唐瓷形狀生動有勁，輪廓變化多端；宋瓷雅緻而曲線優美；明瓷堅固耐用。普通的唐瓷碗，碗口向外翻轉，其橫切面顯出中空；側面輪廓低矮，碗側邊線條直而斜，碗足粗，腳緣闊。典型的宋瓷碗為圓錐形，側邊線條彎曲，碗腳小，腳緣窄，形狀優雅，但容易翻倒。明瓷碗側面輪廓像一個平放圓圈的下半截，碗腳很闊，碗上部側邊線條筆直，下部稍微水平地向內彎曲至碗腳頂端，腳緣呈方形或稍似斧形。必須記得，某些形狀是某時期以後或以內才開始出現的，如發現於宋朝及以後時期的梅瓶，發現於唐朝至明朝期間渣斗。怪狀的花瓶，如雙連瓶，三連頜、及轉心瓶，多數是清朝產品。

瓷胎的特點是堅硬、有不吸水性；以指輕敲時發出鐘聲；鋼刀尖不能把它劃花。這些特色是由高嶺土與白墩子塑性的混和後，用攝氏一千三百度以上的高溫燒之，然後讓它逐漸冷却而形成的。陶器是用低火力黏土或混有沙的黏土加熱燒成；而石胎瓷則是將成分相似的黏土加高熱燒成，但不須加熱至攝氏一千三百度。陶器和石胎如不加上釉，就會吸收水分，而且可以用鋼刀尖劃花。

根据西方國家關於瓷器的定義，潔白是必要條件之一；我國認為所有以高火力燒成的高嶺土器皿，不管其顏色如何，都屬瓷器。因此，我們可以說，青瓷是世界上最早的雛型瓷器。這種瓷器胎身的顏色有些是灰色、油灰色、淺黃色或灰黑色，有些甚至是白色，但光滑部分都是灰綠色、藍綠色或草青色。

在中國發現的最早期表面有釉的器皿，始於商朝。商器必定是以約攝氏一千二百度的高熱燒成的，否則不會如此光滑。由於青瓷是雛型瓷器，而且因為目前還在生產中，故其種類繁多。早期的青瓷器皿也許是產於浙江和江蘇，但四川、廣東及其他各省（福建、江西、安徽、湖南、山西、陝西、河北、河南等）均有出產，有些是在漢末製造的。必須提到的青瓷品種有著名的南窰如越、龍泉、哥、南宋官、長沙，北窰如耀州、麗水、汝、鈞、北宋官。在西方國家，北青瓷是指耀州和麗水。當龍泉青瓷在中國名傳遐邇時，把酷似龍泉的一切青瓷都叫做龍泉、又把北青瓷稱為北龍泉這種壞習慣就形成了，陶瓷商人多數有這種壞習慣。

据我們所知，最早期的白瓷始於隋末唐初。著名的後期產品有北方製造的邢、磁州、定和遼，南方製造的大部分是景德鎮瓷，其他白瓷產於江西吉州及福建德化和泉州。

陶瓷器的顏色可能是由器皿本身或表面材料形成的，或者是由加在釉底或釉面的物質例如釉藥形成的。普通顏色有黑和褐，因為釉藥含有三氧化二鐵。含有亞鐵的釉藥能產生從淺青至青綠的顏色，青瓷的顏色就是這樣。鈷通常用於釉層下面，當瓷坯和釉藥同時入窰燒製後，鈷能使藍色更加濃厚。一般人以為，鈷釉或青花在中國元朝被普遍使用，釉中的鈷也許是舶來品。這種鈷能產

生濃厚的顏色，但其深淺頗難控制，因而造成「暈積效果」，好像明初瓷器所表現的。同時國產鈷被採用，這種成分能產生淡藍色。据英國專家哈利·嘉納透露，中國鈷含有錳這種雜質，而外國鈷似乎不含錳的成分。据中國方面人士說，十五世紀中葉以後，外國鈷的來源曾經中斷，那時候青花的藍色比較淡。約莫在十六世紀上半葉後期，外國鈷再被採用；使嘉靖青花和萬曆青花呈現深藍色的就是這種鈷，使明末清初這時期（約為1620－1622）的青花呈現淺紫色的也是這種鈷。清朝的康熙藍是十足的深藍色，它是技術上的最高成就，在純白瓷的襯托下形成鮮明的對照。當時使用的鈷完全是國產，品質最佳。

釉藥其實是有色玻璃，其顏色隨火力熱度而改變。這種情況限制了釉藥的三類用法。（Ａ）釉藥可以用來塗在上了鉛釉的低火力瓷器上而燒。（Ｂ）它們可以塗在已用高熱處理過的高火力素瓷器上，然後塗一層鉛釉，用較低的熱度再燒一次。（Ｃ）有色釉藥也可以施於被燒過已上釉的高火力瓷器的表面，然後以較低的熱度再燒一次或多次。如果瓷器有多種顏色，例如ＡＢ二種，即使多於或少於三色，我國都稱之為三彩。第三Ｃ類瓷器通稱五彩，不管有多少種顏色。不過通常見到的顏色為藍、紅、青或深淺不同的青、黃和白。唐墓陪葬品，宋遼時代的磁枕磁碟，都是三彩。釉上彩色釉藥在明初時普遍被採用。明朝法花瓷是三彩的一種，由於它上面的圖案是用細瓷條凸起分色的，所以顏色不致混淆，正如花園桶形瓷凳、梅瓶和罐所表現的那樣。明成化年間首創的鬥彩，是以青花為輪廓、高度燒後、加彩在釉上，輪廓之處、用低度再燒。其他一般人比較熟悉的包括釉裡紅和矾紅。

盡量鑑定種種色色的瓷器，參觀博物館，多讀有關瓷器的著作，向人請教，同別人討論。消磨空閒時間的方法很多。如果勤力研究你感到興趣的古瓷，就可以度過許多歡樂的時刻，同時可以獲得有關中國偉大文化成就之知識。

The Foliated Dragon

B.S. MCELNEY

About three years ago I had occasion to read the print of a paper by Sir John Addis which he presented to the 1967 Manila Trade Pottery Seminar entitled 'Some Buddhist motifs as a clue to dating'[1]. In his article, Sir John Addis deals at some length with the peculiar type of dragon which is the subject of this article and which, there are good grounds for believing, entered the Chinese decorative repertoire as a Buddhist motif. The characteristics of the animal are that it has forelegs, one substantially in advance of the other, but no hind legs, and in place of a body it has a scrolled or feathered foliation. In many examples there is an elephant-like trunk and embryonic wings. Generally there issues from the mouth a floral scroll which sometimes terminates in a lotus flower; occasionally the lotus scroll is substituted by a string of pearls. For convenience I propose to call this monster 'the foliated dragon'.

This peculiar type of dragon has long been widely accepted as characteristic of the late fifteenth century, and Sir John Addis concludes in his article that the foliated dragon can confidently be assigned to dates between 1465 and 1540. It is the author's opinion that this view is substantially correct, though the decoration was revived in the late Transitional period and in the second quarter of the eighteenth century for short periods. In his paper Sir John Addis mentions the occurrence of two pairs of these foliated dragons in the semi-circular arch over the central entrance of a buddhist temple in Peking, the Wu T'a Sze (Five Dagoba Temple), which is dated in a cartouche above the central arch of the south front of the pedestal to the first year of Ch'eng Hua, i.e., 1465. He also mentions a blue-and-white bowl in the Shanghai Museum[2] with an authentic Ch'eng Hua mark decorated on the outside with two large and two small foliated dragons.

Sir Harry Garner, in his *Chinese and Japanese Cloisonné Enamels*[3], discusses the foliated dragon and states that 'so far as cloisonné pieces are concerned the internal evidence supporting an early sixteenth-century date is far stronger than the evidence, formerly accepted, which would have placed them in the late fifteenth century.' He also illustrates two cloisonné pieces decorated with the foliated dragon[4] and in (plate 32) illustrates part of a white marble entrance gate to the valley of the thirteen Ming tombs on which the foliated dragon also occurs. This entrance gate is said to date from 1540 but Sir Harry Garner strongly suggests that the panels in question may have been taken from an earlier edifice. The foliated dragons on this gate are similar to those on the authentic Ch'eng Hua pieces and are also similar to the foliated dragons on the Wu T'a Sze arch previously mentioned, so that there seems good reason for dating these panels also to the Ch'eng Hua period.

Since reading the article of Sir John Addis and the comments of Sir Harry Garner I have inspected several dozen pieces decorated with the foliated dragon all emanating from Indonesia and the Philippines, some of quite high quality. I have also recently inspected the covered vase with this decoration and a Hsüan Te mark in the Fitzwilliam Museum, which is discussed below, and four blue-and-white examples, all of Imperial quality, in the National Palace Museum in Taipei.

From the examples I have seen, it seems to me that the time is ripe to attempt to take Sir John Addis' theories and dating for this decorative idiom a stage further.

Much of the material that is available for the purposes of our discussion consists of examples of so-called 'export wares'. However, the prototypes for almost all export wares are probably to be found in the Imperial wares. The following points should be borne in mind when considering Ming export wares. Even with the painters of the Imperial wares there appears to have been a great deal of craftsman specialization, some workmen writing the mark and others doing the border. With the production of export wares, where the strict imperial control was lacking, continuous copying of a popular design or decorative motif tended to result in the painting of the design becoming more hurried and perfunctory after constant repetition. Some writers have suggested the existence of a time-lag between an Imperial marked piece and a piece of export quality bearing the same design. This theory might be valid when discussing designs on earlier wares produced in completely different parts of China, but most of the porcelain produced in the middle Ming period was produced within a relatively small area around Ching-te Chen and there are grounds for questioning the existence of anything but a minimal time-lag before a popular design or border motif was being used on porcelain produced for export.

Any discussions, however, must commence with a short summary of the available specimens of Imperial quality decorated with the foliated dragon. There are four blue-and-white examples and one *tou ts'ai* which must be mentioned. The first is the covered jar in the Fitzwilliam Museum which bears a six character Hsüan Te mark and has a double-stepped base (plate 1). The mark itself, which calligraphically appears authentic, is singularly cramped into a small double-lined circle in the centre of the base. The foliated dragon on this jar is quite unlike any of the Imperial examples mentioned below. In particular the following features should be noted: the absence of horns; two embryonic wings rather than the usual one, when the dragon faces forward; a mane consisting of three wisps rather than a full mane; a pronounced elephant-like proboscus; feline-like feet; and an unusually elaborate lotus scroll. The drawing of this jar is in many ways rather weak, and if it is to be assigned a fifteenth-century date it should in any event be placed in the Interregnum period—that is to say between 1436 and 1465—and probably late in the period. This jar was recently included in a survey of manganese content of cobalt blue of fifteenth-century wares and was found to have an unusually high content for a fifteenth-century piece.[5] It will be noted that the animal has very few dragon-like features.

The second example is a bowl with a six-character Ch'eng Hua mark in a rectangle in its base, in the National Palace Museum, Taipei. This bowl is almost identical with the unmarked example illustrated in Pope[6] (plate 2) and depicts four foliated dragons with a jü-i head border round the base. Two of the foliated dragons have their heads turned to the rear while two face forward. Significantly, the prototype has changed, for the Chinese craftsman-painter could not resist making the animal look more like a dragon; it has claws and mane and what looks like a white horn. The forward-looking dragons have only one embryonic wing, though the others have two such wings. The foliated tail is short and the lotus spray is diminutive.

The third piece is a small *tou ts'ai* jar with underglaze blue foliated dragons, in the Percival David Collection.[7] This jar has a 'T'ien' mark and Yung Cheng copies exist. The foliated dragon depicted on this example is much closer to a true dragon type and has considerable affinities to the animal on a similarly shaped jar with a Ch'eng Hua mark and double-stepped base in the Sedgwick Collection.[8] It differs from any other type of foliated dragon under discussion in having substantial birdlike wings. It is also characterized by having no spray of any kind issuing from its mouth. In general effect it appears rather clumsy. I cannot recall ever seeing this type with true wings among examples of export ware. I believe that it is an experimental type from the reign of Ch'eng Hua, roughly contemporaneous with the second example above, from the National Museum in Taipei.

The fourth example is an unmarked stemcup in the National Palace Museum, Taipei,[9] decorated with two foliated dragons and a flying horse, each with a lotus spray issuing from the mouth. The dragons do not have claws and the foliated tails are elongated and detailed. Another stemcup in the National Palace Museum is similarly decorated but one of the dragons has its head turned to the rear and the claws are just visible. I have not seen another example of the foliated dragon without claws with head turned to the rear and this stemcup seems to represent a transition between the second type described and the type under discussion here.

The last piece is a bowl in the Topkapu Saray with a six-character mark of Cheng Te.[10] In the interior this bowl has medallions and a wide border of complex Arabic script while the exterior is decorated with the foliated dragon amid lotus scrolls. The foliated dragon appears here in yet another form. The body and tail are a long, thin, ribbon-like extension and there are no embryonic wings. The head itself is more dragon-like and there is almost no elephantine snout. This bowl and another piece bearing Arabic script are exhaustively discussed in Volume 36 of the *Transactions of the Oriental Ceramic Society*.[11] It is worth quoting from this article in full:

> Among the few documented blue and white wares of the Ming period at the Saray, according to Miss Osbay, are two

bowls with Chêng-tê *nien-hao,* decorated with Islamic inscriptions in underglaze blue (Plate 37*a* and *b*) which she says are recorded as a gift from the Emperor Chêng-tê to the Emperor Selim I in 1521 (the last year of his reign), and that the gift was accompanied by some textiles, which have since perished. I was unable to satisfy myself whether this was a traditional story, or whether the gift, as I gathered, was actually recorded. Pope mentions a gift of two bowls in 1521 (but does not appear to have identified them) which were said to have been brought back and given to the Sultan by the Moslem merchant Ali Akbar, who had for some time resided in Peking and on his return to Istanbul finished the Khitai Nameh in 1516. This seems a more likely story, but unfortunately the dates do not correspond, if the bowls were presented in 1521. Zimmermann illustrates one of the bowls (Plate 37*b*) on his Plate 52, but makes no mention of its origin as a present from China. All he says in the text is that such a bowl might have been equally well made in China for the Near East or for the indigenous Chinese Mohammedan market. Neither Hobson nor David make any mention of this gift or illustrate either of these pieces. Kahle in the "Eine islamische Quelle über China um 1500" discusses Ali Akbar's visit to China and illustrates a number of pieces of Chêng-tê blue and white porcelain with Islamic inscriptions and among them the same bowl (Plate I*b*) but does not associate it in particular with Akbar's visit to China. Mr. Meredith Owens of the Department of Oriental Manuscripts in the British Museum has most kindly hunted through the *Khitai Nameh* for a reference to these bowls, but without success, but this is like looking for the proverbial needle in a haystack as this work has no index. Whatever the history of these two bowls, they carry the *nien hao* of Chêng-tê, and are certainly of the period. The first is inscribed with the Moslem profession of faith (Plate 37*a*), and the second with verses from the Koran (Plate 37*b*).

It will be noted that according to either version the piece cannot date from before approximately 1515 or after 1521. As a piece made for the Imperial court the painting is well done and probably represents an early example of this type of foliated dragon. Corroboration of the dating of this type of foliated dragon to the latter part of the reign of Chêng-tê can, however, be found independently. At least four large blue-and-white dishes with Portuguese motifs are known decorated with good examples of this type of foliated dragon.[12] Two bear on the reverse the Portuguese coat of arms and upside-down armillary spheres while the other two examples have two medallions consisting of crowns of thorns enclosing sacred monograms. The expedition of Feinao Peres, which was the first real Portuguese contact with China, took place in 1517 and King Manuel died in 1521. The use of his armillary sphere device makes it almost certain that these dishes date to the late Chêng-tê period.

The Imperial examples described above illustrate well the five main types of foliated dragon. There are a number of examples which differ in minor details from the types described but, with the exception of one major variant found only in export wares and mentioned below, all conform to the basic types. Various other examples of the foliated dragon appear in well-known collections. For instance, foliated dragons of the fourth type are depicted in circular medallions found on a well-known series of *tou ts'ai* cups with Ch'eng Hua marks.[13] Other examples of the fourth type appear in a narrow border on the inside of an unmarked blue-and-white stemcup in the Percival David Collection[14] but in these examples there are three strings of pearls coming from the mouths. The interior of the stemcup depicts horses in a downward glide amid clouds around a medallion showing a hermit crab among waves, while the exterior is decorated with lotus and waterweeds rising from a wave design. It seems that the string of pearls, substituting the more common lotus spray, is more frequently used when the foliated dragon is confined within the border. It apparently occurs solely in the fourth type and the major variant mentioned below.

A further polychrome example of the basic fourth type is illustrated in the catalogue of the exhibition 'The Animal in Chinese Art'.[15] In this case, however, the embryonic wings are much more developed and the paws have four small cat-like claws.

In the export wares the second, fourth and fifth main types described above are all found and examples of the fourth (plate 4) and fifth types (plate 5) are illustrated with this article. I have not seen export examples of either types one or three but an example similar to type two but with some of the characteristics of type four was sold recently at public auction.[16]

The fourth and fifth types seem to be the commonest types of foliated dragon found on export wares. A further important variation of the basic fourth type which seems to be confined to export wares, many of high quality, represents the tail of the foliated dragon extensively feathered. A fine example of this variant is illustrated in plate 6. The cavetto of this example of a rather rare lipped shape contains compact, roughly circular, floral sprays of a type usually associated with the Hung Chih period. Another fine example of this variant of type four is illustrated in Sir John Addis' article. This piece has a continuous lotus scroll in the cavetto and the deep undercut foot frequently found in Imperial dishes with the Hung Chih mark. Type four seems to have been in vogue over quite a long period as many examples exist (chiefly in *tou ts'ai*) bearing the Ch'eng Hua mark while other examples are found associated with the interrupted lotus scroll. The interrupted lotus scroll, an example of which is illustrated in the cavetto of plate 7, seems to have come into the ceramic repertoire about 1500.[17] It became increasingly common in the reign of Chêng-tê, progressively superceding the continuous lotus scroll which had been in almost exclusive use before his reign.

Two polychrome examples of the basic fifth type are illustrated in Volume 7 of the Japanese Series (日本雄山閣出版之陶器講座).[18] These examples bear the Chia Ching Imperial mark. Both examples have the foliated dragon among lotus scrolls, which is the decoration with which this type of foliated dragon is normally associated, and in neither case do the animals have horns or lotus sprays issuing from their mouths. An interesting feature of some examples of this type is the reappearance in this period of spindly dragon-like claws (see plate 5). Claws, other than the most rudimentary truncated kind, have been absent in the foliated dragon since the period of the second type. The early examples of the fifth type (typified by the plates with the Portuguese motifs) do not usually have claws but usually do have horns. The export examples of the basic fifth type seem to get progressively coarser and it is clear that the type extended well into the Chia Ching period; examples are known with commendation marks normally associated with middle Chia Ching. But gradually the motif disappeared from ceramic design, partly no doubt as a result of the increasing popularity of Taoism and the corresponding decline in the popularity of Buddhism in the Chia Ching period.

On the basis of the evidence reviewed above the following tentative chronology is proposed for the various types of foliated dragon.

Type 1	pre-1465
Type 2	1465–75
Type 3	1465–75
Type 4	1475–1510
Type 4 feather-tailed variant	1495–1515
Type 5	1510–45

NOTES

[1] See Sir John Addis, Manila Trade Pottery Seminar, 1967, 'Introductory notes'.

[2] See Addis, op. cit. Comparable with pl. 62 in J.A. Pope, *Chinese porcelains from the Ardebil shrine*, Washington Smithsonian Institution, Freer Gallery of Art, 1956.

[3] Sir Harry Garner, *Chinese and Japanese cloisonne enamels*, London, Faber and Faber, 1962, pp. 70 and 71.

[4] Ibid., pls. 31a and 33.

[5] See Adrian Joseph, *Ming Porcelains*, London, Bibelot, 1971, fig. 33 and appendix II.

[6] *Chinese porcelains from the Ardebil shrine*, pl. 62.

[7] *Catalogue of the Percival David Collection*, London, section 5, no. 784.

[8] *Ming Porcelains*, fig. 13.

[9] *Catalogue of the National Palace Museum, Taipei: Blue and white wares of the Ming dynasty*, vol. 3, pl. 6. For an illustration of a similar example see *Ming blue and white*, Philadelphia Museum Bulletin, 1949, vol. XLIV, no. 223.

[10] *Transactions of the Oriental Ceramic Society*, London, vol. 36, p. 58, pl. 37b.

[11] Ibid., p. 48.

[12] One example is illustrated in the catalogue of Sotheby Parke Bernet, 2 July 1967, lot 93; another in the catalogue of the same auctioneer, 24 May 1974, lot 353.

[13] For example, *Catalogue of the Percival David Collection*, London, section 5, no. A745; and Brankston, op. cit., pl. 27a.

[14] *Catalogue of the Percival David Collection*, London, section 3, no. A668.

[15] Catalogue of the exhibition, London, 1968, pl. 28.

[16] See catalogue of the Sotheby Parke Bernet sale, 10 May 1974, lot 28. This example is interesting in that the floral sprays of type 2 have disappeared but the tail is more like type 4. It obviously represents a transitional type before the full development of type 4.

[17] A small imperial bowl with six-character Hung Chih mark illustrated in the catalogue of the Chinese ceramics in the Tokyo National Museum has a carefully drawn interrupted lotus scroll. The writing of the mark links it to marks found on Chêng-tê pieces and argues a late Hung Chih date for the bowl.

[18] Pls. 119 and 121.

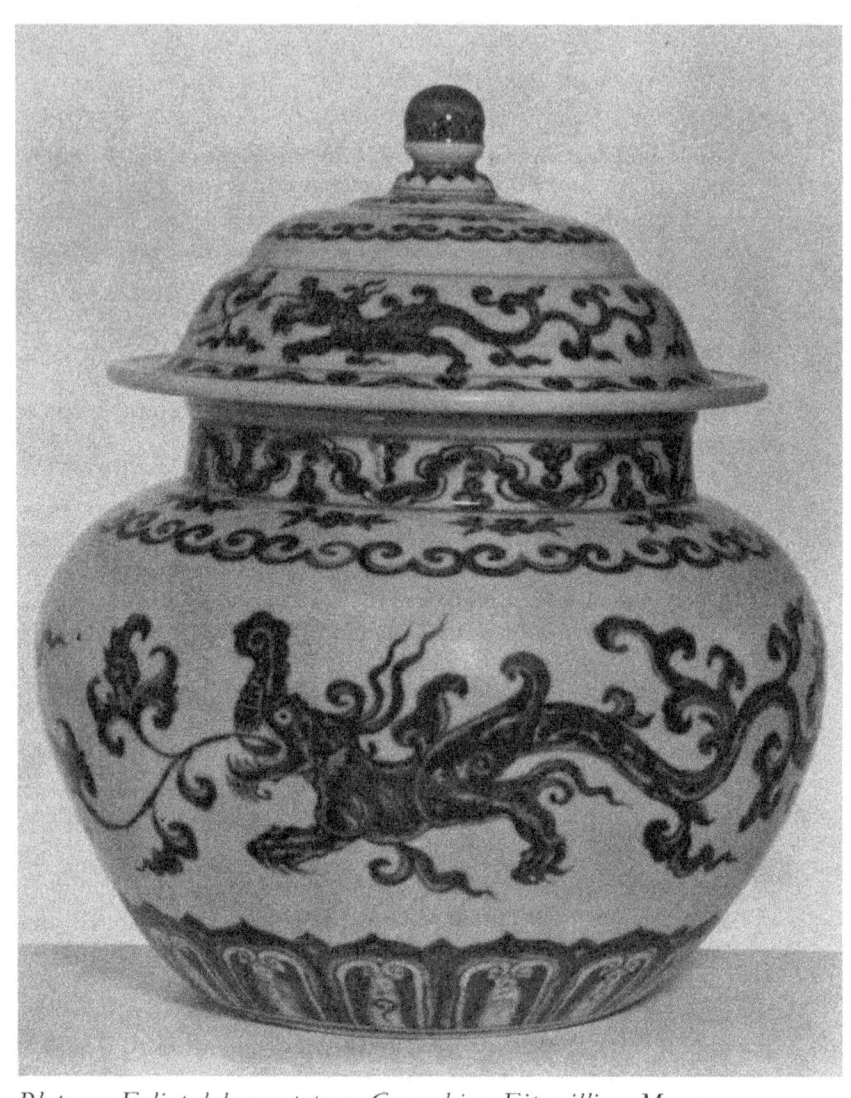

Plate 1: Foliated dragon type 1. Covered jar, Fitzwilliam Museum

ED. NOTE: *Type 3 of foliated dragon not illustrated.*

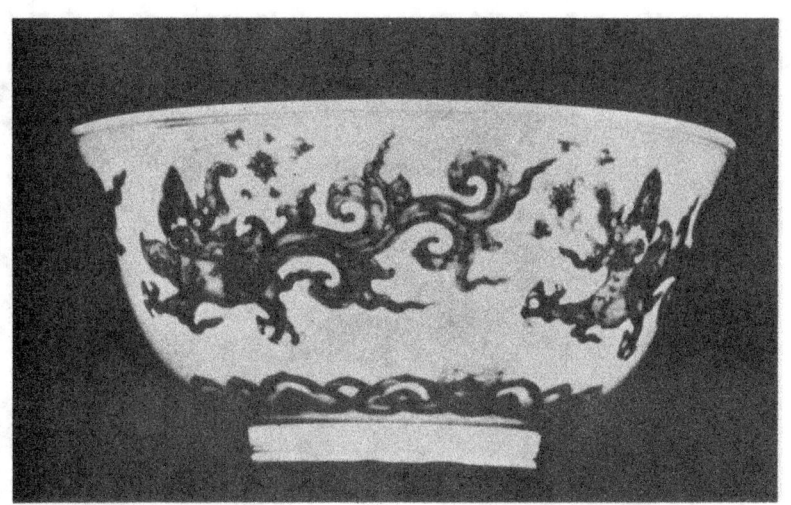

Plate 2 : Foliated dragon type 2. Bowl, Ardebil Shrine

Plate 3 : Foliated dragon type 4. Export ware bowl, private collection

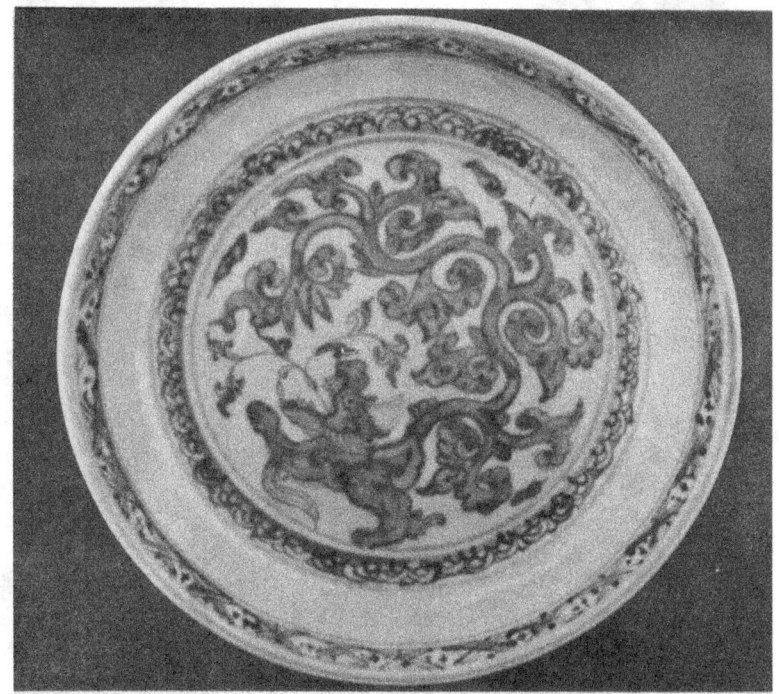

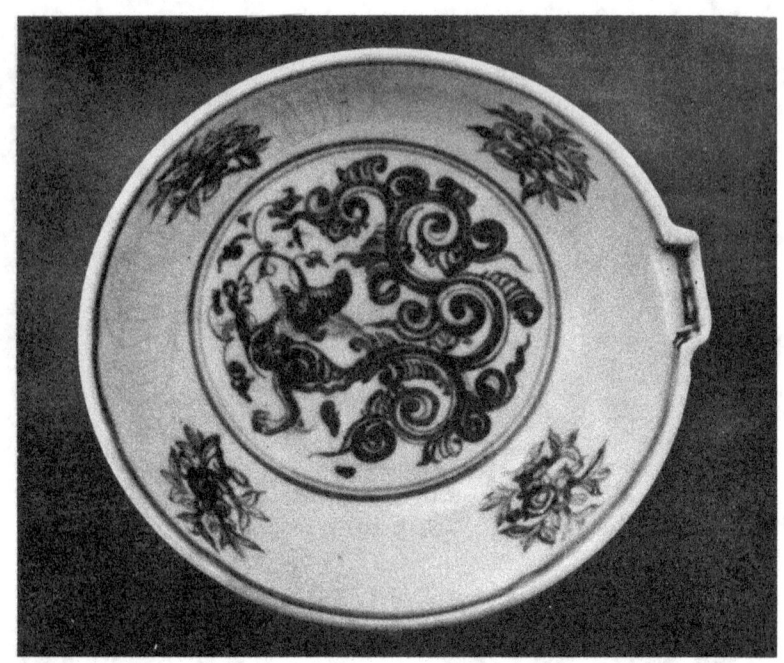

*Plate 4 : Foliated dragon type 4, feather-tailed variant. Export ware
          bowl, private collection*

Plate 5 : Foliated dragon type 5. Export ware bowl, private collection

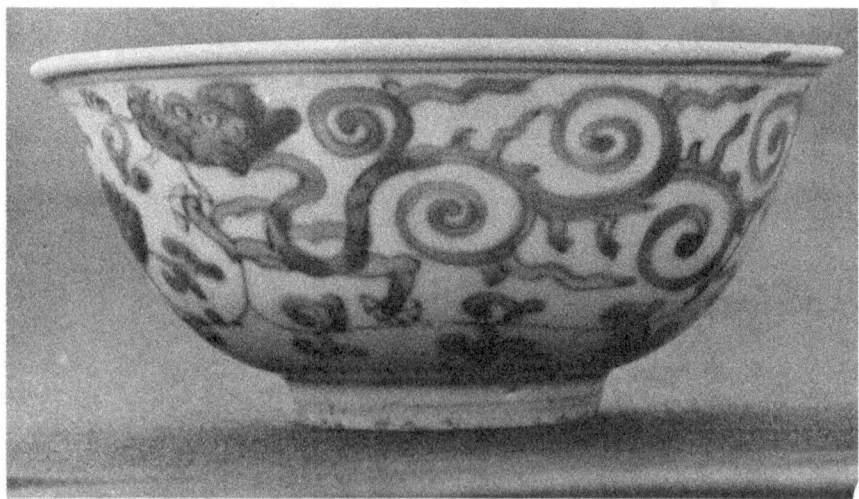

夔龍（多葉尾紋龍） （簡譯）

大約三年前，我有機會讀到一篇約翰・亞廸斯爵士寫的論文，題目是「有些佛教圖案主題可以作爲推斷年代的線索」。這篇論文是他於一九六七年呈交給「馬尼拉商業陶器討論會」的。他的論文詳述了一種形狀特殊多葉尾的龍，而此類龍就是本文的題目。有充分理由相信，龍作爲一種佛教圖案主題而進入了中國藝壇。這種龍的特徵是，只有一對前足而無後足，其中一隻前足與另一隻相距甚遠；有一層漩渦形或羽狀葉紋的東西代替龍身。一般來說，此種龍有一條「象鼻」和一對發育不全的翅膀、龍口都銜了一枝花卉的漩渦形物，此物有時止於一朵蓮花；偶爾，花狀漩渦形物被一串珍珠代替。爲了便於叙述，我把這種龍稱爲『多葉尾紋龍』（ FOLIATED DRAGON ），即夔龍。

　　這種龍向來被公認爲十五世紀末葉的特徵。亞廸斯爵士在其論文中斷定，夔龍出現於公元一四六五和一五四〇年之間。本文作者認爲，上述看法大體上是正確的，雖然多葉尾紋龍裝飾在明末清初以及在十八世紀三十至五十年代復活了短時期。約翰・亞廸斯在其論文中，提及北京五塔寺中央入口處半圓形拱門上的兩對夔龍，記錄指出其雕鑿年代爲成化一年。他也提及上海博物館的一件青花瓷碗，碗上有成化年號，碗外繪有兩大兩小夔龍。

　　哈利・嘉納爵士在其「中國和日本的景泰藍」一書中談到夔龍，他說：「就景泰藍器皿而論，支持它始於十六世紀初葉年代的証据，强於推斷它始於十五世紀末葉的証据。」他也用圖片說明兩件以此種龍作裝飾的景泰藍器皿，又用另一幅圖片解說明代十三陵入口處白石門的一部分（明長陵石牌坊），石門上也有夔龍。据說石門建於一五四〇年，但哈利・嘉納爵士推斷，議論中的石門可能是從較早年代的一座建築物搬過去的。石門上的龍紋似五塔寺拱門上的同樣龍，也類似上海博物館珍藏的成化青花碗上的龍，因此，有充分理由顯示石門建於成化時期。

　　拜讀了約翰・亞廸斯爵士和哈利・嘉納爵士的大作以後，我

57

細看了數十件來自印尼和菲律賓的瓷器，瓷器上都有夔龍裝飾，其中有些品質極高。不久以前我也在費茲威廉博物館欣賞過一個附有宣德年號的夔龍花瓶，又在台北故宮博物館看到四件青花宮瓷。

從我所見過的青花瓷判斷，進一步研究約翰‧亞迪斯爵士理論和推斷夔龍出現年代的時機，對我來說似乎成熟了。

可供討論時參攷用的資料，多數是所謂「出口瓷」的樣本。不過，幾乎所有出口瓷的雛型都可能在官瓷中找到。

探討明代出口瓷時，應該牢記下述各點。雖有官瓷畫家專畫圖案，但似乎還有其他專業人才，其中有的寫年號，有的做邊緣修飾。隨着不受官方控制的出口瓷的生產，製造商不斷抄襲深受歡迎的圖案和裝飾主題，使圖案的描繪越來越馬虎。

討論開始時，必須對繪有夔龍的官瓷作一個簡介。有四件青花瓷和一件鬥彩必須提及。第一件是費茲威廉博物館的有蓋瓶，瓶上載有六字款的宣德年號，並附有二級的底。年號本身被嵌入底中央的一個雙圈內。從年號書法判斷，這件似乎是真器。這個青花上的龍，與下述官瓷樣本上所繪的迴異。下面說的特點要特別注意：瓶上的龍無角；有一對發育不全的翼，而不是常見的一個翅膀；龍首向前；只有三束如鬃的毛，而不是全鬃；有一條搶眼的「象鼻」；足似貓；口噴荷花狀漩渦形物。這個瓷瓶的繪畫，在許多方面都頗為拙劣；如果說它是十五世紀的產品，那麼一定是在一四三六和一四六五年之間或者是在該期後期的產品。不久以前，專家曾對十五世紀瓷器的鈷藍所含錳質作一次測量，上述瓷瓶也是測量對象之一。測量結果証實，這個瓷瓶有極高的錳含量。值得注意的是，瓶上所繪的動物只具有少數似龍的特徵。

第二件青花瓷是台北故宮博物館的一個碗，其底上的長方格中載有六字款的成化年號。碗上繪有四條夔龍，其中兩條頭部向後，另外兩條頭部向前。最重要的是，龍的雛型變了，因為中國工匠兼畫家忍不住要把那頭怪物畫得更象龍；這條龍有腳爪、鬃毛和一隻像白角的東西。頭向前的兩條龍只有一隻發育不全的翼，而頭向後的兩條卻有兩隻類似的翼。葉紋尾巴不長，噴出來的蓮花也顯得細小。

第三件瓷器是「英國大維德博物院藏品」中的鬥彩瓶，釉層下面繪有藍色夔龍。這條龍比較接近眞龍類型，與「英國塞治威克夫人珍藏品」中那個載有成化年號的類似瓷瓶上的動物極相似。它同討論中的任何一種夔龍的最大分別，在於它有巨大的「鳥翼」，而且沒有東西從口中噴出。大體上說，它似乎頗爲笨拙。在我們所見的出口瓷樣本當中，從來沒有這種長着鳥翼的龍。我相信，上述鬥彩瓷瓶是成化年間的一種試製品，約莫與台北故宮博物館那個瓷碗同一年代。

第四件瓷器也是台北故宮博物館珍藏的無年號高脚杯，杯上繪有兩條夔龍和一隻飛馬，每隻動物都吐出一朵蓮花。兩條龍都沒有爪，尾巴很長。該博物館的另一個高脚杯繪有類似的裝飾，但其中一條龍頭部向後轉，龍爪幾乎看不見，除此以外，我從未看過別個無爪而頭部向後轉的夔龍瓷器樣本；上述高脚杯似乎代表着前述第二類型和下面所說那種類型之間的過渡時期產物。

最後一件瓷器是土耳其伊斯坦堡博物館收藏的磁碗，碗上載有六字正德年號。碗內有圓形裝飾和阿拉伯字，而外部則以夔龍和荷花狀漩渦形物做裝飾。這條龍形狀獨特，軀幹和尾巴像絲帶那樣長而薄，沒有發育不全的翼，頭部更似龍，沒有「象鼻」。作爲一件官瓷，圖案畫得很漂亮，也許可以代表這種龍的早期樣本。這一類型的龍，肯定始於正德時期後期。至少有四件具有葡萄牙圖案主題的青花大磁碟，是以這種龍做裝飾的。其中兩件磁碟的反面，繪有葡萄牙盾形徽章和顚倒的渾天儀；另外兩件繪有兩個圓形圖案，每個圖案是由圍着神聖拼合文字的荊冠組成。費納奧·貝雷斯的遠征發生於一五一七年，而馬紐爾皇帝則死於一五二一年。那次遠征成了葡萄牙同中國的首次眞正接觸。渾天儀的使用，幾乎可以証實上述大瓷碟爲正德時期後期產品。

上面說的官瓷表明了主要的五種葉紋龍。有許多瓷器在細微處與上述不同，但除了在出口瓷中發現的一個主要變種外，都符合基本種類。

在出口瓷中可以找到前述第二、第四及第五各主要種類。我從未見過第一種和第三種，有一件類似第二種但具有第四種某些特點的瓷器，最近公開拍賣了。

第四和第五種似乎是出口瓷中最常見的夔龍類型。第四種似乎只限於爲數頗多的高質出口瓷，這類型的一項主要變化在於龍尾有濃密的羽毛覆蓋。

　　綜合上述証据，各種龍的出現年代約如下面所列：第一種爲一四六五年以前；第二種爲一四六五至七五年；第三種爲一四六五至七五年；第四種爲一四七五至一五一〇年；第四種變種（有羽毛尾的變種）爲一四九五至一五一五年；第五種爲一五一〇至四五年。

CHINESE DYNASTIES

Neolithic Period	pre-1523 BC
Shang Dynasty	1523–1037 BC
Chou Dynasty	1037–221 BC
Ch'in Dynasty	221–206 BC
Han Dynasty	206 BC–AD 221
Six Dynasties	AD 221–589
Sui Dynasty	AD 589–618
T'ang Dynasty	AD 618–907
Five Dynasties	AD 907–960
Sung Dynasty	AD 960–1280
Yüan Dynasty	AD 1280–1368
Ming Dynasty	AD 1368–1644
Ch'ing Dynasty	AD 1644–1912
Republic	AD 1912–1949
People's Republic	AD 1949–....

RESIDENTIAL MEMBERS OF THE SOCIETY

Mrs E.L. Alleyne
Mr S.E. Alleyne
Miss Nicole Andrau
Mr G.C. Armstrong
Mrs M. Armstrong
Mr H.H.L. Babington
Mr S.A. Barden
Mr John F. Barrow
Mrs Mary R. Barrow
Mr K.J. Bernau
Mrs Marjorie Bernau
Mrs Mona A. Birley
Mrs Pamela Q. Birnbaum
Mrs M.S. Bordwell
Mr Gus Borgeest
Mr Paul Braga
Mr Brian Brake
Mr Nigel Cameron
Mr G.W. Capell
Mr G.P.T. Carpenter
Mr R.H. Carter
Mr John Charles
Mr Cheung Sing-hoi
Mrs Jerry Coan
Mr Jerry Coan
Mrs Patti Chow
Mr Philip Chu
Miss Winnie Chung Po-Kam
Miss J.V. Cockell
Mrs Mary Coffey
Mrs Paul Colinet
Miss Eileen Davidson
Mr A.I. Diamond
Mrs I.R. Diamond
Mr E.C.N. D'Oliveira
Mrs Hope Donald
Mrs Christine Downer

Mr Michael Edwards
Mrs Lucille Evans
Mr Sam I. Feldman
Miss Paula Fleming
Mr L. Foldes
Mrs P.C. Foldes
Mr A.H. Forsyth
Mrs Nancy T. Francis
Mr Kenneth H.C. Fung
Mr Fung Shiu-lam
Mr Timothy J.B. George
Mr Hugh Gibb
Miss Lydia Go
Miss C.M. Goldney
Mr Andrew Graham
Mr J.H. Grieve
Mrs Suzanne-Louise Grieve
Mrs Elizabeth Heatherington
Mr R.I.C. Herridge
Mrs Grace Ho
Mr Walter Hochstadter
Mrs Mamie Howe
Mrs E.A.P. Hownam-Meek
Dr Rayson Huang
Mr P.E. Hutson
Mrs P.E. Hutson
Mrs Rosemary A. Inglis
Mr Ip Che
Mr Vincent Ip
Mr W. Irik
Mr Aladin Ismail
Mr William Godfrey Izard
Mr David M. Joyce
Mrs Philippa Kelly
Mr C.G.W. Kennedy
Mrs C.G.W. Kennedy
Mrs Ann Kerbs

Mr Larry Kerbs
Mr R.S. Kilburn
Mr Dunt King
Mr G.J.H. King
Mr James H. Kinoshita
Mrs Jean Kirkwood
Mr David G. Kohl
Mr Kazunoki Kunizuka
Mr Simon S.M. Kwan
Mrs Rowena Lack
Mr T.C. Lai
Dr Veronica Lam
Dr Michael Lau
Mrs Lau Poh-chit
Mr Lee Charm-fun
Mr J.S. Lee
Mrs Terese W.F. Lee
Mrs P. Leonard
Mr Justice Patrick F.X. Leonard
Mrs D.K. Lewis
Dr Choh-Ming Li, K.B.E. (Hon)
Mr Raymond Li
Mr H. Kenneth Liu
Mr K.S. Lo
Mrs Robert K.L. Lo
Mr Louis Lo Sai-keung
Professor Brian Lofts
Mrs Jean Loo
Mr C.C. Low
Mr Lu Li
Professor Ma Meng
Mr I. Macaulay
M/S Tike B. Macchetti
Mr Duncan J.H. Macintosh
Mrs Somsri Macintosh
Mrs Elsa Maggs
Mrs C. Manley
Dr Barbara Mao
Dr Philip Mao Wen-chee
Mrs Barbara Marion
Mr Stephen Markbreiter

Mr Alan Mason
Mr Peter W. Matthews
Mr Warwick S. Matthews
Mr George A. Mendenhall
Mr J. McCarlie
Mrs P.M. McCarlie
Mr Brian Shane McElney
Mrs E.D. Miller
Mr Robert Fenwick Miller
Mr Richard J.E.H. Mills-Owens
Mrs Bagwanti Mohan
Mr Ng Kai Yuen
Mr Peter Emile Ozeuf
Miss P. Nye
Mr John Hugh Pain
Mrs Alice Y. Piccus
Mr Robert P. Piccus
Mrs P.M. Pridham
Mr Richard E. Radez
Mr James G. Robinson
Mrs Joanne Robinson
Mrs Doreen E.J. Saddler
Mr Gordon F. Saddler
Mrs Irene Saunders
Mrs Laura H. Sherman
Mrs Vera T. Shiu
Miss Toni Smith
Miss Anna Victoria Siu
Mr Siu Tsun-tak
Mrs Angela D. Szeto
Mrs Laine Talamo
Mr Laurence C.S. Tam
Mr G.E. Taylor
Mr Paul Ti Po-Shing
Professor David Todd
Mr Andrew Tse
Mrs Tseng Chun Wai-yee
Mrs Priscilla Tso
Dr Tso Shiu-chiu
Mrs Nguyet Tuyet
Mr Richard Wang

Mr John Warner
Miss Ann M. Wilkinson
Mrs Joy Wong Ling-shang
Mr Edwin Wong
Judge T.L. Yang

Mr Yuen Chi-chew
Mr N.M. Yuen
Mrs Adrian Zecha
Mrs Doris Zimmern

(As at October 1, 1974)

NON-RESIDENTIAL MEMBERS OF THE SOCIETY

Mr David P.L. Chan
  Singapore
Mr J.E. Clemens
  Malta
Mrs B. Cullings
  England
The Viscount Errington
  Singapore
Mr F. Hickley
  Singapore
Mrs P.F.I. Hickley
  Singapore
Baron De Koenigswarter
  Philippines

Mr John Munro
  Australia
Mrs B.J. Oline
  Japan
Mr James L. Rea
  Philippines
Mr Alfred P. Rochelle Thomas
  United States of America
Mr James P. Rooney
  Thailand
Mr Michael Smithies
  Indonesia

(As at October 1, 1974)

1976

THE ORIENTAL CERAMIC SOCIETY OF HONG KONG

COMMITTEE 1975-76

President:	Dr Philip Mao Wen-chee
Vice-President:	Mr B.S. McElney
Hon. Secretary:	Mr Duncan Macintosh
Hon. Chinese Secretary:	Dr Michael Lau
Hon. Recording Secretary:	Mrs E.L. Alleyne
Hon. Treasurer:	Miss C.M. Goldney
Hon. Editor:	Mr R. Jones-Parry
Committee Member:	Dr Ip Yee
Committee Member:	Professor B. Lofts
Committee Member:	Mr Edwin Wong

EDITOR'S NOTE

The *Bulletin* is the official annual publication of the Oriental Ceramic Society of Hong Kong. While it is intended that the *Bulletin* should serve to put on permanent record a selection of the addresses presented in the annual programme of the Society, other contributions and suggestions for forth-coming issues will be welcomed.

R. Jones-Parry

CONTENTS

The Role of the Potter in the Discovery and the Development of Metallurgy in Ancient China— with Particular Reference to Kiln and Furnace Construction

NOEL BARNARD

Unlike the major metallurgical cultures of the West which owed their knowledge of metals, in the first instance, to the lithic industry and thus the characteristic 'smithy' aspect attending manufacturing methods throughout the greater part of their later development, the beginnings of metallurgy in China were very much an off-shoot of the ceramic industry which was at a highly advanced state at that time.

It was the potter who influenced the design of the furnace, the crucible, clay model preparation, and the making of sectional moulds. In the earliest manifestations of metal manufacturing that have come to light over the last five or six decades of archaeological discovery, there is virtually no evidence at all of copper or bronze artifacts constructed by metal-working procedures — particularly in the case of the few rather primitive-appearing knives, awls, spatulae, etc. that have been recovered from aeneolithic sites such as Ta-ho-chuang (大何莊), at Yung-ching (永靖) and Huang-niang-niang-t'ai, Wu-wei (皇娘娘台, 武威) in Kansu.

The casting of containers of more complex shape, amongst which *chia* and *chüeh*-wine-cups (斝、爵) seem to have been the earliest types attempted, was effected by assemblies of clay sectional moulds and cores whose sophistication in design and construction may be claimed to out-rival the comparatively meagre attainments in piece-mould casting technology elsewhere in the Ancient World. It is true that knowledge of metals and of casting methods arose much later in China. However, the evidence available to us indicates most persuasively that the

1

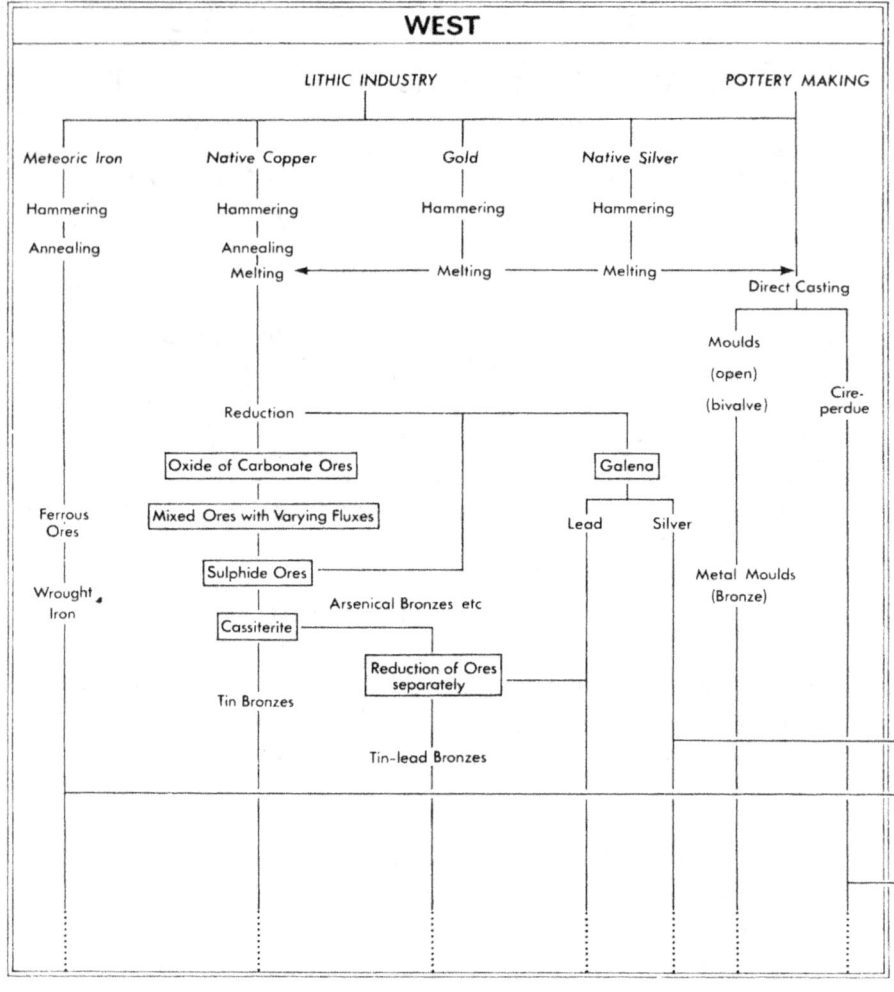

Figure 1 A diagrammatic rendering of contrasting aspects of the origins and development of metallurgy in the West and in China. Particular attention is directed to the pre-Metal Age motivating factors—the lithic industry in the West and the ceramic industry in China. This Table is reproduced from Barnard & Sato *Metallurgical Remains of Ancient China* (p. 69, Table 6) where in the data is fully discussed. In this diagram horizontal broken lines indicate possible instances of technical influences from the West. The different horizontal levels of the data in the two sections of the diagram may be regarded significant chronologically in a rather generalised way.

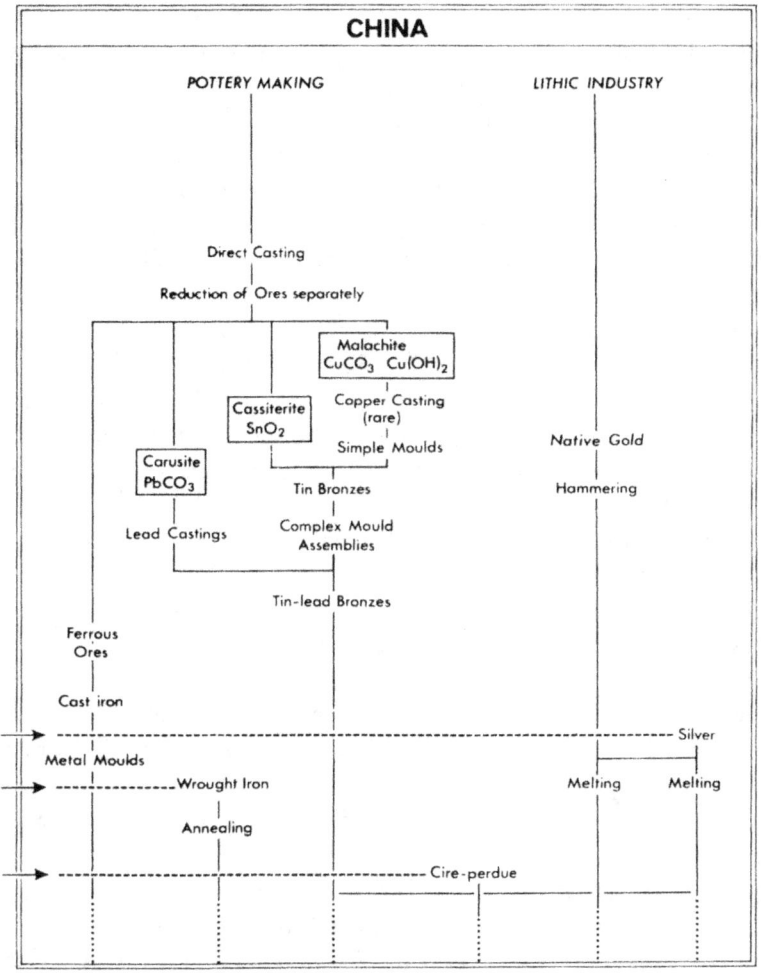

discovery was in all probability an indigenous one.

Any consideration of the question of the origins of metallurgy in China and of its development over the first two millenia, at least, must involve the student in an investigation of the several highly relevant facets of the ceramic industry prior to the conjectured date of discovery of metallurgy (*circa* 2000 B.C.) and the nature of innovations that took place during the Chinese Bronze and Iron Ages. At the same time it is necessary that the student should familiarise himself with the general history of metallurgy in the Middle East and Europe. Accordingly, in this short appraisal of the significant role of the potter in the discovery and development of metallurgy in ancient China we may usefully consult, first of all, the general picture of the divergent lines of development in China and in the West as depicted diagrammatically in Figure 1. Then with this overall view of the situation in mind we may the better appreciate the importance of the potter in the Chinese scene. As the subject in all its essentials is a particularly involved one we shall concern ourselves in this paper mainly with the kiln and its development from Yang-shao to Han times. From the comparatively extensive data relating to the potters' kilns we are able to supplement the lesser understood aspects of the metallurgical furnace and, indeed, arrive at a fairly reliable reconstruction of the bronze-casting furnace in Shang and Chou times.

Excavations conducted over the last decade have yielded valuable information regarding the structures of kilns in Yang-shao, Lung-shan and Shang strata in various sites. Perhaps, one of the best reported kiln sites of Yang-shao date is that of Pan-p'o-ts'un (半坡村) near Hsi-an (西安), Shensi. The kiln structures were often of small scale and, as the reporters observe, only one or two large pots, or four to ten small pots could have been fired at once (*Hsi-an Pan-p'o*, p. 157). Two early types (Nos. 5 and 6) are represented by the more complete remains of No. 6 comprising the fire-chamber and two upward sloping heat-channels (flues) leading to the firing platform. Walls of the kiln were found baked hard and vitrified, resulting in a green-blue colour on the surfaces and red inside to a depth of 2-10 cm. A further type is represented by Nos. 3 and 4; the former is the most complete in many structural details (Figure 2), in particular the nature of the grate which has the ten small heat-vents opening from three flues — one at the rear and one on either side. The grate (or floor) of the baking-chamber is approximately a metre in diameter and located a couple of metres away from the present edge of the fire-chamber opening. The long tunnel-like structure of the fire-chamber is characteristic of other Yang-shao kilns; the fire chamber ranges from 0.7-1 metre in width and is about 80 cm in height. A third type of kiln, No. 2, is of vertical construction

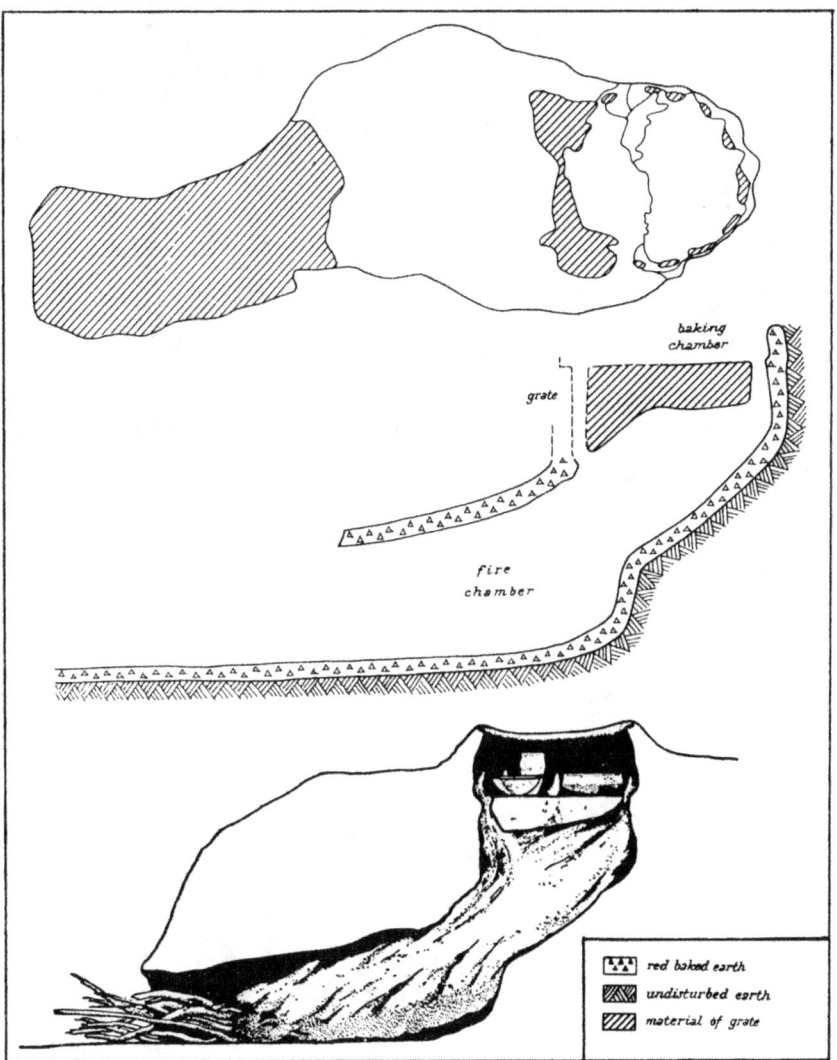

baking
chamber

grate

fire
chamber

red baked earth

undisturbed earth

material of grate

Figure 2   Plan and section of Kiln No. 3 (of Yang-shao date), Pan-p'o-ts'un, and a suggested reconstruction (after *Hsi-an Pan-p'o,* Figs, 116 & 118).

with the fire-chamber entirely fashioned by excavation into the natural yellow soil; only a single narrow heat-vent opens in the baking-chamber floor on which a pair of low pillars are

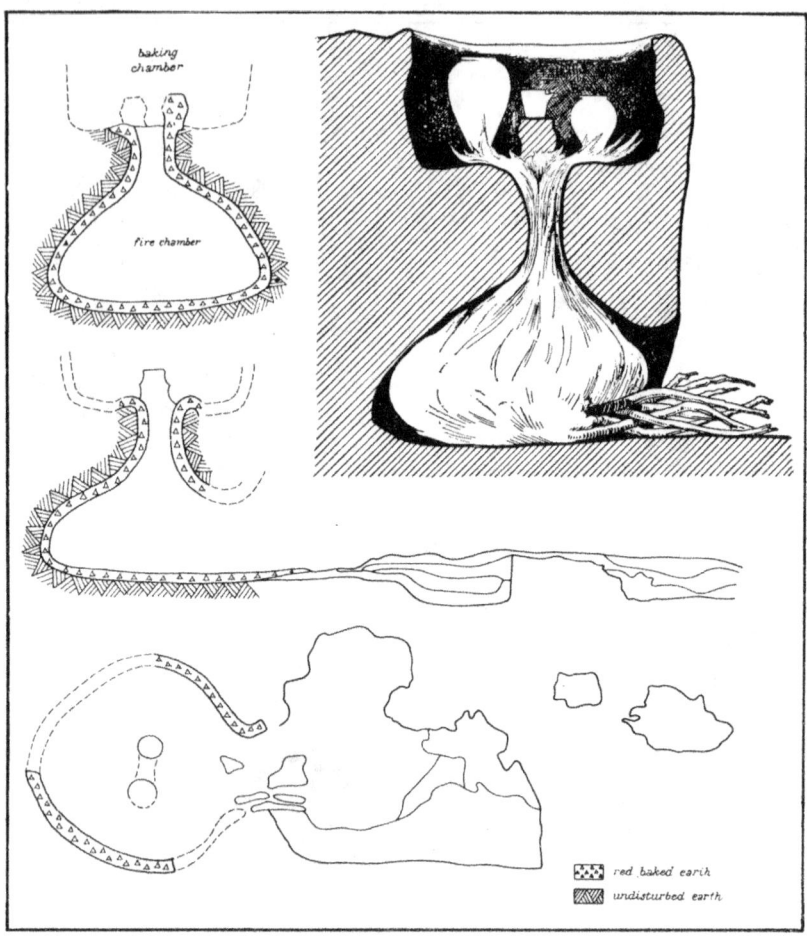

Figure 3   Plan and section of Kiln No. 2 (of Yang-shao date), Pan-p'o-ts'un, and a suggested reconstruction (after *Hsi-an Pan-p'o* Figs. 117 & 118).

constructed alongside the heat-vent opening (Figure 3). These may have been designed to spread the heat more evenly, or simply to place the unfired pottery on — so suggest the reporters (p. 160). However, the possibility that the pillars may have supported a grate should be kept in mind.

In each case the Pan-p'o kilns were basically constructed as excavations of the natural earth; in other Yang-shao kilns this

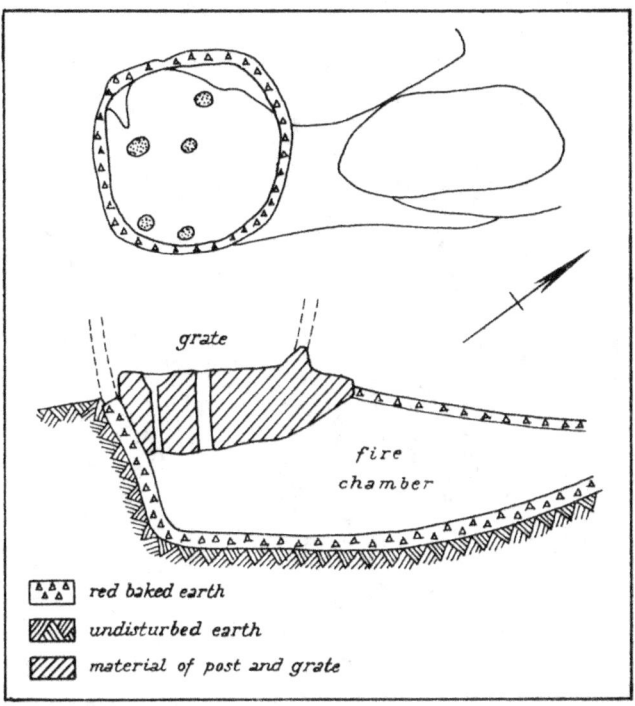

Figure 4 Plan and section of the P'ing-lu-hsien kiln (of Yang-shao date) with grate and heat vents (after *K'ao-ku* 1960.8:6).

feature is also apparent. A Yang-shao kiln excavated at P'ing-lu (平陸), Shansi shows not only the incorporation of a grate but also a horizontal extension of the fire-chamber door along the roof of the tunnel-like fire-chamber (Figure 4). One other Yang-shao kiln has been reported and illustrated in some detail. It was discovered at the Lin-shan-chai (林山砦) site near Cheng-chou. The fire-chamber is comparatively deeply excavated below the original ground surface, the lower part of the baking-chamber with heat-channels was also fashioned in the natural earth. The deep fire-chamber seems decidedly a feature proclaiming this kiln to be of a later stage of development than those with the shallow elongated structures but its lack of a grate poses a problem—possibly the heat-channels and the vented grate plus flues were originally two separate developments which only oc-

7

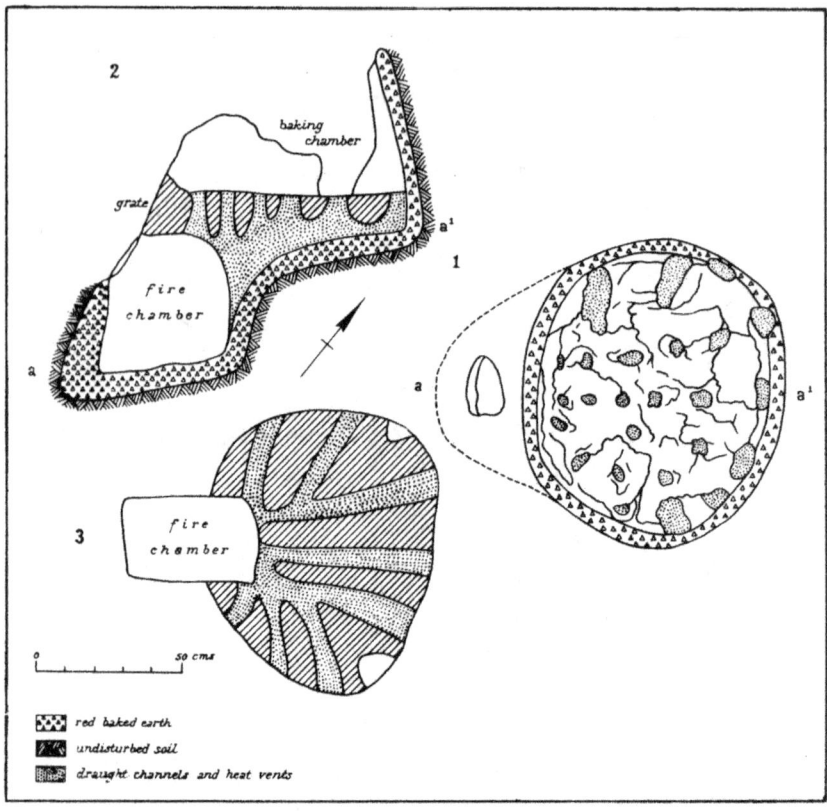

Figure 5 Plan and section of a Lung-shan period kiln at the Miao-ti-kou site, near Shan-hsien (陝縣). Honan (after *Miao-ti-kou yü San-li-ch'iao* (廟底溝與三里橋) pp. 19-22).

casionally came to be combined within the one kiln? (Figure 5).

It would appear thus that in Yang-shao times kiln designs reflect aspects of a period of innovation and experiment. Three kinds are known from presently available reports; one of these (Figure 4) is in principle far in advance of the others in terms of the general picture of structural evolution. The others with their tunnel-like fire-chambers may be classed as a more primitive version. The tunnel-like structure came to be dispensed with as the fire-chamber was gradually lowered below ground level to form a pit. As a consequence, provision had to be made to direct the heat more effectively into the higher baking-chamber — heat-

8

channels were the means adopted by some kiln constructors. The addition of a grate with heat-vents and flues was found by other kiln builders to effect much the same result. But with the addition of these two units, either separately or in combination, the depth of the fire-chamber had to be further increased and its former tunnel-like structure gave way to an open, rather steep-sided pit which was hollowed immediately alongside of, or just partly under, the baking-chamber. In Lung-shan sites the kilns are practically all found with both flues and vented grates and a well-defined fire-chamber (Figure 5). As in the Yang-shao examples, heat-channels only were still employed to some extent, but in the kilns with grates the heat-vents (usually in combination with flues) became an integral part of the grate unit. The major distinction to be observed between Yang-shao and Lung-shan kilns is the much deeper fire-chamber of the latter together with its consequent effect upon the other elements in the structure — the latter now, as a matter of course, had to be modified to suit the deeper fire-chamber and its tendency to move more and more under the baking-chamber area; thus heat-vents and flues were combined to become single functional units.

A kiln of Lung-shan date which was found in a comparatively complete state in the T'ang-ch'üan-kou (湯泉溝) site near Yen-shih (偃師), Honan (*KK* 1962.11: 562–563) has features which anticipate the structure of Shang period kilns. The fire-chamber and baking-chamber were in vertical position and separated by a grate smaller in diameter than the baking-chamber and held in position by six lumps of straw-grogged clay lodged between the edges of the grate and the baking-chamber walls; these left six openings functioning as heat-vents and flues, while in the centre was a single heat-vent. The grate rested on two oval-shaped narrow-waisted pillars and was affixed to them with blobs of straw-grogged clay. Both the vertical positioning of baking-chamber and fire-chamber and use of pillar supports for the grate are more generally characteristic of Shang kilns.

Kilns of Early and Middle Shang (Figure 6) exhibit the full development of a post to support the grate while the fire-chamber has infiltrated practically right under the baking-chamber. The

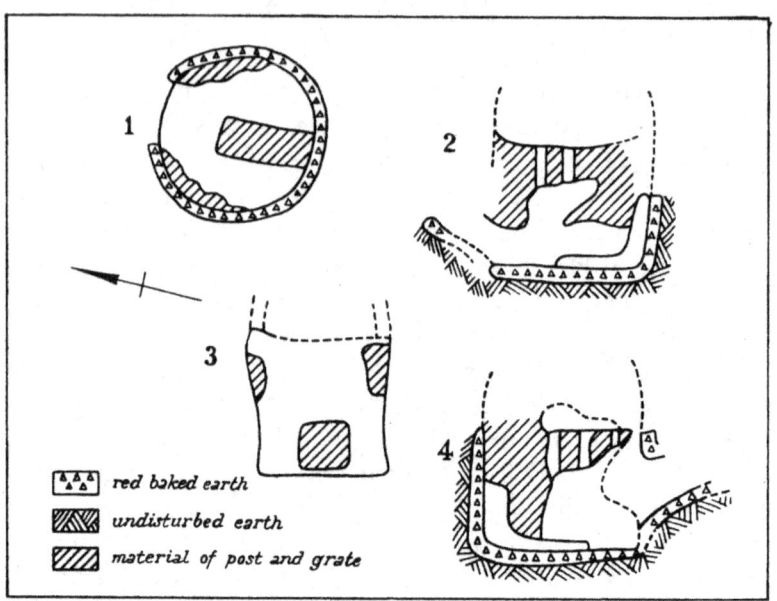

Figure 6   Lower Middle Shang kiln (No. C11E110, after *Wen-wu* 1957.10:59) excavated at Ming-kung-lu, Cheng-chou.

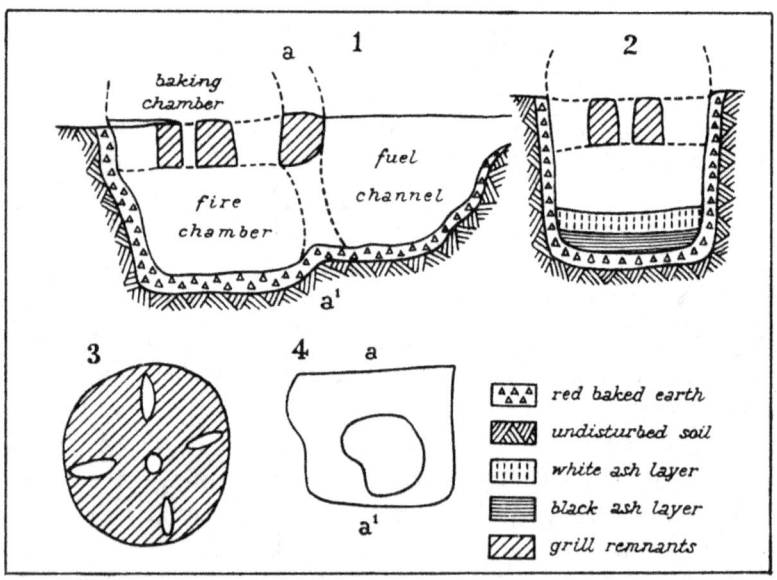

Figure 7   Late Shang kiln (No. C20E8, after *Wen-wu* 1957.10:59) also excavated at Cheng-chou (Pi-sha-kang).

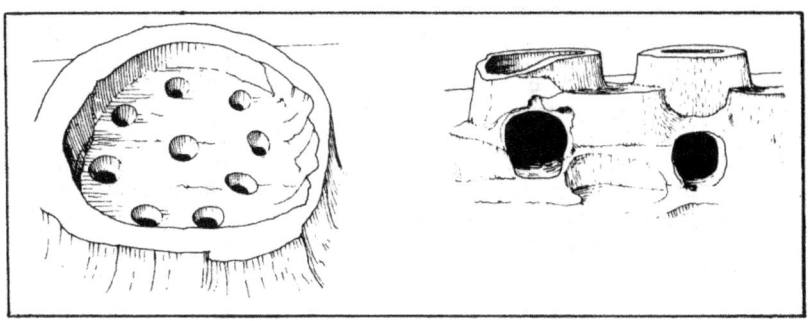

Figure 8   Two views of Late Shang period kilns (Nos. 3 and 4) at Chien-kou-ts'un, Han-tan (drawn after photographs in *K'ao-ku* 1961.4: Pl. 8).

Lower Middle Shang example, discovered in the Ming-kung-lu (銘公路) area, represents most of the general features of the fourteen kilns examined in this find; in most respects these later kilns differ little from that of the Early Shang phase. The grates averaging 25–30 cm in thickness are supported by posts and perforated by 'several tens' of heat-vents averaging 10 cm in diameter (*WW* 1957.10: 59). Many ash-pits around the kilns contain unbaked and baked pottery sherds, heaters, décor stamps, etc. (*KKHP* 1957.1: 57). In Late Shang the baking chamber is found placed completely above the fire-chamber. The post was often no longer required because the grate was fashioned to remain in position without support as in the Pi-sha-kang (碧沙崗) example (Figure 7). Two Shang kilns similar in construction with the fire chamber and baking chamber in vertical line were investigated at Chien-kou-ts'un, near Han-tan (邯鄲) in Ho-pei (*KK* 1961.4: 201). It was noted that the walls rose only a short distance above the grate and it appeared as though the structure was, this far, a permanent one (Figure 8). When the pottery was to be fired, it was placed in position on the grate, and a domed wall was then built up of coils of clay, or by clay slabs, from the shallow permanent wall level.

Somewhat more complex forms of kiln were excavated at Ch'ao-yen-chuang (曹演莊) near Hsing-t'ai (邢臺) in Hopei in 1954 and reported in some detail with photographs (*WW* 1956.12: 53–54, and *KKHP* 1958.4: 45–47). Three Shang period kilns were found. Kiln No. 1 appeared to be associated with a Late Shang stratum and Nos. 2 and 3 with an earlier (Upper Middle Shang?) level. Some details of No. 1 were discernible but reported in a rather hazy way. However, a particular point of interest in the description is the presence of a 'kiln-door' in the sense of an opening to allow access to the baking-chamber. This would imply a permanent dome cover (cf. the Greek vertical kiln, Figure 9). Kiln No. 2, at Ch'ao-yen-chuang, similar in essentials to No. 3, was the more complete and of a rather complicated construction. It comprised a round flat-bottomed pit dug to a depth of 28 cm below the ground surface with walls built up of plastered straw-tempered clay to a thickness of 6 cm forming the baking-chamber. The fire-chamber was tunnelled 54 cm below the grate surface and hollowed out into a pear-shaped space and was then lined inside with straw-tempered clay. Its inside measurements were: length 160 cm, width 135 cm, and height 57 cm. The floor of the fire-chamber was thus in the shape of a horse-hoof with its sides rising upwards; where the sides connected with the wall of the baking-chamber, a narrow ledge 4 cm in height and 12 cm wide encircled halfway around the fire-chamber wall. The opening of the fire-chamber was also hoof-shaped, 63 cm in height and 42 cm wide and facing the east.

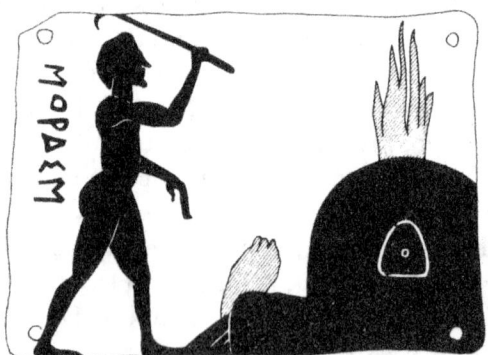

Figure 9   The dome-shaped structure of a Greek vertical kiln with kiln door at side, represented on a black-figured clay plaque from Corinth, sixth century B.C. (redrawn after *A History of Technology*, Vol. 1, p. 392).

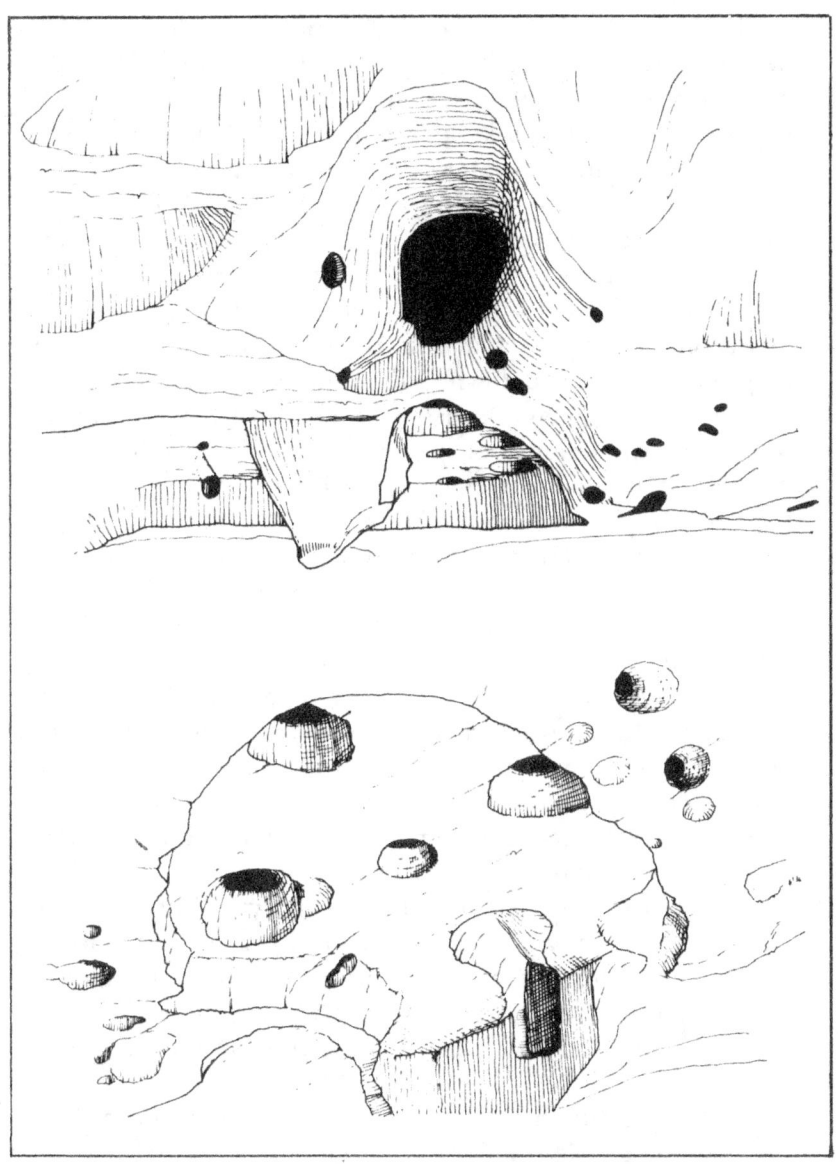

Figure 10 Two views of Kiln No. 2, Ch'ao-yen-chuang, Hsing-t'ai, drawings based upon very poor quality photographs in *Wen-wu* (1956.12:53–54). This Upper Middle Shang kiln, and others found nearby exhibit complex internal structures involving "smoke-holes", dampers, etc.

The grate was 152 cm in diameter and 50 cm thick with six heat-vents, one in the centre almost square in shape, 16 × 17 cm, and the others hollowed around the perimeter of the grate touching against the baking-chamber walls (Figure 10). The latter were oval in shape averaging 24 × 25 cm. The heat-vents were cut downwards to form flues connecting with the fire-chamber. In the upper sections, and sometimes in the centre sections of the flues were found clay dampers for controlling the heat. Seven 'smoke-holes', as the reporters term them, were located in the kiln wall and some around the outside of the kiln wall — these branched downwards to connect with the heat-vent flues within the grate. Diameters ranged from 8 to 12 cm. In some cases two or three of the 'smoke-holes' joined below the ground surface to form a single stem which then connected with the flues. Near to the 'smoke-holes', and also to the flues (and located at various distances) were found a total of 16 round holes of approximately the same size as the seven 'smoke-holes'. They were filled with black/grey earthy material — their function could not be assessed.

Although no vestiges of a 'kiln-door' remained, the reporters have suggested that one section of the kiln wall ledge towards the north which did not appear to have had the wall extended upwards, and where there were no 'smoke-holes' in the flat area outside the extant wall ledge, may have been the access opening in the baking-chamber dome.

Remains of charcoal amongst the ashes indicate the fuel to have been derived from wood. Of most interest amongst the ceramic remains was a number of moulds used to form the leg area of ceramic *Li*-cauldrons — I assume the term (鬲腿) *li-t 'ui* would be descriptive of what is termed 'inter-leg core' in bronze casting parlance.

It is unfortunate that a really detailed study was not made of this pottery establishment as it is quite evident that several features of exceptional importance which are apparently not preserved (or not reported) in other sites, were present. Not only are the kilns the vertical type of Middle and Late Shang, but the complex nature of the baking-chamber, grate, heat-vent flues, and 'smoke holes' would seem possible of assessment if more detailed investigation had been undertaken. The presence of dampers to control the furnace blast — possibly operated by some means through the so-called 'smoke-holes' or, perhaps, the other 16 holes — offers most important though tantalizing evidence on the technical progress attained. But all this must remain incompletely appraised here until some further similar site is discovered and the details more fully and authoritatively reported.

With the location of the grate immediately above the fire-chamber and forming a complete ceiling, flues extending in a diagonal direction were no longer needed. The upward movement of heat was now accelerated more effectively by natural draught and required no urging as hitherto along horizontal or diagonal passages. The heat-vents became more regular in shape and decreased in numbers, and were more evenly spaced around the grate forming usually a petal pattern. The aim towards a more even distribution of heat, as shown in the arrangement of the vents, probably indicates aspects of the artisans' attempts to control more efficiently the high temperatures attainable in the kilns. As to any extensive application of the complex 'smoke-hole' + damper + heat-vent-flue system of the Ch'ao-yen-chuang kilns, other instances are yet to be discovered. Generally, it would appear at present, that less involved kiln designs were favoured.

Two examples of Western Chou kilns have been described in some detail; one (kiln No. 5) in a group of ten kilns excavated west of Lo-shui-ts'un (洛水村), near Ch'ang -an, (長安),Shensi is practically identical in structure to the Pi-sha-kang kiln (Figure 7); vertical positioning of the baking-chamber and the fire-chamber and the lack of a pillar to support the five-vent grate. Interestingly, it was observed that amongst the usual wood and grass ash remains in the fire-chambers throughout this group, there were considerable quantities of animal dung ash. Roofing tiles (illustrated in the report) were produced in several of the kilns as well as the usual types of household pottery. The excavators refer to a kiln (No. 1) they excavated near Ma-wang-ts'un (馬王村), Ch'ang-an, in 1959 (*KK* 1963.8: 412, note 7) in order to support their views on the nature of the baking chamber construction in the Lo-shui-ts'un examples. Although the Ma-wang-ts'un kiln has not been reported elsewhere, the few details recorded in this note are especially important: ". . . the kiln was comparatively complete. When excavated, the baking-chamber was found filled with red-fired earthenware pieces of straw-tempered clay which had fallen in. Furthermore, upon the basis of the curvature of a remaining section of the baking-chamber wall (about 70 cm high) it was evident that it was originally a dome-like shape and in the centre was a hole acting as a chimney." The second kiln (Figure 11) derives from the K'o-hsing-chuang (客省莊) site also in the vicinity of Ch'ang-an (see *Feng-hsi fa-chüeh pao-kao* Fig. 1 for a useful map of these famous sites) — three kilns were excavated and the one reported in detail was found in a circular dwelling site (H172, *op cit.*, p. 172). The two others were of identical construction. As may be noted in the plan and sections, the K'o-hsing-chuang kiln has marked affinities with the Lung-shan San-li-ch'iao (三里橋) kiln and the Chien-kou-ts'un (澗溝村) No. 1 and may thus indicate that two general types of construction continued through Shang into Western Chou times: (a) kilns with vented grates placed partly or wholly over the fire-chamber, and (b) kilns with no grate but a platform (or hearth) with heat-channels, rising from the separately positioned fire-chamber. So far, Shang examples seem to be exclusively of the former type. The second form of kiln, however, may have been the prototype for the horizontal kiln with rear chimney which dates from Chan-kuo times. It would seem upon due study of the description of the K'o-hsing-chuang kiln (H172), and the diagram, that the placement of the smoke aperture is one tending towards the rear. But there is, of course, no suggestion here that anything approaching the construction of a 'chimney' as in the Chan-kuo period kilns (Figures 14 and 15) is to be implied. Fuel employed in the K'o-hsing-chuang kilns was almost entirely straw, the ashes of which predominated; only a few vestiges of wood charcoal or wood ash were present. In each of the kilns discussed so far vitrification of the interior surfaces of the kiln structures is noted in practically every case, thus evincing the general attainment of high temperatures and this with fuels of various kinds.

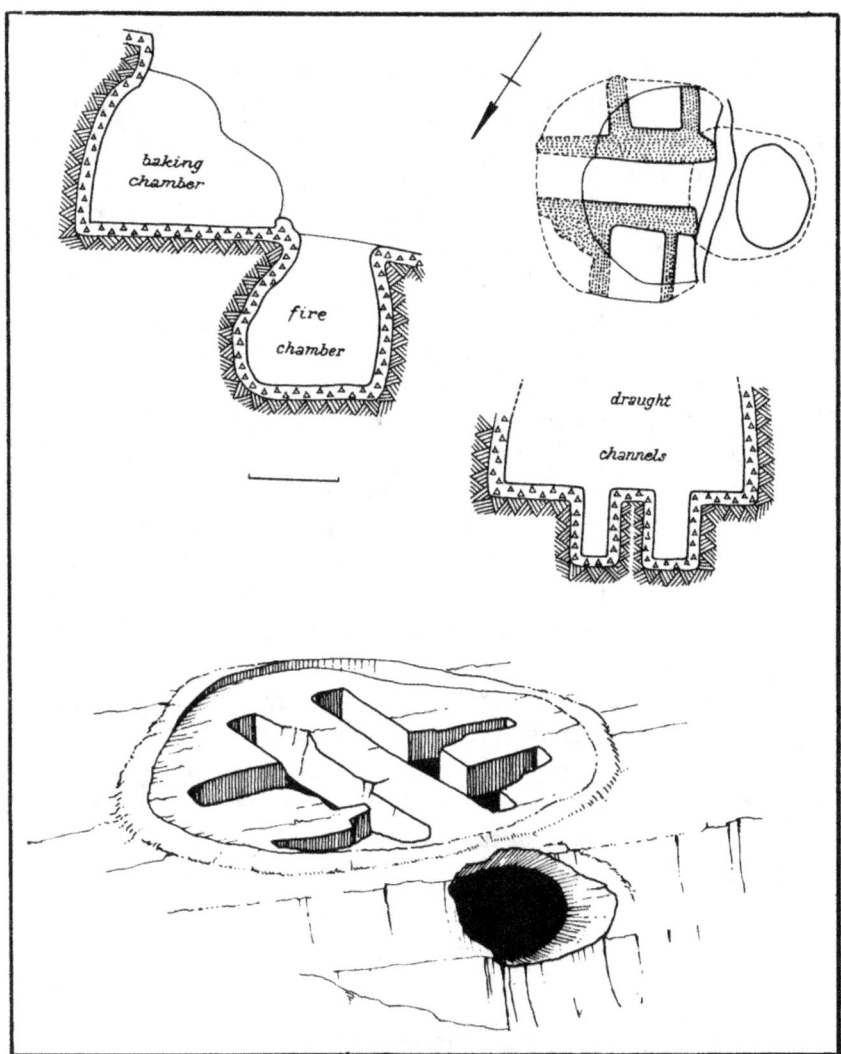

Figure 11   Plan, section, and sketch (from published photographs) of Kiln No. H172, K'o-hsing-chuang, Ch'ang-an (*loc. cit.*).

Simple though the structures were, temperatures as high as 1400°C have been assessed in the cases of kilns in pre-metal pottery culture sites. Yoshida Mitsukuni (吉田光邦) in his study of ancient Chinese metallurgy (*Tōhōgakuhō* (東方學報) [Kyōto] Vol. 29, 1959, p. 58) suggested this maximum figure upon the basis of the chemical composition of the fired pottery and the characteristic vitrification of the clay lining of the kilns. The walls of the fire-chambers and the baking-chambers have often been observed to have attained a high degree of hardness while the interior surfaces usually have become glazed with a husk of vitrified green-tinged clay. Interesting evidence of the fierce heat achieved may be observed in the shape of 'wasters' amongst some of the pottery products from Middle Shang levels unearthed at Cheng-chou (Figure 12). Scientifically excavated porcelain sherds of Western Chou date have recently been subjected to laboratory examination (*KK* 1960.9 48–52) and the firing temperature of 1200°C (±30°) has been fairly precisely determined. Fragments of the materials studied when heated to a temperature of 1300°C, for instance, resulted in the glaze melting and spreading erratically — this test would seem to imply that fairly effective control was possible while the general evidence available would seem to allow us to assert that, at least as early as Lung-shan times, it was indeed, well within the temperature attainments of pottery kilns to melt copper.

All pottery kilns reported from pre-Shang levels are in general principles of construction reverberatory furnaces; in Yang-shao sites some kilns are perhaps to be regarded as marginal cases when precise classification is attempted. These may be admitted, however, to have a fairly distinct division between the heat source and the baking-chamber as far as the overall plan of the structure is concerned — the elongated fire-chamber would not only serve

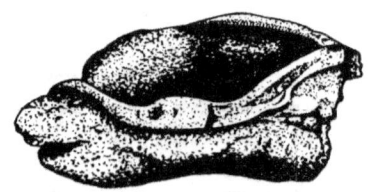

Figure 12   Example of a ''waster'' from Middle Shang levels at Cheng-chou (drawn after *K'ao-ku hsüeh-pao* 1957. 1: Pl. 7). The cone refactoriness of clay (i.e., the temperature at which clay softens, probably *circa* 1300°C — see *Metallurgical Remains of Ancient China*, p. 36).

to keep the burning charcoal separated from the contents of the baking-chamber, but would also function quite effectively in drawing a strong natural draught through the fuel into the baking-chamber. Pottery fired by the simple 'hearth' or 'smother-fire' technique is sometimes found in the most primitive Yang-shao levels, but little information exists as to the nature of the stacking method involved.

A tentative scheme of kiln evolution is proposed in Figure 13 based upon available data such as we have considered in the preceding paragraphs. It may be valid to compare this with a similar evolutionary scheme after that compiled by H.H. Coghlan ('Some Fresh Aspects of the Prehistoric Metallurgy of Copper', *Antiquitaries Journal*, Vol. XXII, 1942). Whether we may accept the interesting variation of the grate development manifested in these two sequences as providing a feature of some significance, however, will remain a problem of some magnitude for some time yet. Nevertheless, the invention of the grate, which in the West may have originated in the Caspian-Mesopotamian area, may well have been independently reinvented somewhat later amongst the pottery cultures of China. Although the invention seems to be connected with kiln construction in its beginnings in both cultural spheres, it is quite obvious from a technical point of view that two quite different problems motivated the respective inventors. The Mesopotamian potter was concerned right from the outset with a vertical structure and sought in an early stage to raise both fuel and pottery articles above the floor by means of the grate and later placed the grate intermediate between fuel and baking-chamber. In China the most elementary form of kiln so far reported followed the configuration of the ground and was partly excavated to form an almost horizontal structure — the evolution towards a vertical alignment of baking-chamber and fire-chamber was accompanied by heat-channels at first then developed the combination of flues and grate. The former was to assist in directing the horizontal (or more usually diagonal) passage of heat to the baking-chamber, while the latter offered better separation of the burning fuel and also a means of decreasing the distance between the heat source and baking-chamber. It may be

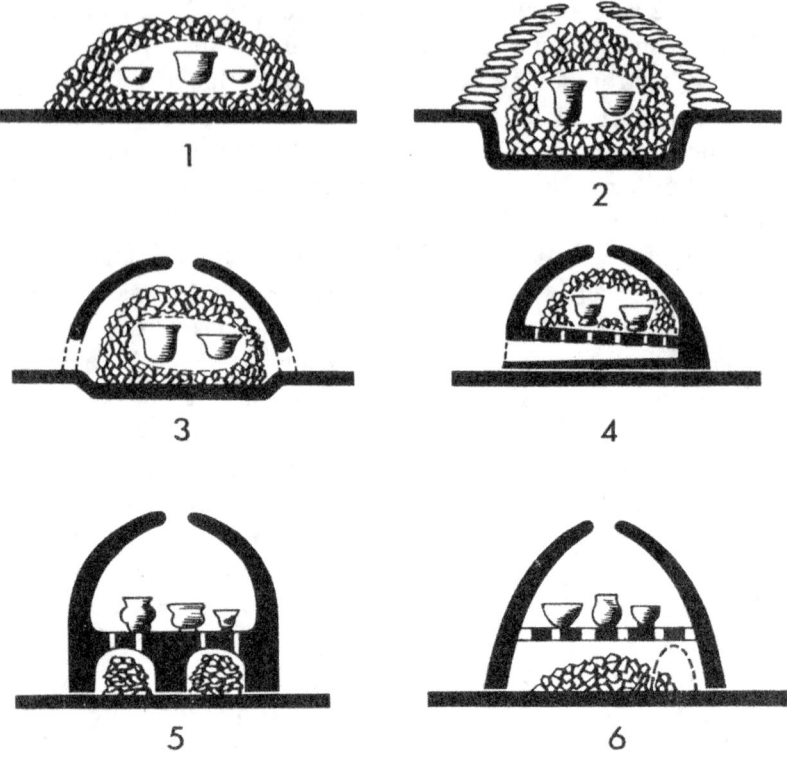

Figure 13   Kiln evolution in China (A-F) and in the West (1-6). The latter are based upon data in R. Ghirshman's *Fouilles de Sialk* (see H.H. Coghlan, *op. cit.*). In drawing attention to these variant structural approaches, it should be appreciated that a more exhaustive investigation into the "Western" data would be needed to confirm the contrasts as pictured above.

observed, too, that the evolution from horizontal to vertical kiln structures in ancient China involved not only the movement of the fire-chamber towards the baking-chamber, but also the lower placement of the former in relation to ground level. In other words, the Chinese potter constructed his kilns largely by excavation to effect the vertical arrangement which in the West (particularly the ancient Middle East) was simply achieved by an upward building from the ground surface — a characteristic method of brick-using cultures.

20

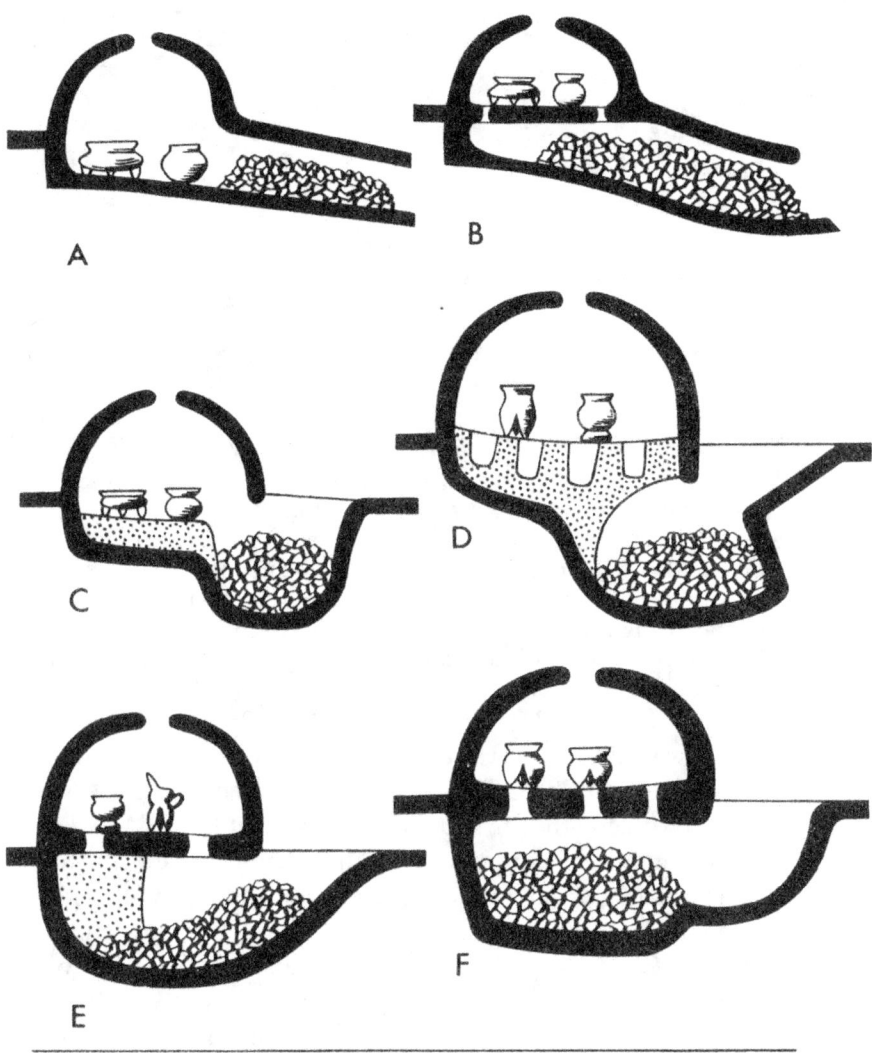

Kilns of the Chan-kuo period manifest a marked structural change and are well represented in the Wu-chi-ts'un (午汲村) site near Wu-an-hsien (武安縣), Hopei (*KK* 1959.7: 338–342) but unfortunately no diagrams have been published and some points in the reporters' descriptions are difficult to interpret precisely (drawings in Figure 14 are based upon the poor quality photographs). Nevertheless, it is sufficiently clear that the

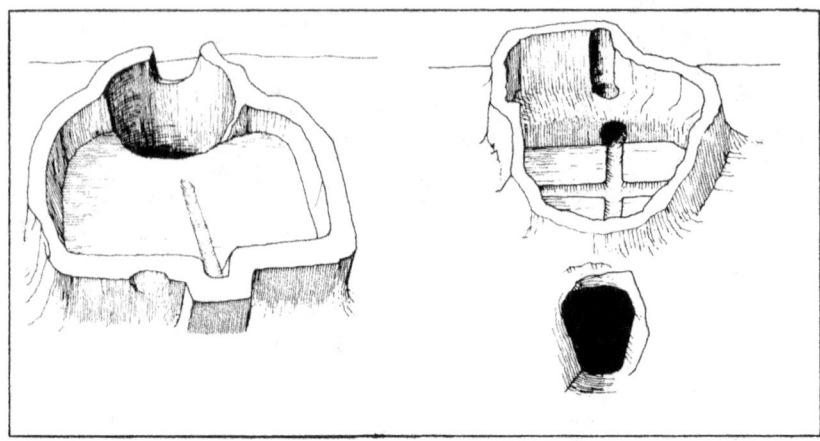

Figure 14   Drawings based upon published photographs of several of the Wu-chi-ts'un kilns (after *K'ao-ku* 1959.7:338-342). Chan-kuo period kilns of this type comprise the earliest examples so far reported in China, or elsewhere in the Ancient World. The use of ''chimneys'' in the rear kiln wall and sometimes connecting heat channels fashioned along the baking chamber floor comprise a marked change in kiln design which has persisted in China until recent times. Similar types in the West appear amongst Roman remains of somewhat later date.

vertical assembly which was apparently firmly established, from Shang to Western Chou times no longer prevailed. The grate was dispensed with and the fire-chamber became a pit located between the fire-chamber opening and the baking chamber platform; fire channels leading to 'chimneys' fashioned at the rear wall of the baking-chamber are seen as especially significant innovations. Two of the Chan-kuo period kilns, Nos. 1 and 2 (T44 and T26), are accompanied by sufficient description to allow a reasonably reliable reconstruction of the major elements in their design; plans and elevation of both are presented in Figure 15 and these may be compared with the drawings in Figure 14 based upon the original photographic reproductions (*op. cit.*, Pl. 8, opp. p. 357). Kiln No. 1 (T44) is 200 cm in overall length and 165 cm in width, the greatest height of the remains is 80 cm. The fire-chamber door faces the east and the fire-chamber comprises a funnel-shaped excavation 90 cm wide and 80 cm deep; it does not extend beneath the baking-chamber platform thus indicat-

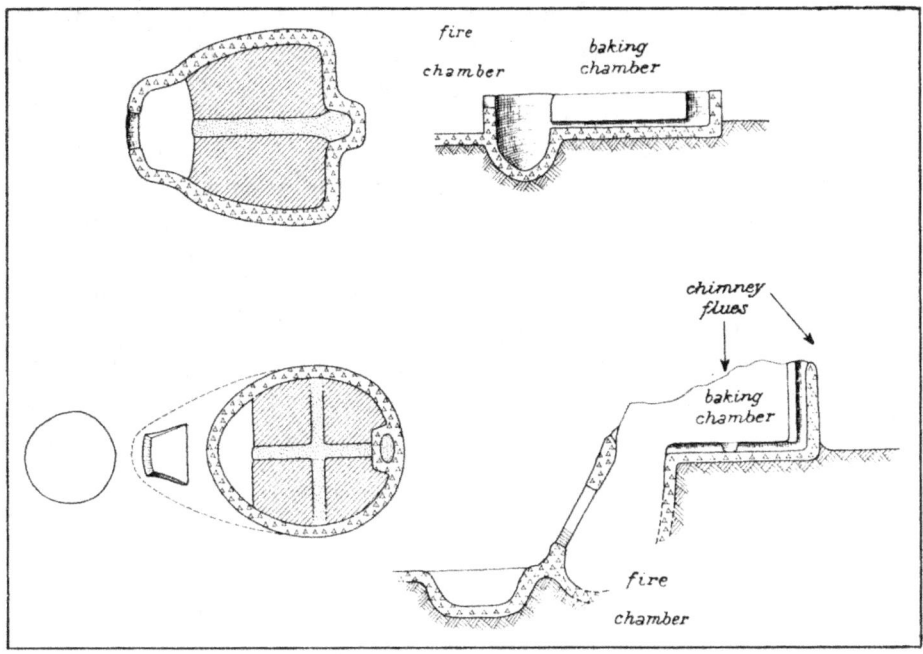

Figure 15   Reconstructions of two Wu-chi-ts'un kilns (Nos. 1 and 2: T44 and T26) presented here as plans and sections. These are based upon details recorded in the report and the published photographs.

ing an abrupt change in plan from the earlier kilns we have surveyed. A shallow heat-channel runs lengthwise along the platform to meet the U-shaped outjutting section of the rear wall which obviously functioned as the chimney base. The inside surfaces had vitrified to a green-grey colour and throughout the 10–20 cm thickness of the walls and floor of the kiln the heat-hardened clay structure had turned red. Traces of wood charcoal indicated the nature of the fuel employed while the preponderance of *Tou*-pedestal-bowl sherds suggested the type of pottery fired. Kiln No. 2 (T26) differed in some respects. Its overall length was 227 cm and width 140 cm; the fire-chamber door 30 cm wide at the bottom and 45 cm high. The highest remnant of the structure measured 165 cm. A single chimney connected with a deep cross-shaped heat-channel.

Other kilns ranging from Chan-kuo to Han date in this

complex are reported with varying amounts of detail. In general they have much the same principles in structure as shown in Figure 15; each one has a chimney and when enclosed as in the case of T26 an opening is present to receive the heat-channel — a feature which is common to them all. The baking-chamber walls are, in most cases, perpendicular and the ground-plan either rectangular, circular, or oval. In the rear walls most of them have the remains of one chimney only, but there are some with as many as three. In such cases the individual chimneys meet together to form a single large unit (see Figure 16).

None of the earlier kilns seem to exhibit specific components in their structure which might have given rise to these new

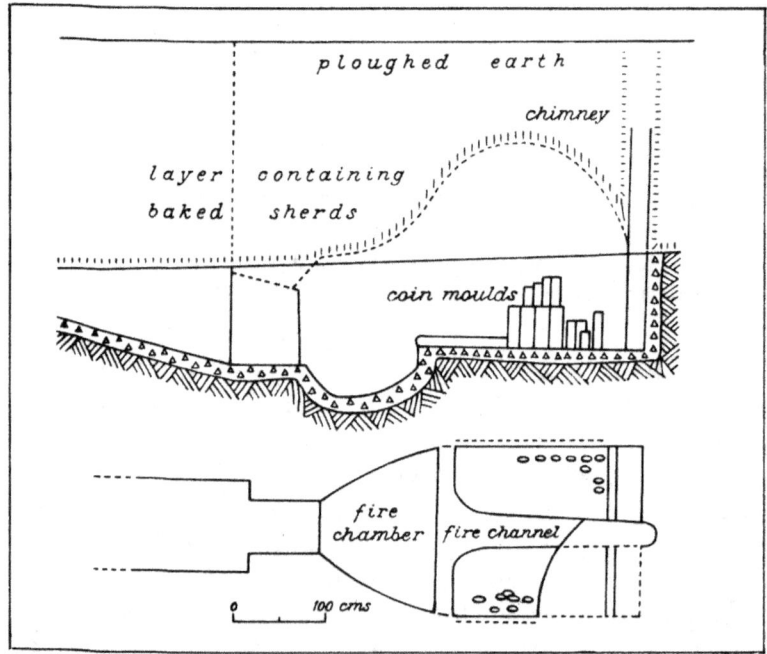

Figure 16   Han period kilns illustrating the continued development of the horizontal kiln type with rear chimneys. Above: Hsin Mang (新莽) period kiln used for the baking of coin moulds; excavated in the northern suburbs of Hsian (after *K'ao-ku* 1965.5:243–251). Opposite: A Late Western Han kiln (No. 2) also excavated at Hsi-an (after *K'ao-ku* 1964.4:180) — used in the manufacture of bricks, eaves-tiles, etc.

24

developments. Although during the general period (Ch'un-ch'iu -Chan-kuo) when this type of kiln construction appears, numerous outside influences were entering and modifying Chinese art and craftsmanship, yet one is hard-put to point to any contemporaneous — or more important, any earlier — non-Chinese horizontal kiln type that might be claimed to have motivated so marked a change in design. The placement of a chimney, or chimneys, at the rear wall of the kiln and the location of the fire-chamber at the front of the structure with heat-channels directing the heat along a horizontal line to the chimney base and thus promoting an efficient degree of circulation throughout the baking chamber, are, in effect, features which would normally be expected to precede the design of the more sophisticated horizontal kilns such as those in Figure 16. The Wu-chi-ts'un Chan-kuo structures are self-evidently the ancestors of the Han period horizontal kilns in this Figure. Why the new approach to kiln design occurred is a matter that requires further investigation (necessarily accompanied by considerably

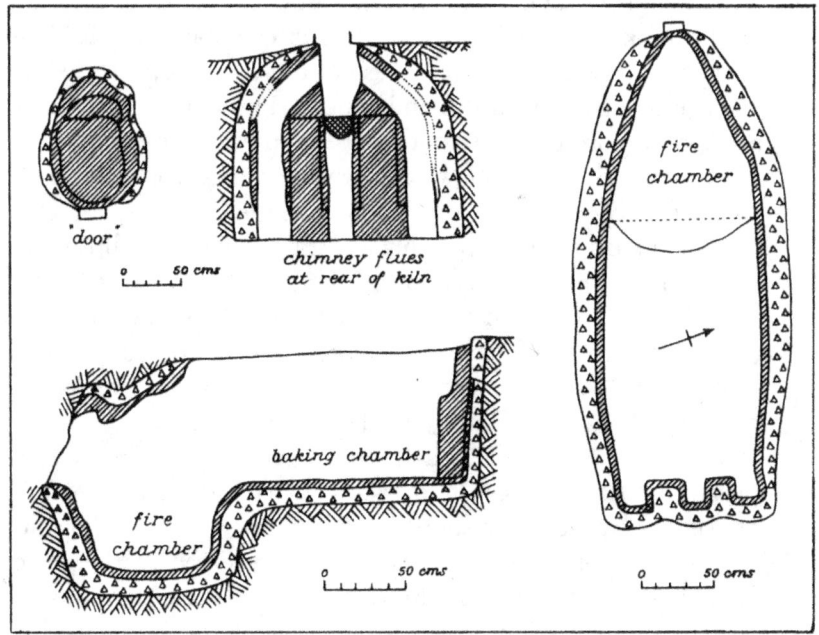

more research than I have attempted here) in non-Chinese areas for comparable kiln structures that may be contemporaneous with, or earlier than, the Chinese examples briefly surveyed here. They may be dated with due caution *circa* 600-300 B.C.

The horizontal kiln of the Han period, it is tentatively suggested, was far in advance of the few known instances of kilns built on the same general principles in other areas of the ancient world. In vertical structures, as already observed, a problem of some magnitude attends the regulation of draught. Some method of baffling the vertical, or near-vertical kiln is necessary, so as to equalize temperature and atmosphere between the two vertical chambers. Possibly the ancient Chinese achieved sufficient control by quite simple means which, however, cannot be reconstructed upon the limited basis of presently available data and the present lack of active experimental data that could be obtained from reconstructions of the ancient kilns. The rarity of 'wasters' from pottery sites and the early production of porcelain and glazed ware provide ample evidence of well regulated firing procedures effected in the pre-Wu-chi-ts'un type kilns.

In the horizontal kiln, the heated gases are thrown down from the dome-like roof structure and, after circulation in the baking-chamber, proceed to the open base of the chimney, directed by channels along the baking-chamber floor. This indirect method of exit allows more efficient control of the interior temperature by simply governing the inflow of air through the door of the fire-chamber. In certain elements of structure, the Chan-kuo and Han horizontal kilns manifest possibly direct links with the Lung-shan types, e.g. in the front location of the pit-like form of the fire-chamber, and also the general practice of excavating the foundation of the complex below ground level. The heat-channel is no doubt descendant from the flues employed in both Yang-shao and Lung-shan kilns, while the diagonal heat-channel system in the Western Chou K'o-hsing-chuang example would appear to offer evidence of an even stronger connection — but there is no chimney. The source of the chimney, however, in this particular complex cannot at present be traced back earlier than the Wu-chi-ts'un examples. Its invention, or introduction, had obviously rendered obsolete the function of the vented grate.

Heat-channels and connecting chimneys of even greater complexity may be studied in the case of the Wang Mang (王莽) coin-mould baking kiln excavated at Kuo-chia-ts'un (郭家村) in the northern suburbs of Hsian, 1958 (*KK* 1965.5: 248–249) wherein a total of five chimneys are incorporated in the structure (see Figure 17 for further details). From Han times it is interesting to observe upon cursory study of T'ang, Sung and Ming examples how the principle of the horizontal kiln has remained virtually unchanged.

With this brief sketch of the nature and evolution of pottery kilns we may now consider ourselves reasonably equipped to attempt a number of interpolations from the comparatively

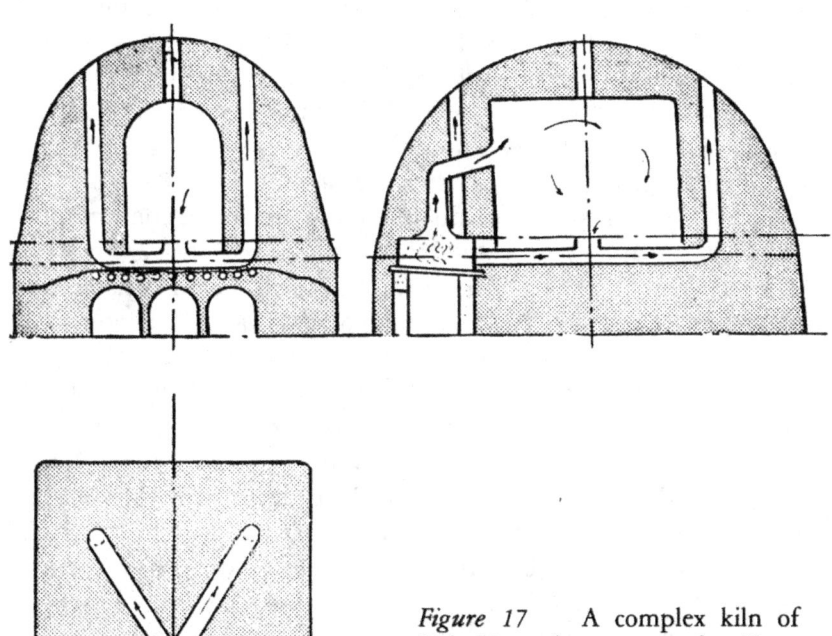

Figure 17 A complex kiln of Hsin Mang date excavated at Kuo-chia-ts'un, Hsi-an with five chimneys and of a particularly ingenious design to effect good circulation and regulation of the furnace draught. Used for the baking of coin moulds (after *K'ao-ku* 1965.5:243-251).

27

meagre evidence relating to the construction of bronze casting furnaces.

Only three bronze casting sites have as yet been reported in sufficient detail to allow some reconstruction of the furnaces to be attempted. The earliest of these is associated with Lower and Upper Middle Shang remains at Cheng-chou. An area of 1,050 square metres was the larger of two places uncovered that were clearly foundry sites. More than a thousand piece-mould fragments were found as well as crucibles, copper ore, slag, charcoal, etc. (*KKHP* 1957.1:56). In the smaller site there appeared to be some connection between the casting activities and a building remains. But no description of an actual furnace is given. A main point of interest is the amount of copper ore and slag reported which would seem to indicate that smelting was carried out in the area. The large number of piece-moulds show that casting was effected by the direct method while considerable quantities of charcoal ash indicate the fuel employed. Many fragments of crucibles were found, amongst which, fairly complete examples could be reconstructed (*WW* 1957.6: 73–74).

In the Anyang site remnants of a casting channel connecting traces of a furnace to a casting pit have been recognised (Figure 18). This was exhaustively investigated by Shih Chang-ju (石璋如) during the 13th season of excavation (1936). It comprised a U-shaped trench 850 cm in length, each end of which connected with a pit-like formation and the whole complex was constructed so as to effect a small degree of slope. At the western end of the channel the depression was oval-shaped, 450 cm in length and 200 cm in width. Beneath a confused layer of pounded earth appeared the rim of the pit 101 cm below the present surface level. The bottom of the pit extended 236 cm below the ground level and was filled with dark coloured ashy-earth amongst which was found a considerable quantity of charcoal, pottery sherds, animal bones, mould fragments, and bronze residue. The pit to the east was more circular in shape 398 cm × 310 cm, the rim 120 cm and bottom 304 cm below the ground surface. It was filled with black ashy-earth and contained also charcoal, bronze residue, mould fragments, pottery sherds, and animal bones — in this pit mould fragments were particularly

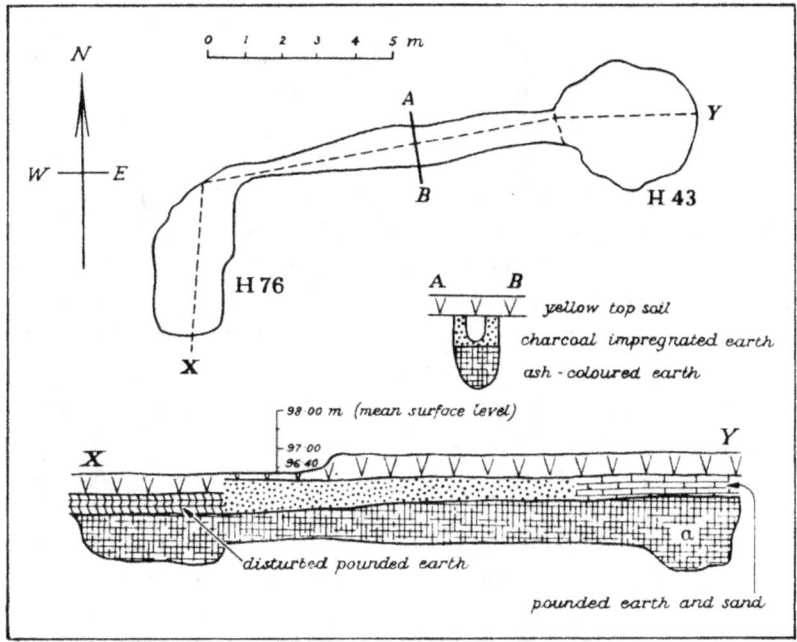

Figure 18   Plan and section of remnants of a Late Shang bronze casting complex at Anyang (after Shih Chang-ju, *BAS* 1955:124). The reconstruction in Figure 19 is based upon this.

numerous, a feature which led Shih to regard it as the casting pit, while the western depression was taken to be the furnace location. However, it may be noted that the cross section accompanying the report and the above measurements applied to it would appear to imply that the slope is downwards from east to west! The present surface level above the western pit moreover, is markedly lower than that above the eastern pit. Obviously the molten metal would have been prepared at the higher level and there, of course, must have been located the furnace. The shape of the channel remains, too, would seem to bear out this interpretation. From the eastern pit the channel commences with a width of about 80 cm which is more or less maintained until it approaches the lower pit. Here it narrows at 20 cm and then swings sharply southwards to enter the casting area. Both the sudden turn of the channel and its diminished width located at a point close to the depression containing the mould-assembly inlets appear to be devices planned to control the rate and volume of flow of the molten metal prior to its entry into the mould-assembly inlets.

The mould-assembly would be located in the western pit at a depth allowing the pouring-cups of the sprues to lie slightly below the lower level of the casting channel. During the pouring of the molten bronze the founder must take extreme care to control, so far as he is able, the circumstances attending the flow of the liquid metal. Too great a momentum of flow and consequent fall into the casting cavities of the mould-assembly results in excessive entrapping of gas bubbles — the slower the rate of flow, the less penetration of these into the molten metal and the shorter the distances will the bubbles have to rise to effect their escape. A relatively high ('super-heated') pouring temperature and a low pouring speed, and in the case of large castings involving considerable volumes of metal, the multiplication of pour by means of several separate streams of entry, are factors which in combination promote good quality casting. These points will be elaborated further in a separate study; in the present foundry complex, however, one may sense the ancient artisans' awareness of practical considerations of this sort.

In the furnace, the crucible charged with molten bronze would have been in readiness for tapping or pouring. The channel, constructed as a long semi-circular trough, rested in a bed of burning charcoal and with further amounts of burning fuel piled along both its sides. In the casting pit awaited the mould-assembly probably similarly heated by glowing charcoal. Upon releasing the molten bronze the metal travelled along the channel, its ease of flow maintained by the localised heating all along its path. At the turn of the narrowing channel the rate of flow would have been sufficiently checked so that the molten metal would then run at a slower but fairly steady rate into the channel divisions leading to one or more pouring-cups and the gating system of the mould-assembly. Such would be the procedure for large castings; Figure 19 comprises a reconstruction of a furnace for large-scale melting of bronze with a channel; it is drawn to scale upon the basis of the crucible placed within it.

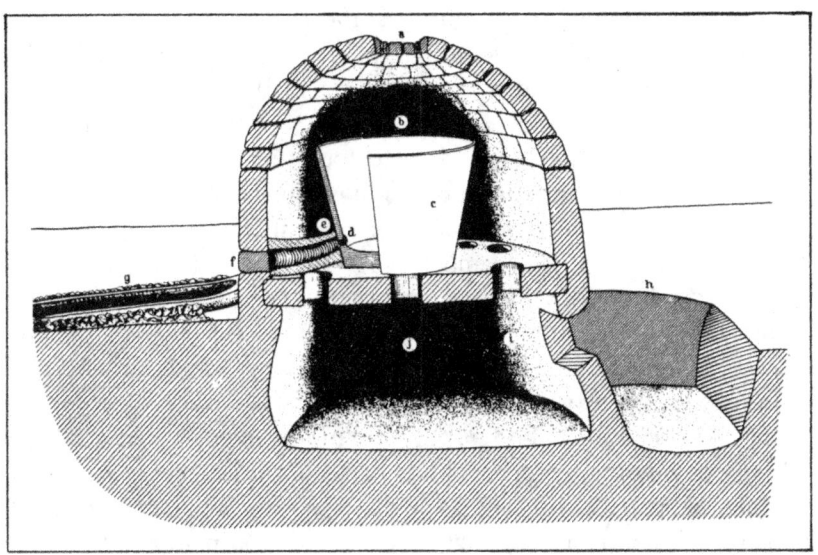

Figure 19   Reconstruction of a large scale bronze melting furnace of the Late Shang period. The structure is drawn to accord in scale with the bucket-shaped crucible inside. This, in turn, is a reconstruction based upon crucible fragments excavated at Anyang (see *K'ao-ku* 1961.2:67–68). The crucible, if filled, would hold approximately 186 litres (= 1,650 kg) of molten bronze. Such large castings as the Ssu-mu Wu *Fang-ting*-cauldron （司母戊方鼎 ） (875 kg) would have been carried out in furnace complexes of this type. Tapping of the crucible would be necessary but archaeological evidence of such a device (e, f) has yet to be found (see *Metallurgical Remains of Ancient China*, pp. 40–45).

A similar casting channel was observed during excavations of Miao-pu pei-ti （苗圃北地） in 1960 — the site located about a kilometre south-east of Hsiao-t'un (*KK* 1961.2: 67–69). In this area building remains associated with the production of crucibles and piece-moulds were found. Inside the confines of one building were sherds of Late Shang type pottery and a number of mould fragments; close to the foundations was a large quantity of broken crucibles and many more mould fragments. Several other building remains in the area contained piles of mould fragments. However, no details of furnaces were reported.

31

A third foundry site which is Eastern Chou in date was discovered in 1959 at Hou-ma (侯馬), Shansi, and has been reported in some detail in several issues of *Wen-wu* (1960.8/9: 7-14; 1961.10:31-34; and 1962.4/5:37-42). The furnace structure is described. There were four furnaces found, all in badly damaged condition, but the following general features were clearly evident: the furnace was round in shape, the diameter of the bottom of the fire-chamber about 70 cm, and 35 cm above was trace of a grate containing perforations each about 10 cm in diameter. In the bottom of one of the furnaces was noted a heap of fired hand-made earthen slabs which obviously had been used in the construction of a hemispherical vault-like structure to form the baking chamber. The evidence here conveniently clarifies this long outstanding enigma of both kiln and furnace construction, while the furnace structure as a whole appears beyond any doubt identical in principle to that of the pottery kiln. Fragments of crucibles were discovered. They were made from a sand/clay mixture and had been fired to a light red colour; both on the interior and exterior surfaces traces of bronze residue could be discerned.

Bronze-casting furnaces, curiously, comprise the least satisfactorily reported aspects of ancient Chinese metallurgy — archaeological discovery has not succeeded in clarifying directly more than a few essentials in their construction. For the most part we must seek, as we have already attempted, relevant data from the pottery industry of antiquity which has been the more intensively investigated and which, not unexpectedly, has contributed much to both the discovery and the development of metal-casting technology in China. Study of iron-casting remains, which although of much later date, does assist in some measure in confirming such matters as the general efficiency of furnace design, the range of, and control, over the high temperatures attainable and, most important, this comparatively new industry does demonstrate the highly advanced nature of metallurgical knowledge that permitted the versatile metallurgists of ancient China to discover iron-casting at so early a date. To propose independent discovery of non-ferrous metals and certain associated metallurgical practices (i.e. direct casting) a millenium or more earlier must be considered reasonable — particularly when all other directly relevant evidence points in this direction.

This paper is based largely upon the considerable corpus of data presented in the section entitled 'Pottery Kilns and Bronze Casting Furnaces' *(pp.27–40) in the author's* 'Origins of Bronze Casting in Ancient China' *(pp. 1–75) which forms part of his contribution to Barnard and Satō Tamotsu* Metallurgical Remains of Ancient China *(Nichiōsha, Tokyo, 1975). As a full list of references appears in our survey, a bibliography has not been prepared for the present paper.*

中國古代冶金術的發現與發展中陶工的地位
——兼論燒窯與鑄爐的構造

作者：巴納

中國冶金文化不同於西方，在西方由於冶工們早已擁有對金屬認識的知識，因而使到鑄造製作方法得到極大發展。中國方面冶金術乃是從當時高度發達製陶工業演化過來的。燒爐設計，爐床，配製泥土模型與及模型坏模製作等皆受陶工們的影響。過往五六十年來考古發現，顯示最初期的金屬製作并沒有包括所謂金屬加工法在內——在甘肅省永靖的大河莊和武威的皇娘娘台等遺址中發掘出土的原始期冶鑄的刀、錐、匕等俱是。

在鑄造最早期且較複雜的容器如斝和爵，採用高度技巧的塊范法，較之西方更勝一籌。雖然中國的金屬冶鑄技法發展較緩，但其根本源自中國本土却在在可証。

如要探討過去二千年來中國鑄冶術的起源與它的發展問題，我們得要注視有關較早於鑄冶術發現前的陶工業發展幾個事實，和中國青銅與鐵器時代興革的性質。同時，又得要對歐洲與中東鑄冶術一般歷史認識。根據圖一顯示，我們知道了東方與西方的冶金術發展情況。這樣才能更了解中國陶工所佔重要的任務。本文只論及由仰韶至漢代燒窯及其發展，由於有了關於陶窯較廣泛豐富資料，雖然我們缺乏研究鑄冶鍊爐詳情，便能深入可靠地明瞭商周時代的青銅鑄冶爐構造。

從過去十年來發掘中，我們獲得了有關仰韶，龍山與商代遺窯地層及其燒窯的構造等寶貴資料。山西省西安附近半坡村的窯址或許是仰韶時代的最佳遺址。據報告稱，那燒窯構造是屬小型的，可以每次燒製四隻至十隻小瓶或是一隻或二隻大瓶。五號與六號是較早期的燒窯，內部組成包括有火膛與二條向上傾斜通往烘室的火道。窯壁已被燒焦硬化，外層成藍綠色，內裏紅色。圖二圖中三號與四號窯以三號最具結構上的詳細資料。窯內爐床裝有十個小的通火孔道與三個大煙囱連接，一個在前，另左右各一。烘室內爐床約一公尺長直徑，位置離火膛口數公尺外，仰韶燒爐特式是它的長條通道形的烘室結構，烘室面積變化由0.7至一公

尺闊度，高度約80公分。第三類型的窰(二號)是屬直立形構造，烘室是從天然黃土裡掘成，室內地上只有一條狹窄的通火孔道與二條低支柱(圖三)，據稱這設計可平均散熱或可擱置未經燒製陶器。另一可能那支柱是用以支撐承著爐床用。

　　每個半坡窰都是基本上從天然泥土中掘製而成。其他仰韶窰也是一樣。在山西省平陸發掘的仰韶式窰顯示出結構上不只有爐床，且在隧道型烘室頂上設有一度長長的門。(圖四)

　　鄭洲附近林山砦的另一座仰韶窰據報它的烘室是深藏於地面下泥土中掘成，烘室下半部和火道也是泥土製成的。那深深的烘室似乎確定了它比淺窄長型結構燒窰爲更後期的結構。但是因爲它缺少了爐床而引起一個問題——可能火道與附有囱通的爐床分成是二種個別發展，而巧合地同時會出現在同一燒窰中。(圖五)

　　由此看來仰韶式燒窰反映出那是一個改革實驗時期建造。從最近發表報告中，三種燒窰之一(圖四)它在結構改良方面比其他進步良多。附有隧道形烘室一類可視爲屬較原始類型。隧道形設計漸漸地被入地式鑿成穴洞形的代替。結果，因爲採用陷地式結構，建造燒窰工人便得要找尋方法將火引進到較高位置的烘室中去。

　　由於烘室漸次深藏土中，前時的隧道型結構改變了爲傾斜型露口穴洞，於是建窰工人增建了一座附有散熱小道的爐床與及烟囱，（圖五）龍山窰址中的燒窰全部俱設有烟囱，散熱爐床與及完善的烘室。正如仰韶式的例子，火道間有被採用，但爐床單位的主要結構包括散熱的通火小道，通常與烟囱相連。仰韶窰與龍山窰主要不同的地方在於後者之烘室較深陷。因此緣故，結構上改革令到整座燒爐設計將通火道與烟囱連成組成一完整單位。

　　在江南省偃師附近渴泉溝發掘出來一座龍山窰，算是較完善無缺的。它有著商代燒窰結構。火膛與烘室成直立形，由一座被烘室圓徑較小的爐床分隔其中，爐床則由六條稻草混泥製成土柱支撐黏牢著烘室牆壁上。這樣那六條土柱的洞口可當作通火道用。此外另有二枝橢圓形窄腰式的草泥土柱承撐著該爐床。商代燒爐窰特徵就是這樣的直立垂直式設計安排爐床處在火膛與烘室間由土柱支撐組成的。

商代早期及中期的窯(圖六)顯示著火膛建在烘室直接底下，爐床則由柱樑支撐著。在銘公路地區所發掘的商代中後期燒窯是為此類經驗查過十四個窯的代表。它的大部份情況跟商代早期的窯差不多。爐床厚度平均約25至30公分并由數十支柱穿過每條約10公分直徑的通火小道支撐著。很多還繞燒窯附近的灰穴留有燒過與未燒過的破陶片，窯具，圖紋印等物。於商代末期，烘室已完全建於火膛上面而爐床則不需用支樑支撐了。見圖七碧沙崗窯。河北省邯鄲附近澗溝村二個窯都用火膛與烘室成垂直線的同樣建造方法。據知它們窯壁與爐床距離空間極小(圖八)。燒陶時，陶器放在爐床上，然後用泥板或泥條蓋在其上做成一個圓拱形的頂覆蓋着。

1954年在河北省曹演莊和邢臺附近所發掘燒窯中，其構造則較複雜。在那裏發現了三種商代不同的燒窯。據紀錄資料，第一號窯似乎與商代後期的一般，第二號與第三號的是屬較早期。有關第一號的詳情仍可辨別，惜報告却很模糊。其中一點較值得注意的是窯室裝有窯門，直通烘室內去。這可說是一個永久性的圓拱頂蓋物(圖九)。曹演莊的第二號窯與第三號主要相同，只為較完整與複雜些。它有一個藏於地底下28公分的平底圓形洞穴，烘室壁以草泥堆製厚約六公分而成。火膛通道築在爐床54公分之下，引到一個梨形內裡砌有草泥間條的空間。內裡的面積是:長160公分，闊 135 公分，和高57公分。火膛內的地面成馬蹄形，四週向上連接到烘室去，其上有高約 4 公分橫12公分的突出部份環繞火膛室內的牆壁，火膛洞口亦成馬蹄形，高63公分，橫42公分，朝向東方。

爐床直徑 152 公分，厚50公分，通火道六個，中間的火道幾乎成四方形，為16公分乘17公分。其如的空心火道築在爐床四週與烘室壁相連（圖十）。那些火道是橢圓形，平均尺寸是24乘 25 公分。火孔道向下切成火口與火膛接合。火口上部(有時是中部)裝設有泥隔離器來控制火力。根據報告，窯壁上內外共有七個「煙孔」，這些「煙孔」直徑約 8 至12公分向下連接到爐床裡的通火孔道的。有時在地底下二三個「煙孔」串連起來組成一條通道跟火口連

接一起，在火口與煙孔附近，共有與煙孔直徑相同面積的洞穴共十六個。它內裡裝滿黑土，但其作用還未能估計。

雖則沒有窯門痕跡的存在，但根據報告，窯壁向北的一面上沒有凸出的壁架，同時那兒亦沒有發現煙孔，故很可能那便是烘室半圓形頂蓋出入孔道。

遺留下來的灰爐混有炭枝，表示燃料就是木柴。在遺留瓷片中有著許多瓷模（鬲腿），以為製造瓷器的鬲腿型用途。

很不幸的，我們未能得到有關這陶窯詳盡的資料，雖然明顯地這裡有其他窯址未能發現的貴重資料。如果詳盡的研究，不難發現更多有關商代中期與末期的垂直型燒窯，與及烘室爐床，通火孔道，煙孔等物之複雜成因。有關運用泥隔離器來控制火力方法，它可能在煙孔中操縱或是與其十六個洞穴互相關連。這些都是最重要的待考據的專門觀點，留待將來發掘有同樣的窯址的時候去研究。

因為爐床築在火膛上，它便變成天花頂板，所以用不著斜線形的火口孔道。而火力因天然通風關係向上漸次加烈，故無庸像於平行或斜線通道式的火道加以控制火力。燒窯內極猛烈火力之平均分散可從通火孔道之形狀及其數目多寡加以調節。至於煙孔與泥隔離器與火口系統之應用仍待研究。一般來說，看來簡單設計燒窯較為普遍受歡迎。

二座西周燒窯的資料較詳盡。第五號窯是於山西省長安附近洛水村西面發掘出的十個窯址之一，與碧沙崗燒窯(圖七)建造上完全相同：內裡火膛與烘室成垂直形與及內裡沒有支撐的五孔通火孔道爐床。有趣的是從遺下來木材與草料灰爐中，發現了相當數量的獸類糞灰。其中數個燒窯還發現有除了家用陶具外還有屋頂磚瓦破片。1955年於長安馬王村發掘的窯(圖一)可作為對洛水村窯的烘室結構的參考証明。雖然在其他地方找不到一些像馬王村窯的資料，以下的紀錄是非常重要：「……那窯是比較上完整。發掘時，烘室內裝滿跌下去的以草泥製成燒成紅色的陶器。此外，根據烘室牆壁（約70公分高）遺跡，它原來是一座圓拱形當中作煙囪用的洞孔。」第二個窯址（圖十一）則於長安附近客省莊發現。那兒發掘了三個燒窯，其中報告詳盡的是屬圓形建築。其他

二個構造相同。據圖形與部份遺跡來看，客省莊窰跟龍山三里橋窰與澗溝村窰顯著雷同，故可說這二類以下結構流傳於商代至西周期間：（甲）有通孔道爐床的燒窰全部或部份建造於火膛上，（乙）沒有爐床只有平台與火道與火膛相連的燒窰。現在可以說商代的燒窰只屬前者，後者可能是屬於戰國時代平橫式附有煙囱的燒窰典型。

依據研究客省莊窰及其圖片所得，其煙囱位置有建築在後面的趨勢。當然這并不意味說這與建造戰國時代燒爐(圖十四、十五)有關。客省莊窰所用的燃料幾乎全是稻草和少許用柴或樹灰痕跡。據以上所曾討論過燒窰內牆表面所見，我們有理由相信那些燃料可產生高度的氣溫熱力。

雖然結構簡單，這些在金屬前期陶器文化時代的燒窰遺址中曾有高達攝氏1400度之熱力。吉田光邦於東方學報談論古代中國冶金術研究中提及燒瓷時化學分析與及燒爐內泥土間格特點，却信可產生達這高熱火力。火膛與烘室裡的內牆因曾受高熱而高度硬化，而內層表面通常變成青色陶化的泥壁。從鄭州出土的中商時代(圖十二)的陶器製品顯示它曾受高度火力所製成。又據西周時期的陶片最近受實驗室試驗，証明火力應有攝氏1200度之多。以研究用的破片加熱至攝氏1300度時，則瓷釉熔解四散，這項實驗提示了龍山時代燒陶火力，可高達到將銅溶化的境地。

商前期間全部陶窰一般是反射爐式構造，仰韶燒窰或許不能決定它的類別。無論怎樣，它們明顯不相同的分野在於整體構造結構內熱力來源與烘室之差異。長形火膛不只將燃燒著的木炭與烘室內器皿分隔，并可有引導天然通風功能以加強火力。有關最原始式的仰韶窰內簡單爐床燒成陶器的技術方法，我們所得資料甚少。

圖十三所載燒爐改革是根據所得資料製成。我們可將它與 H. H.Coghlan 氏所編寫的文字作比較。二者所提及之爐床改革仍有待將來之考証。西方國家所發明之爐床可能是繼中國陶瓷文化期後的獨特發明。雖然爐床發明似乎與早期燒窰結構有關，很明顯地從技術初期觀點看來，二者各具其不同的困難。

西方米索不達米亞陶工最初利用垂直式結構，用爐床將燃料

與陶器提離窯裏地面，後來才將爐床築在燃料與烘室中間。中國燒窯最初的形式是依地形建造起來，部份由土地中掘空而成使能做成一座平衡橫式的結構，後來改革了爲將火膛與烘室作垂直式設計，再後建造爐床與火口孔道。前者效用在乎引領熱力橫過到烘室去，而後者能更佳的將燃料隔離幷減少熱力能源與烘室間的距離。我們亦可這樣說，中國古代燒窯由平衡橫式改建爲垂直式，不只牽涉及將火膛移近烘室，而亦將火膛建在地面上去。換言之，中國陶工將泥土發掘洞穴而製造垂直式燒窯，但西方則簡易地在地面上築起燒窯，這是用磚的文化特徵。

戰國期所建的燒窯具有明顯的結構上改變，其中以河北省武安縣午汲村窯址可爲代表。不幸沒有可用的圖表，而報導出來的資料也難以正確地演譯。雖然這樣，很明顯地自商迄西周時代垂直式已不再出現。爐床取消了，火膛改變爲位置在烘室與火膛口之間的穴洞。後煙囱相通的烘室內牆火道有著特別顯明的改善。戰國時代窯（一號與二號）附有足夠的資料來說明它的設計改革。圖十五是平面圖與視角圖。它們可與圖十四的照片草圖比較。一號燒窯全部長度是 200 公分，闊 165 公分，最高的高度則是80公分。火膛門向東，火膛內有著90公分闊與80公分深的煙囱形坑穴。但這穴幷不會穿過烘室地台。這顯示了早期燒窯的突變改革。平台裏藏有一條狹窄的火道與 U 形的後牆相連而成爲煙囱的底部。窯裏內壁已被燒成灰青色，窯的10公分至20公分厚度牆壁與平面泥土都被燒成紅色了，柴灰與碗形陶器碎片顯示出當時用的燃料與陶器製品類別。二號燒窯略有不同，它的全部長度爲 227 公分，闊度 140 公分，火膛門底部30公分闊，高度爲45公分。一個單式煙囱是與十字形火道相接連。

戰國到漢代的燒窯，一般說來都與圖十五的結構大致相同。每窯都有一煙囱。烘室內牆壁，大多數是垂直的，地面則是長方形或橢圓形狀。後牆上多數有煙囱的痕跡，但亦有多至三個煙囱的。在這情形下，每條煙囱連結起來組成一個大的組合（見圖十六）。

沒有一個早期的窯顯示特別的結構設計引發後期的新改革。雖然建造此等燒窯同期，中國美術與工藝都受了外來的影響。煙

囪的後移與及火膛在前座的位置使到橫式通火道加強火力流通的設計特色可能先於橫式建造燒窯前發現。

漢代橫式燒窯是比古代其他地區所建造原理相同的燒窯更先進。在垂直式結構中，通風調節問題必成難題。中國古代的人可能對此獲得足夠的控制方法，但以現存資料來推論，實難明其經過與方法。早期製成的陶瓷器皿實足以証明當時燒窯的火力控制十分良好。

在橫式燒窯中，熱力氣流由圓拱形屋頂引導下去，圍繞烘室經火道孔而到達煙囪的出口。這樣的間接的氣流運輸較易控制窯內的溫度，因為只要從火膛入口調節空氣進入便可。

從某些結構因素關係來看，戰國與漢代橫式燒窯顯然與龍山式可能有直接的關連。舉例來說，火膛前座的洞穴形狀和在地下掘製窯坑的構造等便是，毫無疑問火孔通道是從仰韶及龍山窯的火口改進過來的。西周客省莊窯的傾斜型火道更顯出它的強烈關連，那就是沒有煙囪。煙囪的起源不能追查到午汲村更前的時代了。煙囪的運用及其發明曾很明顯地令到火道爐床失却功能。

西安北面近郊郭家村發掘出王莽錢幣燒窯內裏的火道與其煙囪更為複雜。其內有煙囪五隻結成一組（見圖十七）。自漢以來，有關唐，宋各朝代的簡略研究獲得結論是橫式燒窯原理歷久不變。

有了以上粗略的陶窯性質報導與改革資料我們現在便可嘗試探討鑄銅爐問題。

我們只有三個冶銅遺址提供足夠的資料以研究此類爐的構造。早期於鄭州遺跡中的發現是屬於商代中上與後期的建造。其中大者遺址有著1,050方公尺面積，超過一千塊的陶模碎片與及小爐，銅鑛，鐵渣及木炭等物留在那兒。在那較小的遺址內似乎可見鑄造活動遺物與及一所建築物，但却沒有鍊爐的確跡。值得注意的是那些銅鑛和鑄造廢料的數量顯示著那兒是曾有過冶鍊這一回事。從大量鑄模碎片可知曾採用直接鑄冶法，而相當數量的木炭顯示以此為燃料。其中鍊爐碎片尚可供製作較完整之模型用。

在安陽遺址中發現了鑄爐洞穴遺跡（圖十八）。1936年石璋如在其十三次發掘詳盡報告裏說那址內藏有U形長850公分的溝

坑，每端皆與洞穴形的空間連接，整座結構築成微傾斜狀。通道西口低陷地方呈橢圓形為450公分長與及200公分闊。距離一層碎土的地面下約101公分就是鑄塲洞的邊沿。鑄塲底部深入地下236公分，其內滿佈黑色灰泥和相當數量的木炭、陶片、獸骨、模型破片，與及銅器殘片。鑄塲穴的東西是較為圓形約為398公分乘310公分，距離地面邊沿是120公分，底部304公分。那兒亦是黑色灰泥隨處，混有木炭，銅器殘片，模型破片，陶片與及獸類遺骸。此中的模型破片特別多，被認為乃是鑄冶塲地，而在西方另一端該是鍊爐所在地。但是值得注意一點乃是從橫剖圖面及其面積尺寸計算，顯示了那傾斜形是由東向西傾下去的。鑄塲的西面地面水平較東面明確的低陷。明顯地，較高的地面為鑄溶鑛物的地方，亦應是鍊爐所在地。根據通道遺跡所示，亦可証明這一說法。鑄塲東西入口通道約80公分闊直達下層為較窄約20公分之通道向南接到鑄製地方。由於通道地形轉接與及其漸減之闊度，那是一種控制調節鑄物鎔液流通的設計。

　　當傾倒鎔化銅液時，鑄匠必須極度小心控制其流動，過度的流動衝力便會引起鑄模內產生過多的氣泡。鎔液流動越慢，則氣泡越能將浮升上表面的距離拉短。製造良好品質的銅鑄因素是須有高溫度的鎔液與及緩慢的流動速度。如果要大量鑄造，則可以將鎔液分成數條支流滙合注入。

　　圖十九表示鍊爐和坑槽供給大量鑄造銅器的用途。在鍊爐中，通槽成長半圓形，放置在炭火上的上面，它的二側堆放燒着的燃料。當銅鎔液流過通槽便藉火力維持溫度，在轉角轉入漸窄槽中的時候，流液轉動緩慢而流入鑄模系統中去。

　　1960年於小屯東南約一公里的苗圃北地塲址發掘中發現了同樣的鑄造通槽，在那裡發現了好些製模破片，鍊爐，和商代後期陶器碎片等遺跡。鑄塲附近有大量鍊爐破片及更多的模型殘缺小片。塲址內其他數座建築內裡藏着整堆的製模破片。然而却欠了鍊爐的痕跡。

　　第三座鑄冶塲是於1959年在山西省侯馬發現的東周遺址。它已經被幾期的文物刊中詳載過。關於鍊爐構造是這樣的記載。當時發現了四座鍊冶爐，全部破毀不堪，但有幾點特徵還清晰顯現

：鍊爐是圓形，火室底部直徑約70公分，其上是35公分，其中孔道每條直徑約是10公分。鍊爐之一其中底部堆有曾經燒製手做塊狀土泥，相信是用以建造烘室內的間隔。這種証據澄清了長久以來有關鍊爐與陶窯構造的謎。無可懷疑的，大體上鑄鍊爐構造跟陶窯原理吻合。發現了的鍊爐破片是由沙粒與泥土混製而成，被燒成淺紅色。它的表裏二面都發現銅片渣滓痕跡。

奇怪的，中國古代冶鍊術對鑄鍊爐最少提及，考古發現不能成功地表明多過數點的建造要素。我們須要從古代陶器工業中找尋重要資料去印證中國鑄冶工藝技術之發現及其發展經過。有關鑄鐵遺跡考究，雖屬後期的事，但可於某些方面幫助証實鍊爐的一般效能，對高熱度的控制量度。尤其要者，這種較新工業高度鑄冶知識容許昔日中國多才多藝鑄冶工匠後來發現鐵鑄技法。

Jade Carving in China

CHENG TE-K'UN
Chinese University of Hong Kong

The Material

Before going into the carving of jade in China a few words should be said of the stone itself. Much has been written on the mineralogical aspect of the material, so a clear definition of the stone is necessary before we try to discuss the technique of its carving.

In China the material is known as *yü* (玉). The earliest versions of the character may be found in the oracle inscriptions of the Shang period when it was in the form of three or four horizontal strokes connected by a vertical one (王). In some cases the vertical stroke ends in two or three branches. In the next millennium or so the character gathered around it several meanings. In *Shuo wen chieh tzu* (說文解字), a dictionary of the second century, it is defined from three different points of view:

"*Yü*: A stone that is beautiful."

"It has five virtues: there is warmth in its lustre and brilliancy, this is the manner of kindness; its soft interior may be viewed from outside revealing [the goodness] within, this is the manner of rectitude; its note is tranquil and high and carries far and wide, this is the way of wisdom; it may be broken but cannot be twisted, this is the manner of bravery; its sharp edges are not intended for violence, this is the way of purity."

"It pictures three pieces of *yü* strung together by a stroke [string or cord]".

The first definition is possibly the original and most common meaning of the character, while the third is a string of jade pendants or beads. The second meaning is evidently a Confucian moralization on the stone which was recognized by Confucius and his followers to be emblematic of their teachings.

In the translation of this character *yü* into English no word could be more fitting than the word *jade*. It is a modern word which appeared in the English language, according to the *Oxford*

Dictionary, in 1727, and may be traced to a Spanish origin. This leads one to suspect that the green stone called jade was first introduced into Europe by the Spanish adventurers from the new world. The stone had also some connections with medicine as it was believed to be capable of curing pains in the region of the short ribs. Strictly speaking, the word *jade* has no scientific meaning whatsoever. But the development of modern science in the last century demanded a more specific definition of it, and jade has gradually come to signify generally two types of stone, nephrite and jadeite. Superficially, these two types of stone look very much like each other, but they were found to be quite different after they had been examined and described by A. Damour in 1863. Nephrite is a calcium-magnesium silicate, a mineral of crypto-crystalline structure, while jadeite is a sodium-aluminium silicate belonging to the pyroxene group of minerals. The latter is an aggregate of small grains instead of the short interlocked fibres of the former and, consequently, it is the harder of the two. These two types of stone are used extensively in the Chinese lapidary. The two words, *yü* and jade, now denote the same materials, nephrite and jadeite.

In the finished product however, a nephrite artifact is oily in its lustre usually described as mutton fat (羊脂), while a jadeite appears vitreous, hence a glassy texture.

To the Chinese, both ancient and modern, *yü* means a beautiful stone and the archaeological material recovered from any ancient sites is so named. Take for instance the *yü jade* excavated at the ruins of the Shang capital in An-yang (安陽) which Dr Li Chi (李濟) tried to determine from the mineralogical point of view. To select jade artifacts for scientific study is a difficult task, because most of the stones are calcified and appear with a soft chalky surface after long burial in the ground. These would be of no use for mineralogical study. Li Chi selects only those which have retained their original texture and colour. He makes a detailed study of a total of 62 specimens and the data tabulated on the following pages provide some information about the material used in the ancient times.

The specimens are described by the shape, the colour, the specific gravity and the hardness. Each entry is numbered. There

NO.	TYPE	COLOUR	SPECIFIC GRAVITY	HARDNESS
1	2-HOLED AXE	GREEN WITH BLACK	2.92	6—7
2	FRAGMENT	BLUSH-GREEN	2.96	5—6
3	FRAGMENT	BLACK	3.02	9+
4	FRAGMENT	WHITE	2.97	7—8
5	FRAGMENT	YELLOW	2.52	5
6	RECTANGULAR FLAKE	IVORY-WHITE	2.81	9
7	SQUARE BEAD	BLUISH-GREEN	2.94	8
8	FRAGMENT	YELLOW	2.74	3—4
9	FISH	PALE GREEN	3.00	6—7
10	?	BLUE	2.96	7—8
11	FRAGMENT	BONE WHITE	2.84	8—9
12	ORNAMENT	WHITE	2.95	8—9
13	ORNAMENT	WHITE	2.92	8—9
14	TRIANGULAR FLAKE	WHITE	2.91	8—9
15	FRAGMENT	YELLOW	3.18	4—5
16	FRAGMENT	WHITE WITH BLACK	2.92	8
17	FRAGMENT	WHITE	2.91	6—7
18	*HUAN* RING	GREEN	2.94	8—9
19	FISH	GREEN	2.95	6—7
20	FISH	WHITE	2.98	6—7
21	FISH	GREEN	2.94	8—9
22	PERFORATED DISC	PALE GREEN	2.88	6—7
23	*HUANG* SEGMENT	PALE GREEN	2.94	6—7
*24	2-HOLED AXE	BLUISH-GREEN	2.96	6—7
25	HUMAN FIGURE	BLUISH-GREEN	2.88	6—7
26	HUMAN FIGURE	WHITE	2.87	9+
27	*HUANG* SEGMENT	BLUISH-GREEN	2.96	6—7
28	*HUANG* SEGMENT	GREEN	3.00	7—8
29	TIGER	IVORY WHITE	2.84	7—8
30	ELEPHANT?	GREEN	2.96	7—8
31	HAIRPIN	GREEN	2.94	7—8

NO.	TYPE	COLOUR	SPECIFIC GRAVITY	HARDNESS
32	HAIRPIN	GREEN	2.94	8—9
33	BRACELET?	GREEN	2.78	8
34	YUAN RING	GREEN	2.95	6—7
35	HORSE BIT	GREY, BLACK, GREEN	2.93	6—7
36	YUAN RING	GREEN	2.99	6—7
37	FISH	TURQUOISE GREEN	2.62	8—9
38	CHUEH RING	GREEN	2.93	9
39	HAIRPIN	WHITE	2.91	6—7
40	FISH	PALE GREEN	2.49	6—7
41	FISH	GREYISH-WHITE	2.96	6—7
42	FISH	WHITE	2.80	6—7
43	FISH	GREYISH-WHITE	2.96	5—6
44	FISH	RICE YELLOW	2.88	5—6
45	FISH	PALE GREEN	2.94	6—7
46	FISH	PALE GREEN	2.97	6—7
47	FISH	PALE GREEN	3.06	6—7
48	FISH	RICE YELLOW	2.80	5—6
49	FISH	RICE YELLOW	2.88	6—7
50	HUMAN HEAD	GREEN WITH BLACK	2.97	6—7
51	HUMAN HEAD	GREEN WITH BLACK	2.95	6—7
52	FISH	GREYISH-WHITE	2.90	7—8
53	FISH	YELLOW	2.86	9
54	FISH	PALE BLUE	2.96	6—7
55	FISH	GREYISH-WHITE	2.90	7—8
56	FISH	PALE BLUE	2.95	6—7
57	FISH	GREY-BLACK WITH WHITE	2.91	6—7
58	FISH	RICE YELLOW	2.88	6—7
59	FISH	PALE GREEN	2.99	6—7
60	FISH	PALE GREEN	2.95	6—7
61	KO DAGGER-AXE	BLUE WITH YELLOW	2.88	6—7
62	KO DAGGER-AXE	BLUE WITH BLACK	2.93	7—8

*FROM THE BLACK POTTERY SITE AT JIH-CHAO SHANTUNG

are 30 specimens in the forms of human figures and animals, such as fish, elephant and tiger; 9 in discoidal forms, such as *yuan* (瑗) and *huan* (環), *huang* (璜) and *chueh* (玦) and others; 8 in the shape of axes, bead, hairpin and other straight and square forms; and 13 fragments and 2' others. Green and white predominate in the variety of colours but yellow, black and blue also occur. 31 pieces are in various shades of green, 17 in various grades of white, 7 yellow, 4 blue and 3 black. The hardness extends from 3 to more than 9, while the specific gravities extend from 2·49 to 3·18.

Li Chi does not attempt to analyse his findings further, so it would be profitable to examine his figures more closely. Although the specimens cover wide ranges of specific gravities and hardness, they are actually concentrated within comparatively narrow limits. Out of the 62 pieces, 47 are with specific gravities of 2·88-3·00 and hardness of 5-9. These are 76% of the total. Jadeite has a specific gravity of 3·33 and hardness of 6·75, so it is obvious from the table that none of the Shang jade specimens are of this material. Nephrite has a hardness of 6·5 and specific gravity of 2·90-3·10. Twenty-three specimens fit these specifications, and, in the absence of further data, may be identified as nephrite. These form 39% of the total.

From the wide ranges of colour, hardness and specific gravity encountered, it is clear that the Shang jade carver used several kinds of stone for his work. He made his choice irrespective of the hardness, requiring only that the stone be fine. He was capable of tackling stone harder than nephrite and jadeite. Twenty-five of the specimens have hardness ranging from 7 to greater than 9; some of them are harder than corundum. The Chinese jade carver has continued to use any type of fine stone for his work throughout the centuries, though nephrite and jadeite have always been most admired.

Prehistoric jade

Li Chi includes in his study a specimen from the prehistoric period. This, No. 24 on the list, was found at Liang-ch'eng-chen (兩城鎮), in Jih-chao (日照) along the coast of Shantung, and more important, from the Black Pottery level. It is a green stone axe with two perforations. The stone has a hardness of 6–7 and a specific gravity of 2·96, similar to those of nephrite. Besides, many jade-like artifacts have been recorded from the neolithic sites in many parts of China, so the beginning of the use of jade in China cannot be later than the late Neolithic period, some 7,000 years ago.

In the neolithic times jade was only a member of the stone family in the lapidary, in fact, a minor and unimportant material. But its hardness, toughness and heaviness together with its colour and fine texture which was capable of taking a high polish soon elevated the material above all other stones. On the other hand, the working of these hard substances might have also been responsible for the improvement of the carving techniques and prepared the way for the continuous development of the art throughout the following dynasties.

Carved artifacts of jade should have been the pride and joy of the craftsman as well as the warrior-nobility. The really fine pieces were rare and costly and their working was slow and laborious. The possession of this type of weapon and ornament would have been the prerogative of chieftains and men of substance.

The jade artifacts recovered from the neolithic sites in China may be classified into two categories according to their functions. The tools and implements include various types of axes, hoes, adzes, chisels, knives and points while the ornaments are usually in the forms of discs, rings, beads and animal forms.

Plate I presents a group of neolithic stone artifacts: a and b, two arrow points, shaped by chipping; c, a slender axe, fashioned by chipping, polishing and perforating; d, a fragment of a partly calcified chisel; e, a heart-shaped pendant made of turquoise and f, a pi (璧) disc with a straight saw-mark.

All these specimens show that the techniques of carving had reached a point where the jade carver could handle such hard substances with ease and the tradition was closely followed in the early historic periods. It is only natural that many of these prehistoric implements and ornaments should have been handed down and continued to be made in the historic times, mainly as ritual and ceremonial objects.

Shang jade

The carving of jade achieved its maturity in the Shang period. The art was so well-developed that it may be regarded as a specialized branch of the lithic industry, producing all sorts of artifacts. Besides tools and implements and ornaments, the Shang carver made all sorts of fittings and ceremonial objects. The finished products show that a number of elaborate processes were employed for some of the marks which were left on the objects permit a closer understanding of the techniques used at that time. There is no doubt that all the techniques of the stone cutter including chipping, pecking, polishing, sawing and drilling was at its service, but jade carving required some more highly developed techniques.

The majority of Shang jades were carved from slabs of stone which had been cut by sawing with sand as abrasive in the neolithic fashion. A large piece of jade was sawn in the neolithic fashion from opposite sides and a step may sometimes be seen where the two cuts failed to meet perfectly and the fault had not been eradicated by subsequent grinding.

Since the Shang people were masters of a mature bronze culture, it seems possible that metal tools were used side by side with the neolithic saw. The most conspicuous development was the use of a rotary disc in cutting. The rectangular blade in Pl. II *a* shows a mark left by this new technique. Unlike straight sawing in the neolithic fashion, it curves in a circular manner showing the action of a rotary wheel. Marks of this type of cutting are quite common on Shang jade artifacts.

The discovery of the use of a rotary disc for hard stone cutting was a logical development. The neolithic Chinese already knew the art of sawing with the help of water and sand. They were also masters of hole boring with the rotary drill. Besides, spindle whorls and pottery wheels were also common. The Shang people seemed to have carried the process a little farther and invented a rotary apparatus for jade cutting which should have been responsible for the development of jade carving into a specialized art.

Apart from the tools and weapons, such as axes, chisels and spear-heads, most of the jade artifacts of the Shang period are small objects carved from thin slabs of stone whose thickness ranges from 2 to 25 mm. These thin slabs were sawn from the original pebbles or rocks and in some cases the pebble surface may still be seen. It should also be mentioned that the Shang craftsman did not hesitate to use damaged materials. Many of the articles in the shape of a fish or animal were adapted from fragments of finished artifacts which had been broken.

Plate II *b* shows a fish leaping into a curve. It has a raised central ridge which has no connection with the shape of an ordinary fish. The article is evidently adapted from a segment of a short cylindrical ring with a circular mid-rib which was slightly retouched to give additional power to the springing.

A thin slab of jade is usually adapted to the shape of the intended object in outline. This is why most Shang pendants and other ornaments have almost always remained in the silhouette which constitutes one of the most conspicuous features in the jade carving of this period. The dragon, the bird, the frog, the hare, the animal mask (Pl. II *c-g*) and the comb (Pl. III *a*) are all shaped in this fashion. They are flat showing mainly the outlines of the artifacts.

The trimming of a jade artifact from a slab is performed in several stages. The straight side or sides of a jade implement are generally cut first by sawing, and the cutting edge or edges are then obtained by grinding, both sawing and grinding being carried out in the neolithic fashion. The implement is then worked from both sides. In most cases the traces of primary sawing were eradicated by secondary grinding, but marks of sawing may occasionally remain on the butt end.

The perforated blade in Plate III *b* serves as a fine example. The three cutting edges are formed by grinding from both sides, while at the butt end the traces of primary sawing, also from both sides, may clearly be seen.

Most of the Shang jade implements are very well shaped and polished, elegant and sharp. With well trimmed cutting edges and fine point as well as its highly polished grooves and ridges on the surface, the *ko* (戈) dagger-axe in Plate III *c* shows the superb skill of the carver's art. In form and efficiency it rivals its counterparts in bronze.

In shaping an article with a curved outline the Shang crafts-man again follows the neolithic tradition first by rubbing the edge of the raw slab on the surface of some coarse-grained stone to form the desired outline and then by indenting to obtain the detailed serration. The artifacts made in this way are usually crude and the surface of the edge has several different planes.

For articles with a more elaborate outline like the bird in Plate III *d*, the various types of indentations at the edge are formed in two stages. Holes of the desired size are first drilled close along the edge and then slits of various shapes are cut from the rim to connect them. This is also a simple neolithic technique. The process can be elaborated into some complicated forms such as the curved beak and the tall crest. The leg and the tail are also separated by the same technique.

In the same fashion the mouth of the dragon in Plate IV*a* and of other ferocious beasts is usually carved by drilling a series of holes which connect with each other in such a way that when the cavity for the mouth is formed, it is surrounded with a row of teeth. Quite unlike those that are perforated in conical section, holes of this type are usually straight in section and seem to have been drilled with a sharp point, harder than the jade stone. There is no doubt that the Shang jadesmith used a drill point harder than corundum in his work, a tool almost as hard as a diamond drill.

The majority of the jade implements of the Shang period as well as discs and rings are undecorated, but most of the animals, birds, fish, insects and human figures are decorated with typical Shang designs on one or both sides. The simplest form of design is usually composed of straight lines carved either by sawing with a straight blade, or by grinding with the edge of a rotary wheel, or by incising with a sharp point. The quality of the lines varies from fine and thin to deep and broad like a groove or trough.

The details of the dragon on the bow-tip (Pl. IV*b*) are decorated with straight lines which are pointed at both ends and thicker and deeper in the middle. They show that the carving was administered with the edge of a rotary wheel.

Incised lines on the Shang jades are also produced by repeated scratching, and traces of individual scratches may sometimes be visible to the naked eye. When a line of this type is viewed under a high-powered magnifying glass, it may be seen to have been worked in sections each composed of hundreds of fine scratches. The details of the cicada in Plate IVc were carved in this fashion. Most of the traces of scratching had been removed by subsequent polishing but a few may be noticed on the picture. The specimen also shows that decorative lines on the Shang jade may be divided into two types, known in Chinese as *yin-wen* (陰文) depressed lines and the *yang-wen* (陽文) raised lines. On one side the details of the insect are carved in *yin-wen* or depressed lines, while on the other, the same pattern is repeated in *yang-wen* or raised lines. It takes two *yin-wen* lines to produce a *yang-wen* line, that is, two depressed lines are scratched with their deeper sides close to each other so that the untouched stone in between them forms the raised line.

Grinding and polishing of the jade surface brings in another type of line developed from the *yang-wen* raised lines. A *yang-wen* raised line is formed first by cutting two *yin-wen* depressed lines on either side of it, then the surface on the outer sides of the two depressed lines is ground away to the same depth as the depressed lines leaving the central *yang-wen* raised line untouched in low-relief. This type of line is generally described in western writings as "thread" carving. The bird on Plate IVd is decorated on both sides in this fashion.

The Shang jadesmith is always ready to vary the linear cutting in width and in quality. A number of very well detailed specimens are carved by patiently grinding and rubbing the surface down into several planes. The animal head on Plate IVe appears in four planes — the horizontal lines on the horns being the highest, then the horns themselves, together with the ears and the eyes, then the head, and finally the incised lines for the nose.

Most of the Shang jades did not receive a finishing polish, and various types of functional marks may still be seen on them. But polishing was already a well-developed technique. A polished specimen has a lustrous surface. The curved bird in Plate Va retains most of the marks of scratching and incising, but on one side the head is so brightly polished that it reflects light.

Perforation was not a problem to the Shang jade carver. The

neolithic Chinese before him were already very skilful in this art and among the jades of this period perforation is common. The holes vary greatly in size and shape and may be drilled from one or both sides. The very hard stone point that he used was capable of making tiny straight holes that penetrated a depth of 17 centimetres.

Sometimes holes were made by tunneling from two directions. The perforation on the human head (Pl. V*b*) consists of two holes drilled from the same surface, going down diagonally so that they meet under the surface. The holes may be either tubular or conical, according to the type of tool used in the operation. The holes on this specimen seem to have been drilled with points of two types: a large one for the circular openings and a smaller one which goes almost horizontally into the tunnel leaving pointed grooves on the sides of the round opening.

Perforation may sometimes be used to produce openwork in decoration. This is done by extending a hole by sawing or scratching it into the desired pattern. The details of the human figure with a tall head-dress in Plate VI*a* are carved in this manner.

The Shang jade carver is just as at home with sculpture in the round as with carving from a slab. Magnificent human heads and figures have been reported from An-yang. Technically the Shang jade sculptures are of two types. One may be considered as a by-product of slab cutting. The fish in Plate VI*b* is carved from a slab, but the artist has brought up the head and the fins to give it a solid appearance.

The hare in Plate VI*c* is detailed on both sides, but the ear has been slit into two halves and the head and legs rounded at the edge. But it is still limited by the shape of the original slab which prescribes the rectangularity of the sculpture.

In the second type, real sculpture in the round, the Shang artist could be as realistic as he wished. The hare in Plate VI*d* shows that the cubical form is almost entirely absent and every detail is so well rounded that it stands as a sculpture in three dimensions.

The buffalo in Plate VI*e* is only 52 mm. in length but the artist succeeds in bringing out not only all the necessary details but also the bearing and spirit of the animal. It is clear that the style of the Shang art is not limited to stylized motifs and subject matter. The ancient artists could express themselves in naturalism if they wished. Many of these sculptural forms are so small that they were far harder to carve than any larger works. They could only be shaped by slow grinding with the help of sand. For such work a rotating tool operated by a lathe was the most suitable apparatus. It is now evident that the Shang jadesmith understood perfectly the value of a rotary instrument and used it to its best advantage. The wheel, the tube and the point which he handled were all operated by a rotary apparatus. It seems likely that the bow drill, the pump drill as well as the treadle lathe were all at his service and they continued to be some of the most efficient implements of the art throughout the centuries.

Chou Jade

The carving of jade in China continued to be developed and improved in the Chou period. In the beginning the art followed the Shang tradition. Plate VII *a* presents a group of jade artifacts recovered from an early Chou tomb at Chang-chia-p'o (張家坡), near Sian (西安), quite far away from An-yang. The subject matter and technique are clearly in the Shang style, showing that there is hardly any difference between the Shang and Chou culture at this stage.

Plate VII *b* reproduces a Western Chou standing human figure from Pai-ma-ssu (白馬寺), near Lo-yang. It is carved from a long wedge-shaped piece of material, the head being bigger and thicker than the feet. The face is round with a pointed chin and some detailed facial features. The headdress has tall projections on the two sides, like a pair of ears. A tailored garment fits the figure tightly down to the legs with no specification for the feet. The details are inscribed in the Shang style by sawing, incising and grinding.

However, the ancient tradition did not stay for long. New techniques were soon invented and a new style began to dominate the art until it reached its full maturity in the Late Chou times.

In the Early Chou times, a large number of ceremonial jades were produced. The long *ch'ang* (璋) sceptre (Pl. VIII*a*) was adapted from a thin slab of stone which had been removed from a core by sawing. As the slab is large in size, thin and even in thickness, it seems likely that the sawing was done not by slicing in the neolithic or Shang fashion but by a metal wire bow with sand as abrasive. The shape is rectangular and it consists of a blade and a handle. The handle projects from the base of the blade with finely sawn notches on both sides and a perforation in the middle. The sides of the handle other than the notched sections are also not quite straight. Both surfaces between the two series of notches are decorated with sawn straight lines which correspond with the notches at the sides. These lines are apparently functionally necessary to produce the two series of notches in perfect symmetrical balance. The series of notches, the straight lines at the handle and the curved sides of the blade all indicate that the artisan knew how to handle a wire saw strung on a bow under great tension. The quality of these of lines is very different from the various types of lines on Shang carvings described above. It seems safe to conclude that the Chou stone worker had a new tool — the wire saw — in his working equipment. This new technique as well as other processes of carving were all greatly improved in the Late Chou period. The skill was now established and all the finely finished products with meticulous designs bear witness of new hard tools. These might have been made of steel as iron was already common at that time.

The carved animal and bird pair in Plate VIII*b* shows the remarkable skill of the Chou jade carver. Both the animal and the bird are carved in open work, each standing on a rectangular bracket by means of which they are chained together with a loose fitting link in the form of an oval ring. The entire group was carved in one piece, and each part is covered with some delicate decorative patterns. Some of the fine and accurate perforations are undoubtedly achieved with a very hard point, possibly of diamond.

Some of the Chou jades still retained the shiny unctuous surfaces, which had remained untarnished even after having been buried for more than 2,000 years. Obviously, the artist had used some abrasives capable of giving a high and lasting polish to the gem stone.

Previous to the Eastern Chou period, jade objects were widely used both in personal ornamentation and for ceremonial purposes. Plate VIII c shows a string of beads recovered from the K'ou (虢) royal tomb at Shang-ts'un-ling (上村嶺) in western Honan. They consist of beads of various types of coloured stone. It is interesting to note that there is a curved bead which recalls some of the perforated animal teeth used by the palaeolithic peoples in north China. It is interesting to note that beads of this sort had attracted the fancy of the prehistoric Japanese who treasured them as family heirlooms, commonly used from the final Jomon (繩紋) around 500 B.C. through Yayoi (彌生) to the Tumulus (古墳) period about 500 A.D. They are known in Japanese as *magatama* (勾玉).

Ornamentation with jade in the Late Chou period was standardized. Official strings of jade pieces were assembled systematically with a *pi* disc in the central position. Some of these have been found together in burial grounds at Hui-hsien (輝縣) in Honan. The assemblage of such a string has been reconstructed by Kuo Pao-chun (郭寶鈞) as in the diagram opposite.

Plate VIII*d* shows a *pi* disc which was used in this fashion. The cross marks which appear on the surface of the jade are simply marks left by the stringing cord in burial. The important role that these jade ornaments played in the official life of the period may be substantiated by the contemporary literary records.

Ceremonial *pi* discs of the late Chou period are usually decorated with fine and meticulous designs. The one in Plate IX*a* has galloping dragons in the centre and around the edge all in open work.

The late Chou jade carver also made utensils, some of which are mounted with gilded bronze fittings. Plate IX *b* is a three-legged *lien* (奩) box, with two handles, one with a movable ring. The wall of the box is decorated with *ku wen* (穀紋) "grain-pattern". The circular cover is set in a gilt bronze rim, on which stand beautiful, naturalistically-modelled bronze birds.

As a whole jade carving in the Late Chou period inclined to break with the past tradition, by favouring objects for secular use.

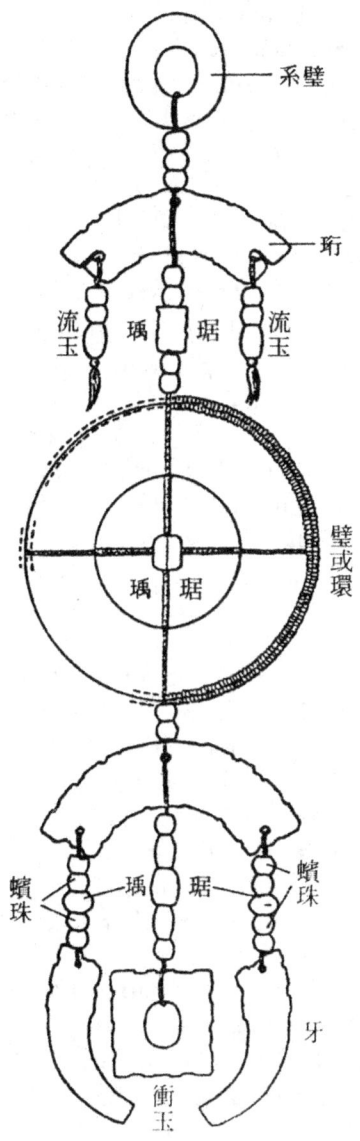

系璧

珩

流玉　瑀　琚　流玉

璧或環

瑀琚

蠙珠　瑀　琚　蠙珠

牙

衝玉

Reconstruction of a Chan-kuo (戰國) *jade pendant with the names of the various parts in Chinese* — 8, 196.

The jade carver came to enjoy a freedom in creating new forms and new patterns. The development was mainly in the direction of increased abrasive efficiency, new forms, improved workmanship and, larger compositions, using jade as a medium of free artistic expression. It seems safe to conclude that Chinese jade carving reached its full maturity at the end of the Chou dynasty in the third century B.C. The technique was already well established. The art became independent and was ready to ally itself irrevocably with the jeweller — a tradition which has continued to be in vogue until the present day.

As a symbol of Chinese culture the carving of jade in China continued without any interruption throughout the following dynasties. The lapidary was forever ready to match the change of style and fashion of the time. The tendency has indeed become more and more elaborate with the years, showing the gradual improvement in the technique and skill of execution. A few examples from each period may be given below to illustrate its long development.

Han jade
The most common jade ornaments of the Han period are fittings of weapons, especially the sword, which uses a triangular piece for the guard, a disc for the hilt and a chape and a finale for the scabbard. The chape or buckle in Plate X *a* is decorated with a mother dragon playing with her cub in high relief. The incised linear design on the side is quite Late Chou in style. The scabbard fitting on the same plate has a curling dragon in low relief and the geometric design on the other side recalls also some typical late Chou pattern.

The Han jade carver was also quite proficient in fashioning figures in the round. The pair of curtsying women (Pl. XI *a*) in the Sidgewick collection, now in the British Museum is well known. The figures were fashioned in the style of Han mortuary figurines.

Recently a jade winged fairy on his horse has been unearthed from the royal burial compound of Emperor Han Chao-ti (漢昭帝). The animal is trotting on a flat platform shaped like a piece of cloud showing that the heavenly being is returning home in the sphere above. (See Pl. XI *b*.) This is a very popular subject in Han art and it shows that the jade carver was ready to serve the fashion of his time because the technique was already sophisticated.

Six Dynasties jades

The Six Dynasties has been regarded in the past as a dark period as the carving of jade is concerned. But archaeological investigation has brought to light some information about the art at this stage. One of the sources is furnished by a few fine stone carvings of Buddhist figures and stelae. The stele reproduced in Plate XII *a* is dated 484 A.D. The carving is close to the style of the stone sculpture of this period so it may be taken as an example to show how the art was adapted to serve the new religion which was beginning to take roots in China.

Some jade animals may also be ascribed to the Six Dynasties by analogy between their type forms and those in stone. Many example to show how the art was adapted to serve the new public and private collections appear to be closely akin to the stone *pi-hsueh* (辟邪) tomb guards of this period in form and in spirit, though always in miniature. One of these has recently been published by the Palace Museum in Peking, (Pl. XII *b*) and two others from the Mu-fei collection are on display in the jade exhibition in London. They are reproduced here in Plate XII *c* and *d*.

T'ang jade

It is well-known that belts were beginning to be decorated with jade plaques in the T'ang times. One of these, a rectangular piece with the design of a T'ang musician may be seen in Plate XIII *a*. The material was first sliced into slabs in the ancient fashion and the decorative pattern, a seated flute player, was carved in low relief. At the four corners on the back are four tunneled perforations which were meant for attachment to the belt itself.

The popularity of the musical pattern in the T'ang times may be illustrated by the small figurine (Pl. XIII *b*). It is in a dancing posture with the left leg curling up behind the right, the right arm up behind the head, and the left placed in front just below the breast. She has a round face and looks almost exactly like those T'ang figurines in pottery and stone as well as in painting. She wears a long sleeved dress and her belt is decorated with rectangular plaques in the T'ang fashion.

Plate XIII *c* is an ox-head ryton cup which calls to mind the metal work of the T'ang period. It shows that the T'ang jade carver did not hesitate to copy other works of art.

Five Dynasties jade

Jade carving in the Five Dynasties may be represented by a group of jade objects from the tomb of Wang Chien (王建), the emperor of Shu (蜀) with its capital in Ch'eng-tu (成都). It is dated 918 A.D. Among the funerary furniture is a jade book comprising a series of slender tablets on which the eulogical essay for the emperor was inscribed. They are strung together with silver cords. The mortuary seal gives the ceremonial title of the emperor. It has a knob in the shape of a crouching animal and the four sides are decorated with the *Ssu-ning* (四靈), Deities of the Four Directions by linear incision. The materials of the book and the seal are both quite advanced in calcification. Rubbings of the latter may be seen in Plate XIV *a*.

In the same plate are the rubbings of a set of eight pieces of jade together with two silver buckles. According to the inscription on the elongated "tail" plaque, the ornaments were carved from a boulder specially for the emperor's belt. The design in low-relief depicts a dragon going after a flaming pearl. The material is better preserved than the book and the seal from the same burial.

Sung jade

The carving of jade in the Sung period may be represented by a large number of cups and vases which are archaic in style. They are usually ascribed to the period on the bases of stylistic analogy. One of these has been published recently by the Palace Museum in Peking. It shows a cup with a dragon handle, recalling the auspicious animal of the Han period. But the cup itself is six-lobed forming a flower of six round petals in outline. See Plate XV*a.*

Another example, a saucer with foliate rim forming a flower of six pointed petals in outline, is reported to have been unearthed in a tomb at Hang-chou(杭州), the capital of the Southern Sung Dynasty. (Pl. XV *b*) The shape and style are both unmistakably Sung; simple, delicate and elegant, recalling a large number of foliated vessels in porcelain and lacquer of the same period.

Sung jade may yet be represented by a number of jade flower ornaments which were beginning to be in vogue in the Sung and the following periods. Plate XV *c* reproduces a rosette of five flowers which are joined to one another into a pentagonal plaque by collecting their stems in the centre. Designs of floral form seem to have begun to attract the imagination of the jadesmith at this stage.

Yuan jade

For the Yuan period there are a number of archaeological finds which show the art in transition from Sung to Ming. A belt slide with pendant loop reported from Inner Mongolia may be taken as an example. The design depicts a goose and a swallow playing among the lotus in openwork framed within a rectangular beaded border. See Plate XVI *a*.

The next example (Pl. XVI *b*) is a large flower disc which may be dated to the 14th century. The design on the front is arranged in three concentric bands. The outer ring is composed of eight stylized peach-shaped petals generally described as the *ju-i*(如意) symbol, a popular design on Yuan and Ming lacquer. The back of the flower illustrates eight overlapping petals radiating from a central disc with the *t'ai-chi*(太極) *yin* and *yang* (陰陽) design, and a tunnelled perforation, which may be used for attachment.

The Palace Museum in Peking has recently published a two handled incense burner (Pl. XVIc). The main decoration on the body is a dragon among the clouds in medium relief and the handles each adorned with a dragon head. It is quite archaic in appearance, but the lattice which serves as the background seems to have initiated a new departure for the decoration of many Ming jade and lacquer works.

Ming jade

Jade carving of the Ming period may first be represented by a group of decorated cups preserved in the Teheran Museum. They have been in the Persian collection since the 15th century. One of these is a dragon handled ewer with raised dragons in high relief on the rim (Pl. XVII *a*). It shows the continuation of the Sung archaic style. Another example of the same style has been published by the Peking Palace Museum (Pl. XVII *b*). As the material is finer in quality than the Teheran specimen, the school of dragons among the waves are better executed in a superior technique.

Jade flower carving in the Sung fashion continued to develop with many more elaborate compositions. Plate XVIII *c*, shows a typical example, composed of a double flower surrounded by a series of auspicious symbols, namely plum-blossom, bamboo, pine, *luan* (鸞) bird, *ho* (盒) box and *pai-ho* (百合) lily. It is executed in openwork characteristic of Ming delicate craftsmanship.

Jade belt plaques continued to be in vogue in the Ming period. They appeared in various sizes and shapes and increased greatly in number, in some cases no less than eighteen pieces being used to decorate one belt. A group of ornaments of this type has been reported from a Ming royal tomb near Peking. A few examples are reproduced in Plate XVIII *a*. The larger plaques are all elaborately carved depicting dragons among flowers in openwork.

A few years ago, the royal tomb of Ting-ling (定陵) yielded a large number of jade utensils which are now on display in the Underground Palace Museum at the site. The two-handled cup with a gilt silver stand is reproduced in Plate XVIII *b* as an example.

Ch'ing jade

In the Ch'ing period jade was applied to many of the purposes that it had served for centuries and also to many new ones. Nephrite from Chinese Turkestan, jadeite from Yunnan and Burma and spinach jade from Siberia reached the capital in large quantities and the great majority of the decorative jades among the furniture of the palaces were made of these materials. The halls of the palaces in Peking still contain thousands of carved jades and many of them have found their way into private and public collections abroad. Some of the objects were purely ornamental: figurines and animals, vessels reproducing ancient bronzes, vases and perfume holders, seals and Buddhist figures and many others.

Plate XVIII*c* shows a large square seal dated 1790 A.D. The knob is fashioned in the form of an animal with two heads, one on each end, and the four sides are covered with long inscriptions.

A Buddha set on a gilded bronze throne and nimbus and decorated with inlaid gem stones from the collection of the late Queen Mary may be seen in Plate XIX *a*. It is reputed to be a work of the 17th century.

The two-handled bowl (Pl. XIX *b*) carved and decorated in the so-called Mogul style with inlaid gold and ruby is a treasure of the Peking Palace Museum. Much of this type of work was produced for the Indian market in the eighteenth century.

The jade vase and its cover in Plate XIX *c* are connected to each other with a chain of 32 links. It is fascinating to note that the vessel was carved out of one chunk of jade into 35 parts and they are all linked together in one group.

The pagoda reproduced in Plate XIX *d* was made in a different way. It is composed of literally several hundred parts, each carved separately and assembled later into this huge structure. The technique of precision carving was indeed at its height in the 18th century. The work was exhibited in the Golden Gate Exhibition in San Francisco in 1938 and it is now a treasure of the University of Oregon.

It was quite common at this stage to have a large boulder carved in one piece to represent a solid landscape in three dimension. The one reproduced in Plate XX *a* furnishes a splendid example. It depicts the activities of Emperor Yü (禹) in water control with some poems composed by Emperor Chien-lung (乾隆) carved on the cliff on the mountain side. A detail of the meticulous carving may be seen in Plate XX *b*. The work is dated 1784 and it is on exhibition in the Peking

Palace Museum.

Modern jade
Finally, Plate XX*c* presents a piece of new jade carved in 1958. It shows a vase entwined with various types of vegetables and insects. All the cucumbers, carrots, crickets and others are in the round and various coloured parts of the stone are used in their respective ways to form the composition.

The carving of jade in China indeed makes a long history. In this brief account of the celebrated tradition, no less than 7,000 years' works have been surveyed ranging from the neolithic period to modern times. It shows clearly that the art has survived throughout the ages as a living tradition. The jade carvers today are ready to produce anything to order. Many of their magnificent works may be seen in the numerous art galleries in Hong Kong.

Bibliography

Andersson, J.G.
1. Researches into the prehistory of the Chinese, *Bulletin of the Museum of Far Eastern Antiquities*, 15, Stockholm, 1943
Cheng Te-k'un (鄭 德 坤)
2. The Royal tomb of Wang Chien (王建), *Harvard Journal of Asiatic Studies*, 1945
3. *Chinese jade*, West China Union University Museum, Guidebook Series, No. 1, Chengtu, 1945
4. T'ang and Ming jades, *Transactions of the Oriental Ceramic Society*, London, 1955
5. The Carving of jade in the Shang period, *Transactions of the Oriental Ceramic Society*, London, 1957
6. *Archaeology in China*, vol. I: *Prehistoric China*, Cambridge, 1959
7. *Archaeology in China*, vol. II: *Shang China*, Cambridge, 1961
8. *Archaeology in China*, vol. III: *Chou China*, Cambridge, 1963
9. Some standing jade figures of the Shang-Chou period, *Artibus Asiae*, Ascona, 1966
10. Jade flowers and floral patterns in Chinese decorative art, *Journal of the Institute of Chinese Studies, Hong Kong*, 1969
11. *An Introduction to Chinese Art and archaeology — the Cambridge outline and reading lists*, Cambridge, 1973
Gray, B., and other,
12. *Chinese Jade throughout the Ages*, London, 1975
Hansford, S.H.,
13. *Chinese Carved Jades*, London, 1968
Institute of Archaeology and others,
14. *Hsin Chung-kuo ti k'ao-ku shou-hou* (新中國的考古收獲), Peking, 1962
Lin Shuo-chin (林壽晉),
15. *Shang-ts'un-ling Kuo-kuo mu-ti* (上村嶺虢國墓地), Peking, 1959
Loehr, M.,
16. *Ancient Chinese Jades*, Harvard, 1975
Nott, S.C.,
17. *Chinese Jade*, London, 1936
Palace Museum (故宮博物院)
18. *Ku-kung-po-wu-yuan ts'ang kung-i-p'in hsuan* (故宮博物院藏工藝品選), Peking 1974
Salmony, A.,
19. *Carved Jade of Ancient China*, Berkeley, 1938
Umehara, S., (梅原 末治)
20. *Kanan Anyo imotsu no kenkyū* (河南安陽遺物之研究), Kyoto, 1941
21. *Shina kōgyoku zuroku,* (支那古玉圖錄), Kyōto, 1955
Wen-wu Editorial Committe (文物編輯委員會)
22. Wen-wu ch'an-k'ao tzu-liao (文物參考資料) 1955

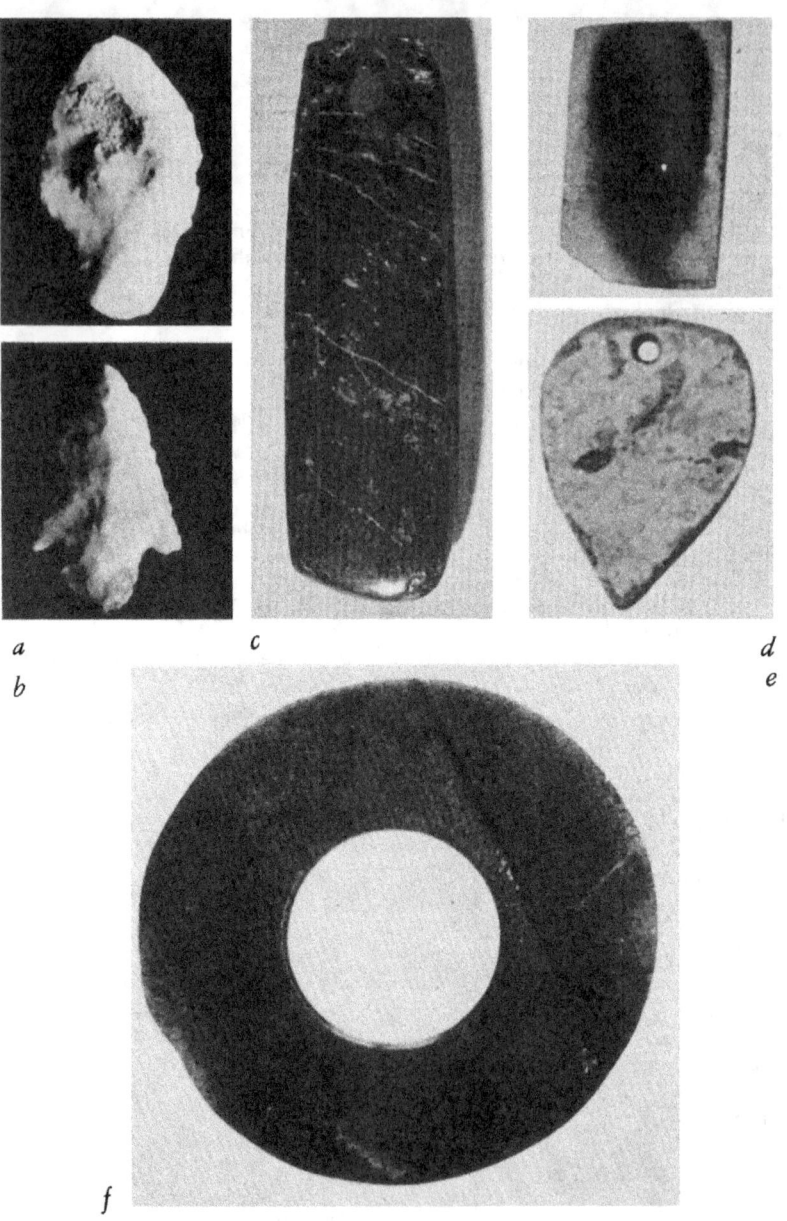

Plate I — Prehistoric jade

(a.) Chipped arrowhead, leaf-shaped, quartz, Pei-tai-ho (北戴河), Hopei, Mu-fei
(木扉) collection. *(b.)* Chipped arrowhead, triangular barbed shape, quartz,
Pei-tai-ho, Hopei, Mu-fei collection. *(c.)* Chipped, polished and perforated slender
axe, nephrite, Mu-fei collection. *(d.)* Fragment of a chisel, nephrite, **1**, Front, Pl. 2,
11. *(e.)* Heart-shaped perforated pendant, turquoise, **1**, Front, Pl. 2, 2. *(f.)* Pi-dis
(璧) with straight saw-mark, nephrite, **1**, Front, Pl. 1, 2.

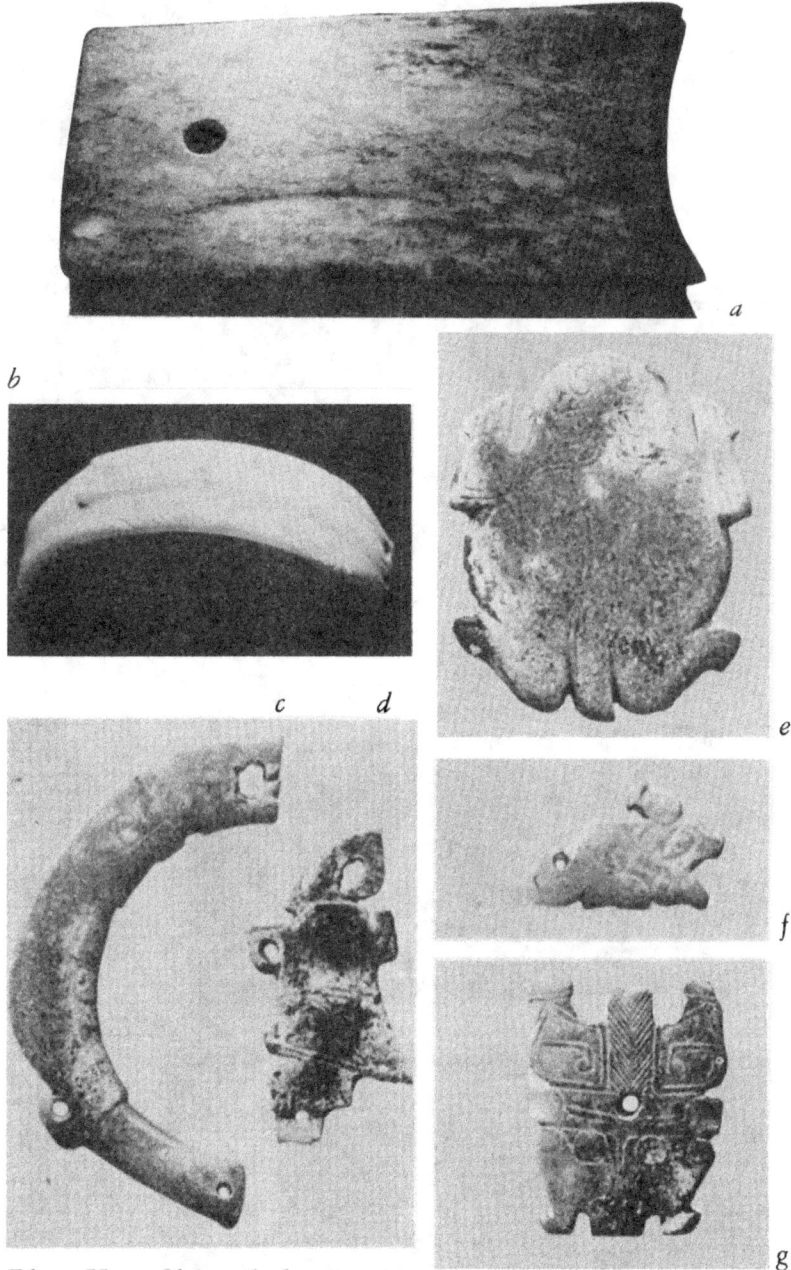

Plate II — Shang jade

(a.) Perforated rectangular blade with circular saw-mark, Mu-fei collection. (b.) Curved fish adapted from a broken ring, **7,** Pl. XIV.d. (c.) Huang (璜) disc segment in the shape of a dragon. **20,** Pl. 27. (d.) Ornamental head of a pin in the shape of a bird. **20,** Pl. 27. (e.) Ornament in the shape of a frog. **20,** Pl. 27. (f.) Incisor in the shape of a bottle-horned hare. **20,** Pl. 27. (g.) Ornament in the shape of a t'ao-t'ieh (饕餮) mask. **20,** Pl. 27.

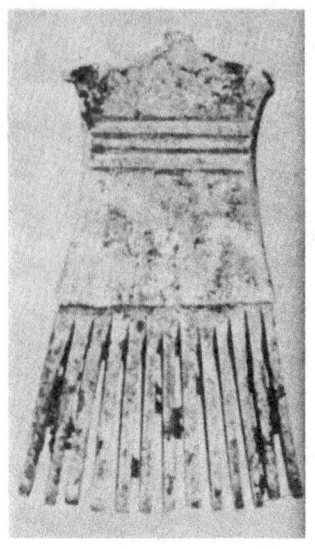

a

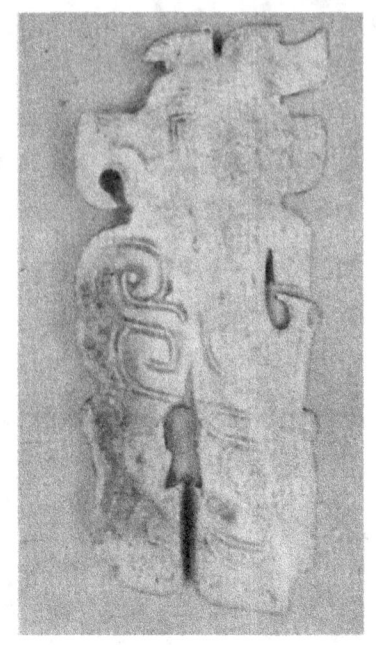

d

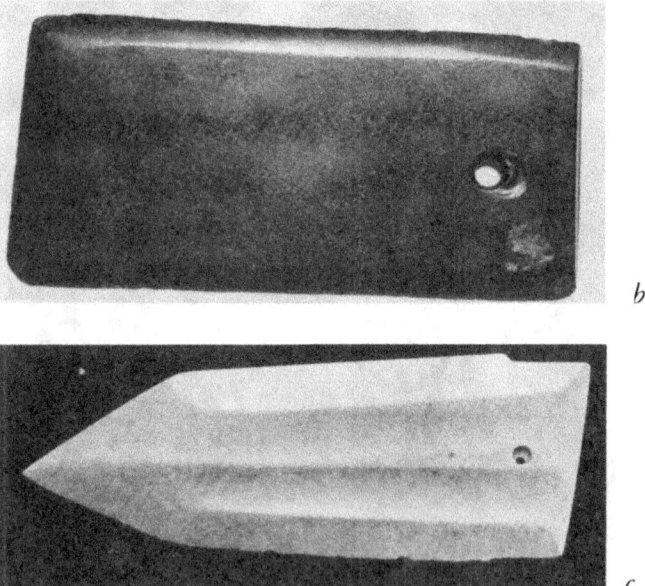

b

c

Plate III — Shang jade

(a.) Comb. **20**, Pl. 27. *(b.)* Rectangular blade with perforations. 7, Pl. XIV. *b. (c.) Ko*
(戈) blade with perforation. 7, Pl. XIV. *f. (d.)* Ornament in the shape of a bird. 7,
Pl. XV. *a.*

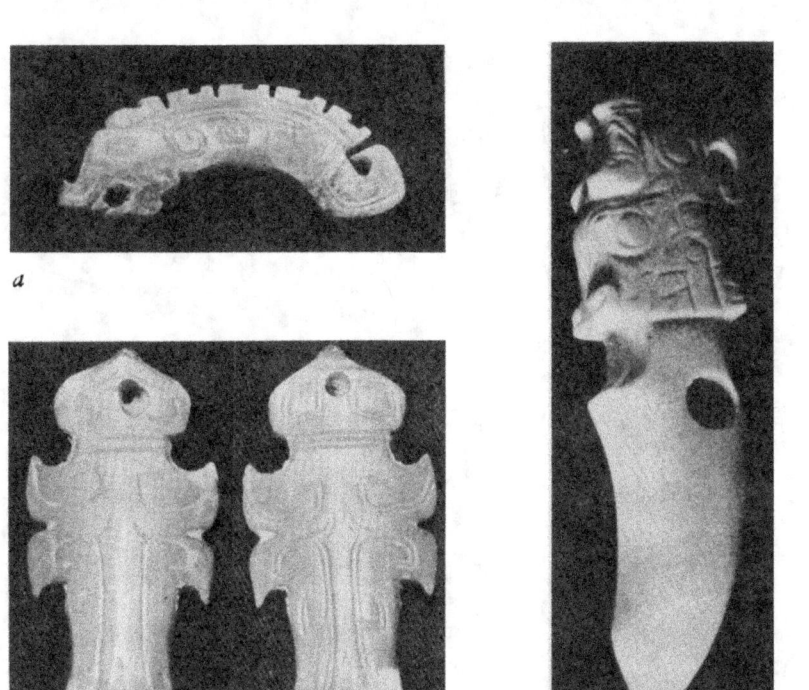

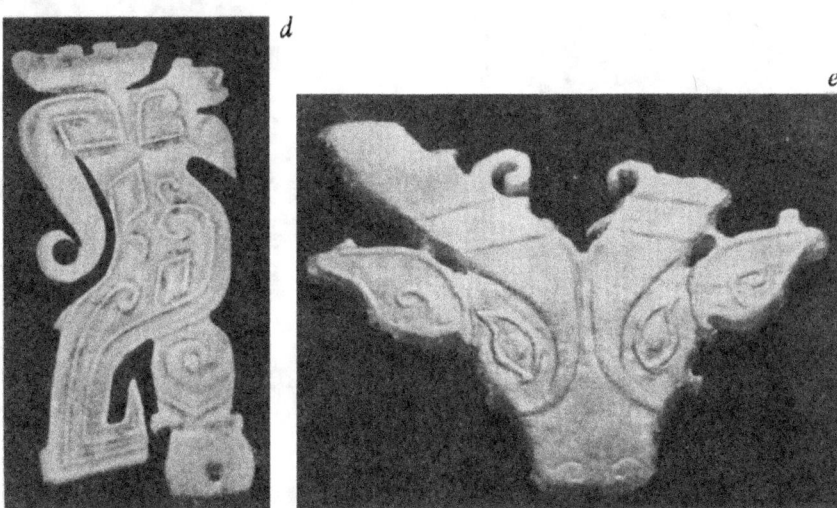

Plate IV — Shang jade

(a.) Ornament in the shape of a dragon. 7, Pl. XV. *d.* *(b.)* *Mi* (弭) bow-fitting with a bottle-horned dragon. 7, Pl. XVIII. *c.* *(c).* Ornament in the shape of a cicada, two views. 7, Pl. XV. *c.* *(d.)* Ornamental head of a pin in the shape of a bird. 7, Pl. XVI. *e.* *(e.)* Ornament in the shape of a goat's head. 7, Pl. XV. *e.*

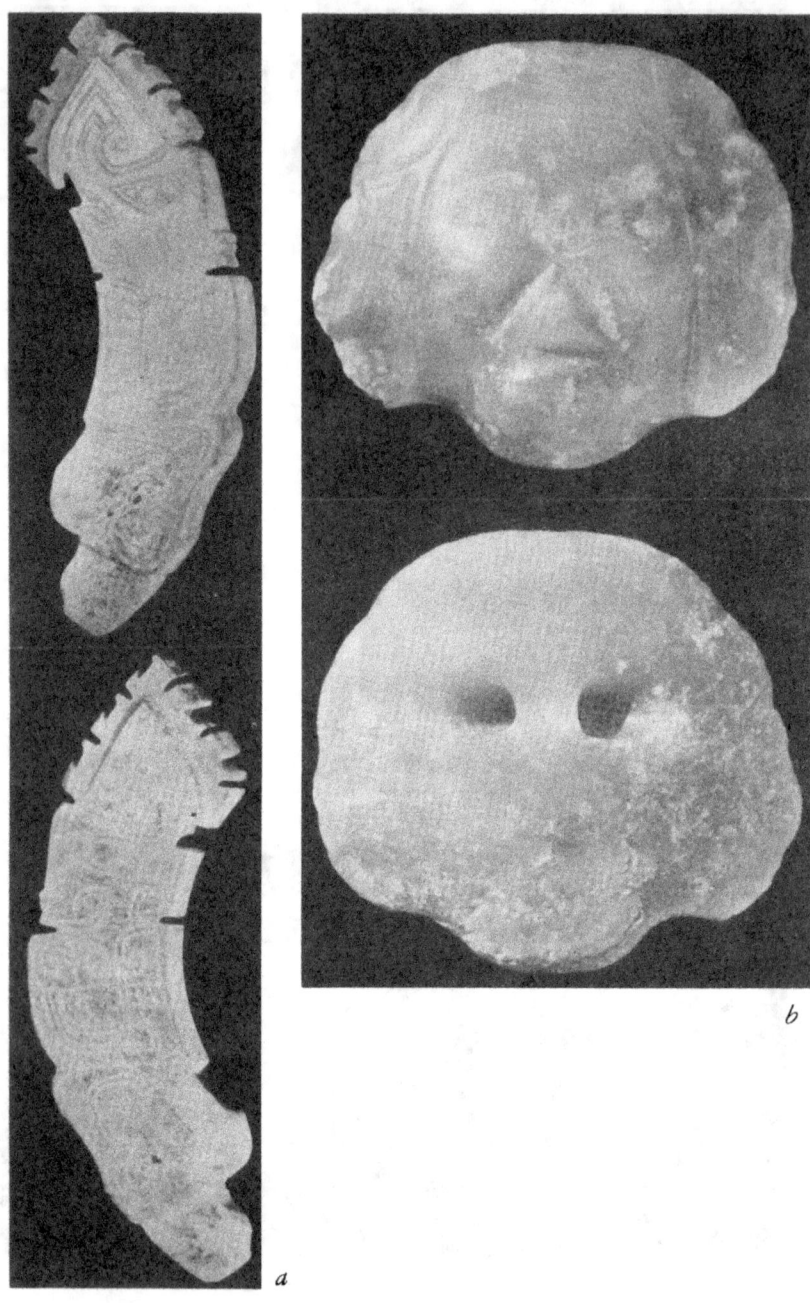

Plate V — Shang jade

(a.) Ornamental head of a pin in the shape of a bird-headed figure, 7, XVI. *b.* *(b.)* Ornament in the shape of a human head with a tunnelled perforation at the back. Mu-fei collection.

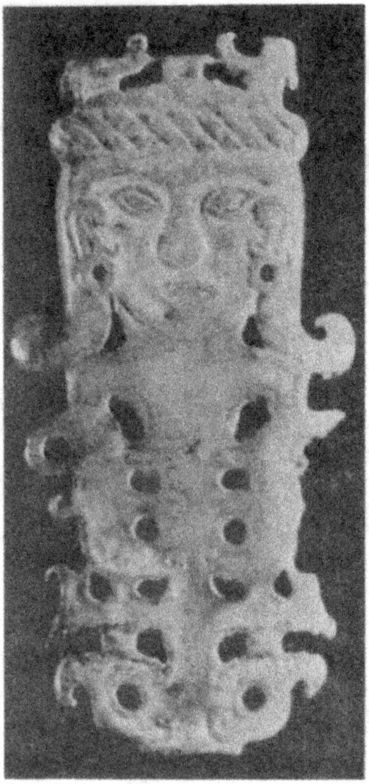

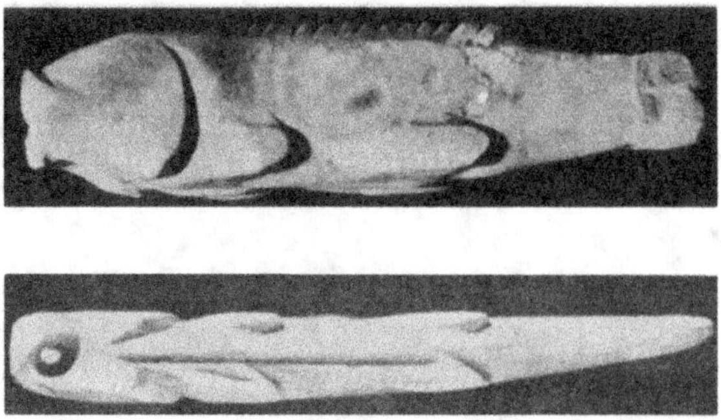

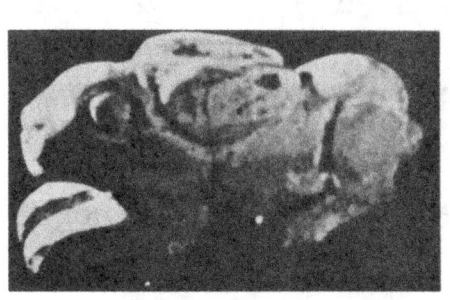

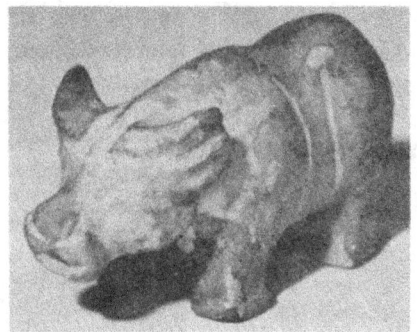

Plate VI — Shang jade

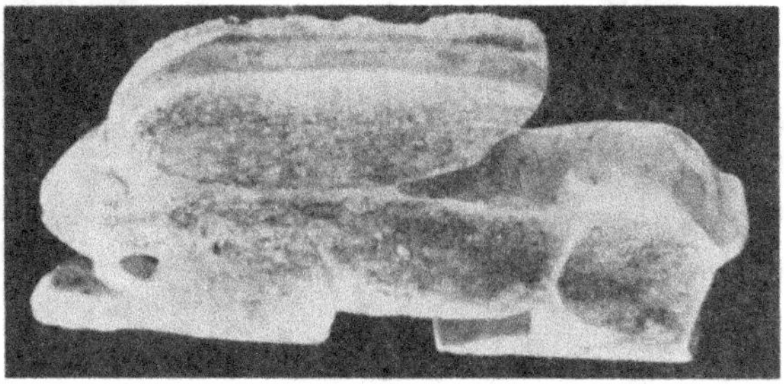

(a.) Human figure in openwork. **12,** Pl.1. *(b.)* Fish in sculptural form, 2 views, **7,** Pl. XIX. *a. (c.)* Hare in rectangular form. **7,** Pl. XIX. *e. (d.)* Hare in rectangular form. **7,** Pl. XIX. *f. (e.)* Buffalo in sculptural form. **7,** Pl. XIV. *c.*

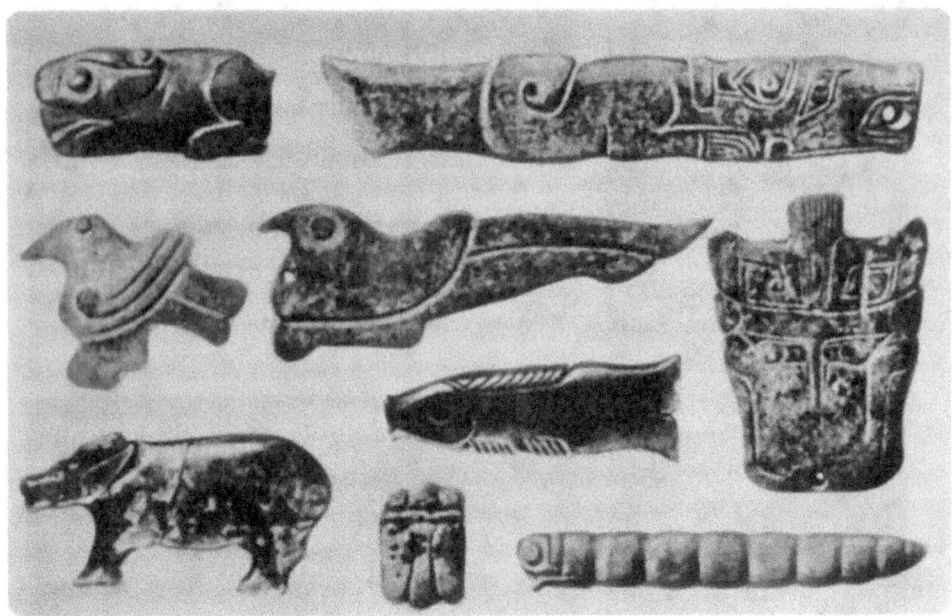

a

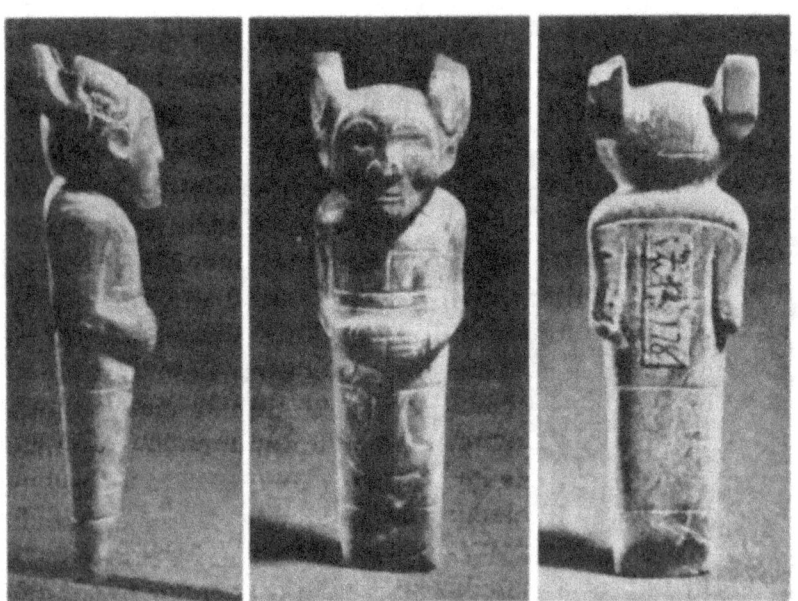

b

Plate VII — Chou jade

(a.) A group of jade artifacts from Chang-chia p'o (張家坡). Sian. **14**, Pl. XXXV 2. *(b.)* Standing human figures, 3 view, from Pai-ma-ssu (白馬寺), Loyang. **9**, fig. 13.

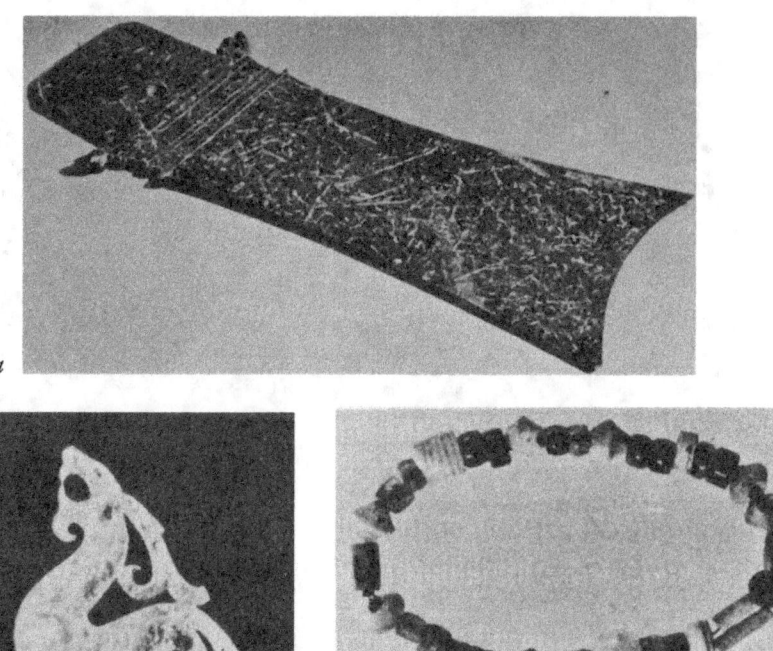

a

c

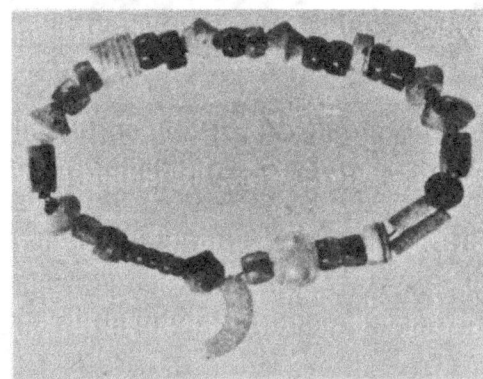

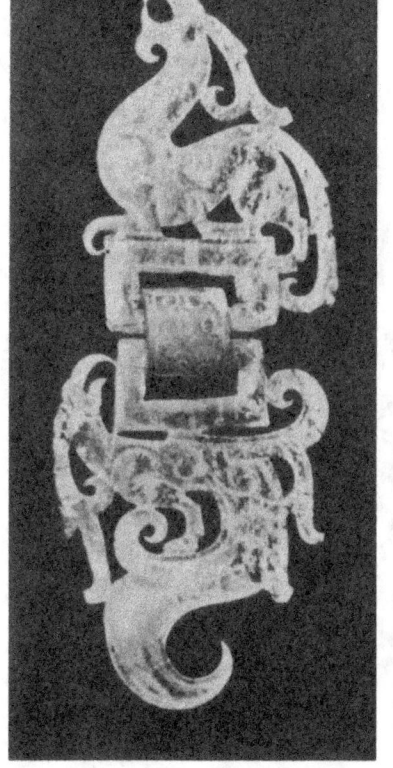

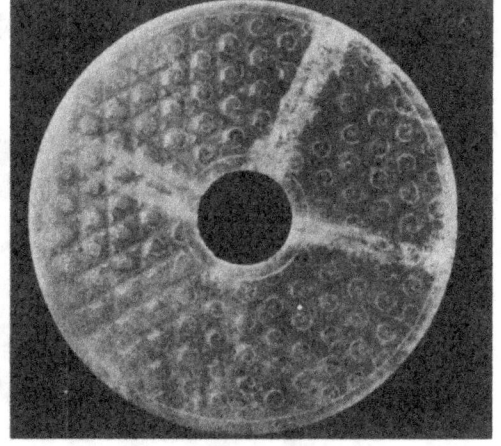

b

d

Plate VIII — Chou jade

(a.) Ch'ang (璋) blade with wire-saw marks, **12,** No. 22 *(b.)* Animal and bird plaques linked with an oval ring. **16,** No. 508. *(c.)* String of necklace from Shang-ts'un-ling (上村嶺), San-men-hsia (三門峽) **15,** Pl. III. *(d.)* *Pi* disc with cord impressions. **8,** Pl. 5a.

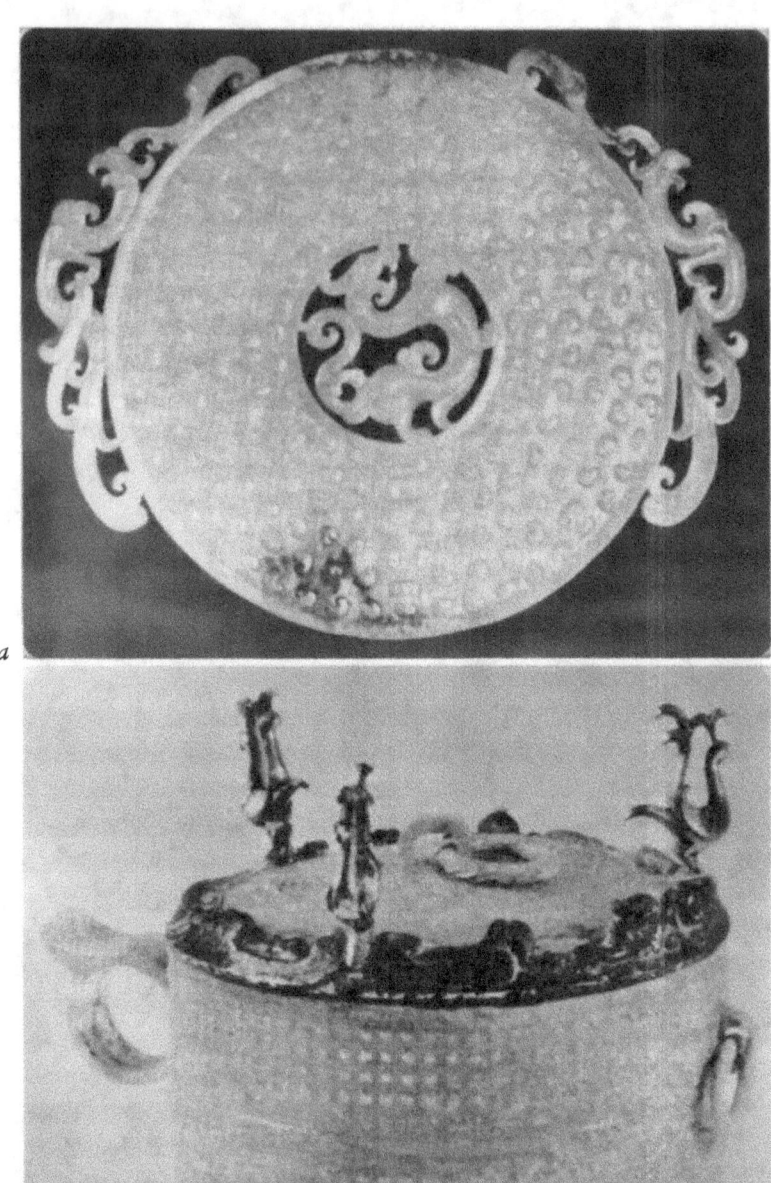

a

b

Plate IX — Chou jade

(a.) Pi-disc with animal and birds in openwork, **18,** No. 10. *(b.) Lien* (奩) box
with gilt mount around the cover. **16,** No. 521.

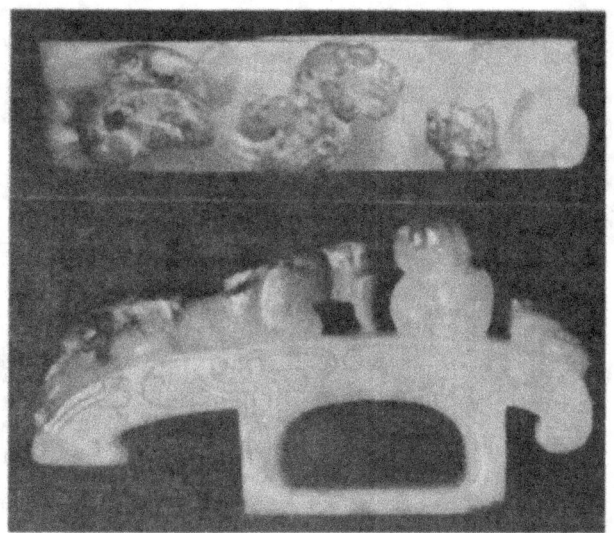

a

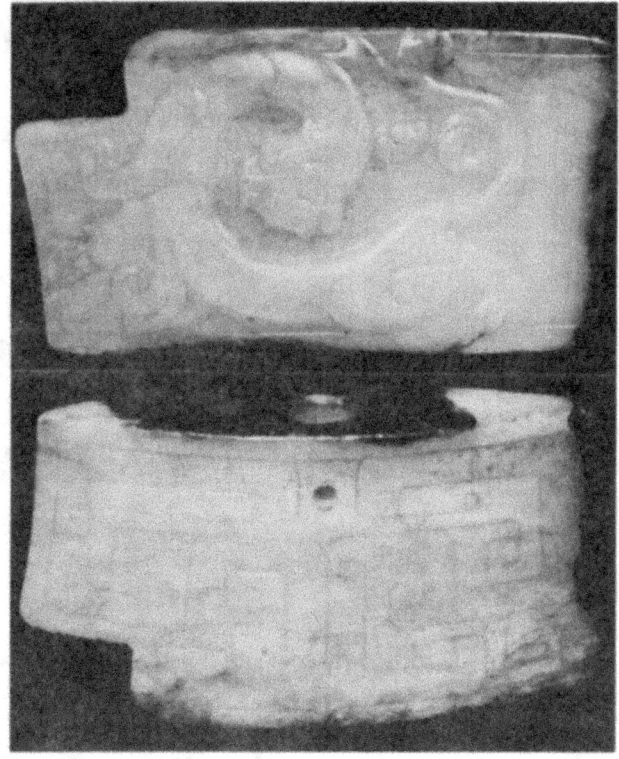

b

Plate X — Han jade

(a.) Sui (璲) scabbard buckle with mother and cub dragon in high relief and incised linear design, two views. Mu-fei collection. *(b.) Pi* (珌) scabbard fitting with dragon in low relief and incised geometric design, two views. Mu-fei collection.

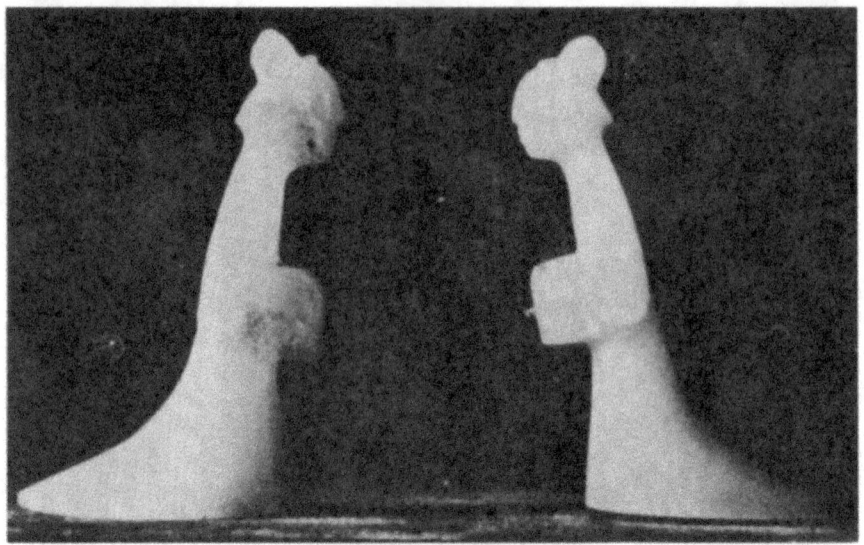

a

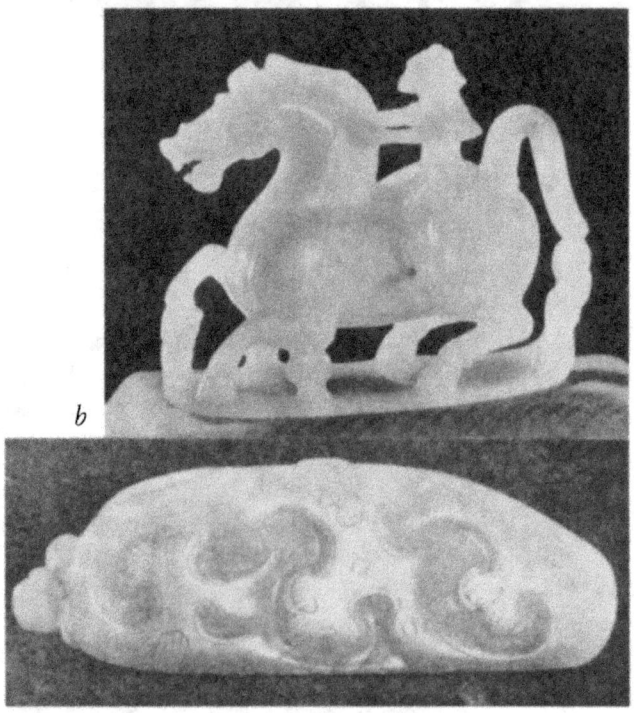

b

Plate XI — Han jade

(a.) Pair of human figures. Sidgewick collection. Now in British Museum. *(b.)* Horse and rider on a flat platform with cloud pattern, from Hsien-yang (咸陽), Shensi. Cambridge Exhibition of Archaeological Photographs from China, 1974, No. 56.

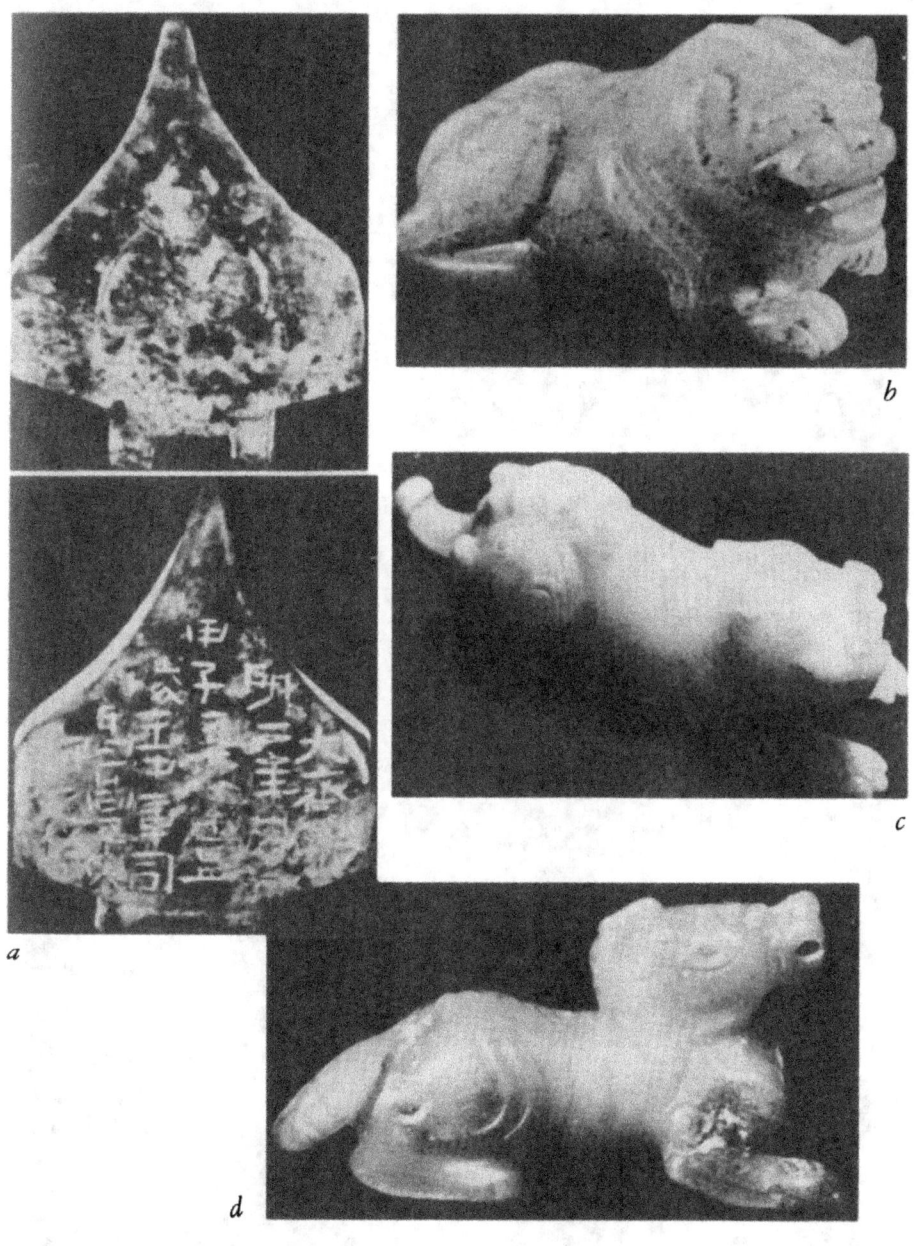

Plate XII — Six Dynasties jade

(a.) Buddhist stele with inscription, dated 484 A.D., two views, **19**, Pl. 70.3. *(b.)* Pi-hsieh (辟邪) animal figure. **18,** No. 19. *(c.)* Pi-hsieh animal figure. **12,** No. 179. *(d.)* Pi-hsieh animal figure. **12,** No. 180.

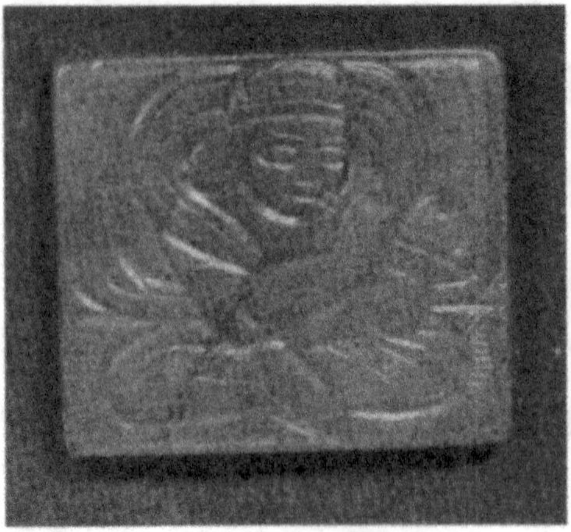

a

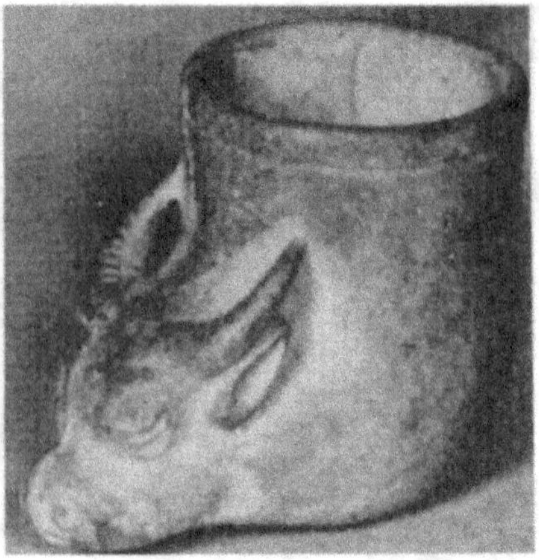

c

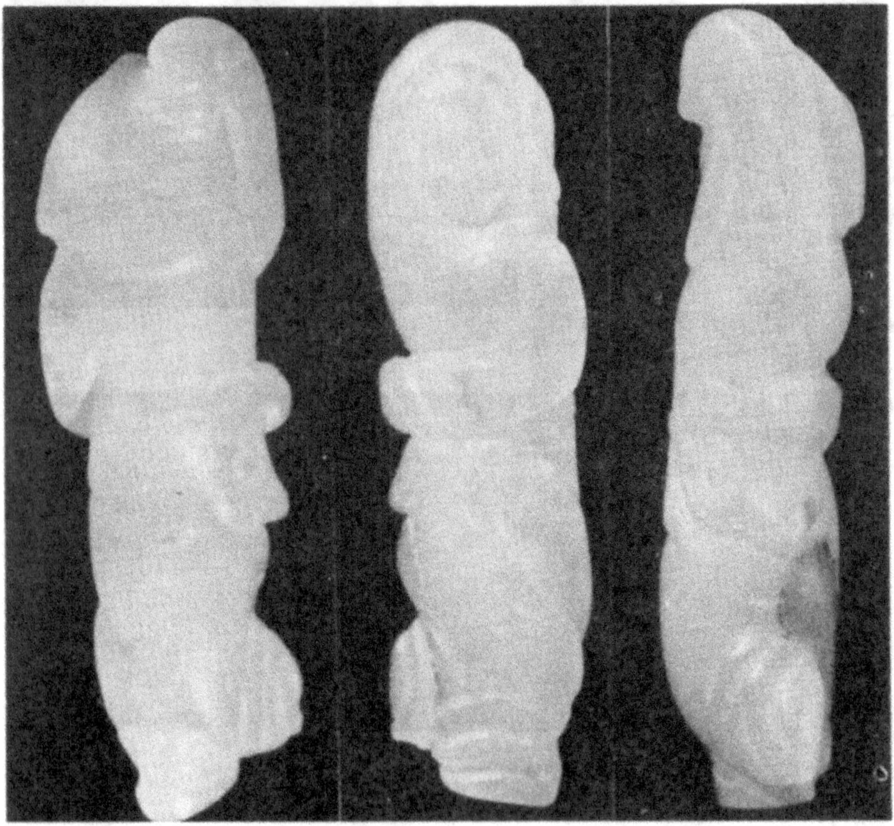

b

Plate XIII — T'ang jade

(a.) Belt plaque with an incised flut player **4**, Pl. 61a. *(b.)* Female dancer, three views. **4**, Pl. 6.3. *(c.)* Rhyton cup with an ox head. Mu-fei collection.

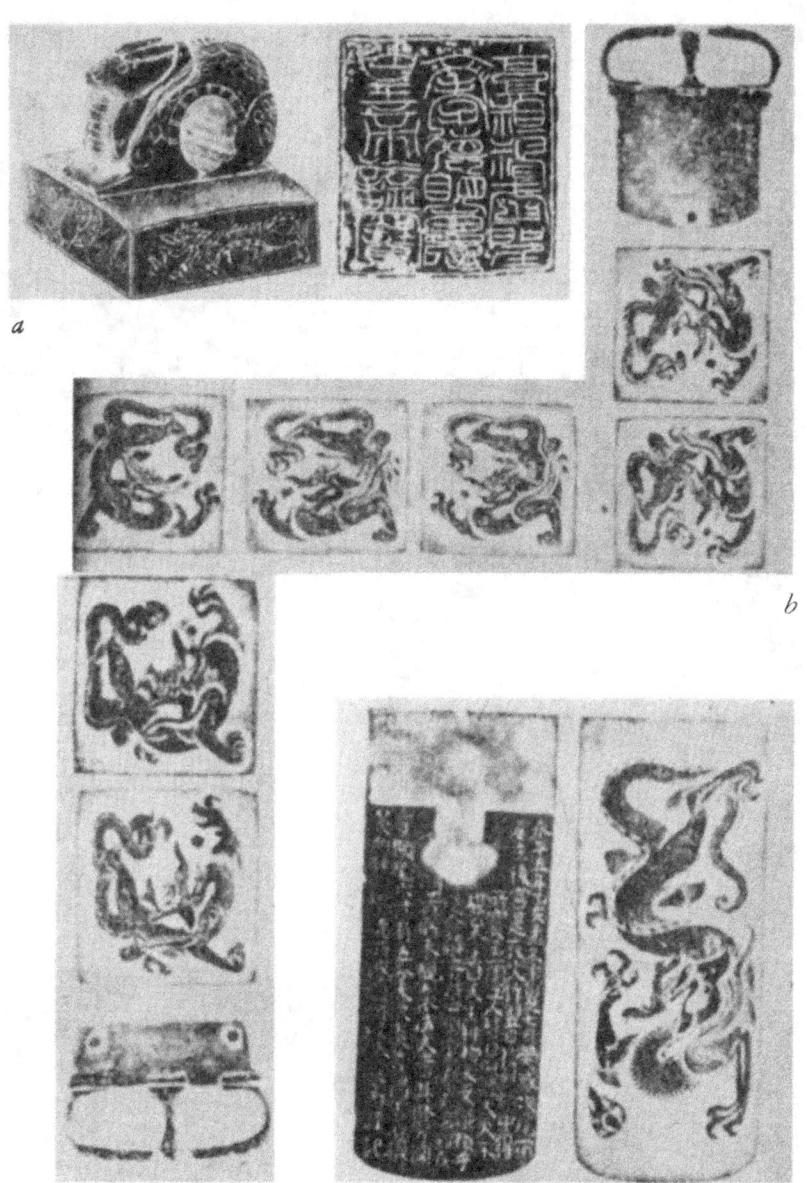

a

b

Plate XIV — Five Dynasties jade

(a.) Mortuary seal of King Wang Chien (王建),with inscription, ink rubbings.
2.*(b.)* Set of belt plaques with dragon designs in low relief and inscription, ink rubbings, **22,** 55.3.7.

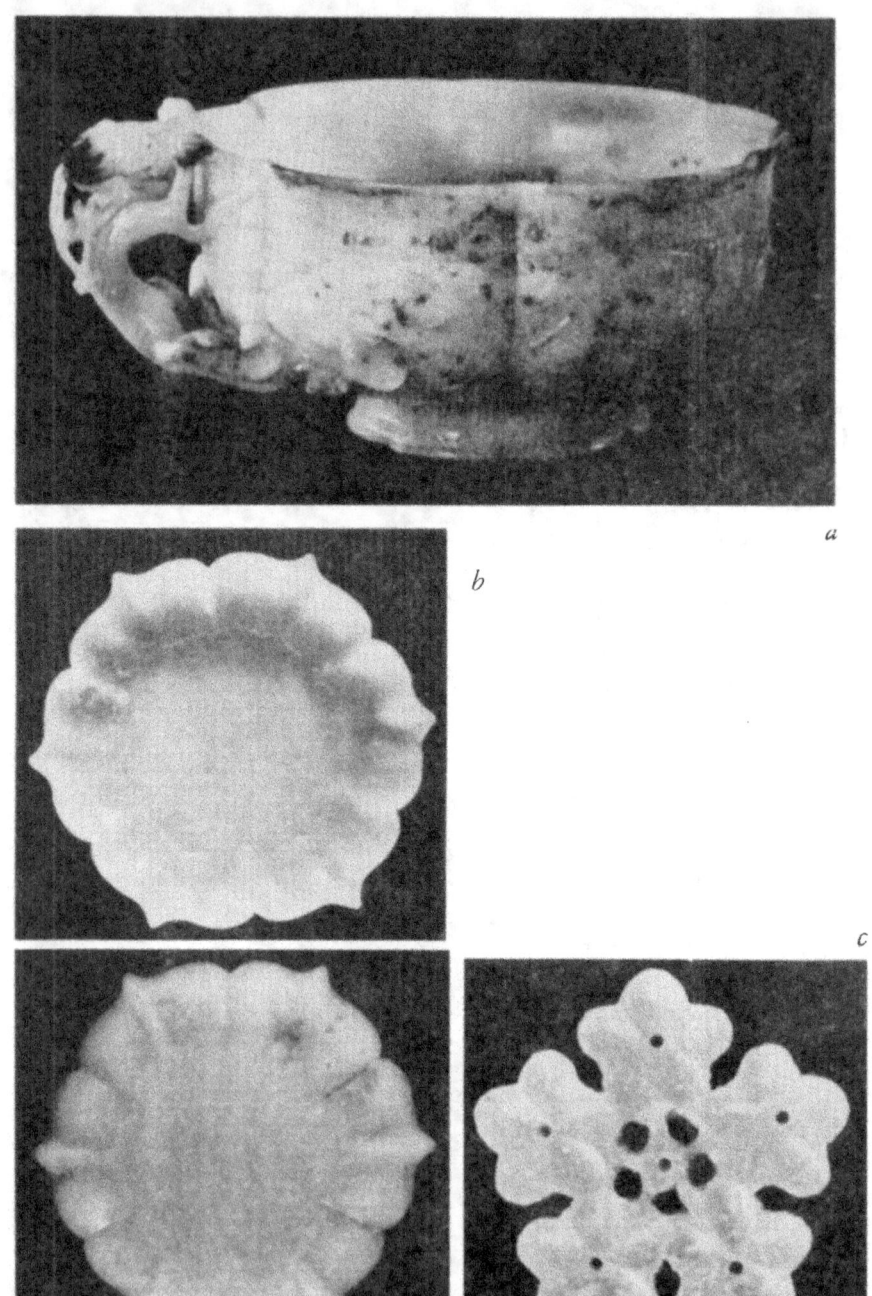

Plate XV — Sung jade

(a.) Sung bowl. **18**, No. 26 *(b.)* Flower-shaped saucer. **10**, Fig. 3*a*. *(c.)* Flower button, **12**, No. 351. *a*.

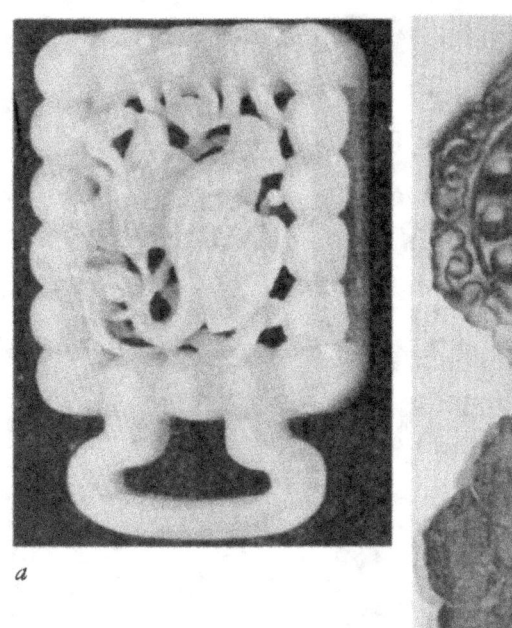

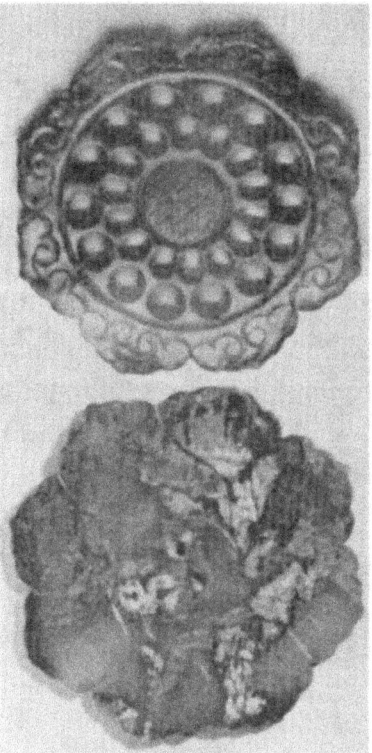

Plate XVI — Yuan jade

(a.) Belt loop, **12**, No. 348. *(b.)* Flower button, with tunnelled perforation in the back. **10**, Fig. 2.*a.* *(c.)* *Lu* (爐) incense burner, with dragon design in medium relief. **18**, No. 29.

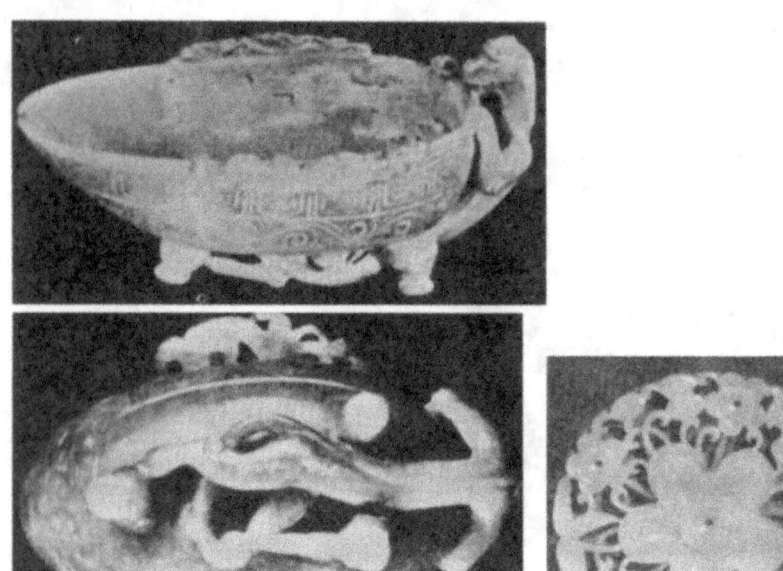

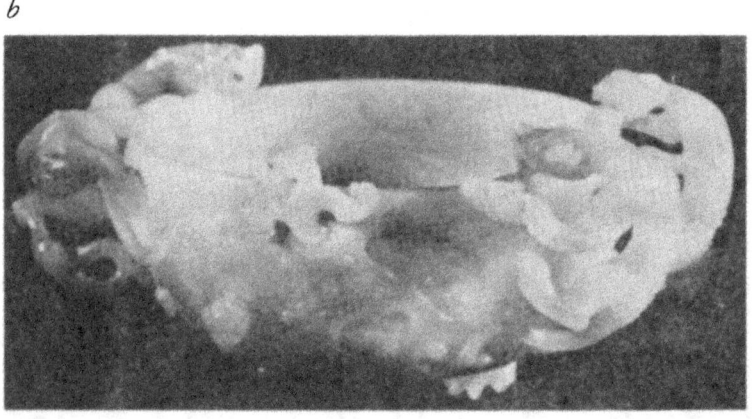

Plate XVII — Ming jade

(a.) Dragon handled ewer, two views. National Archaeological Museum, Teheran after *Transactions of the Oriental Ceramic Society.* **25,** Pl. 4. *a.* & *b.* *(b.)* Oval cup with dragons in high relief. **18,** No. 35. *(c.)* Flower buttons in openwork. **12,** No. 351. *c.*

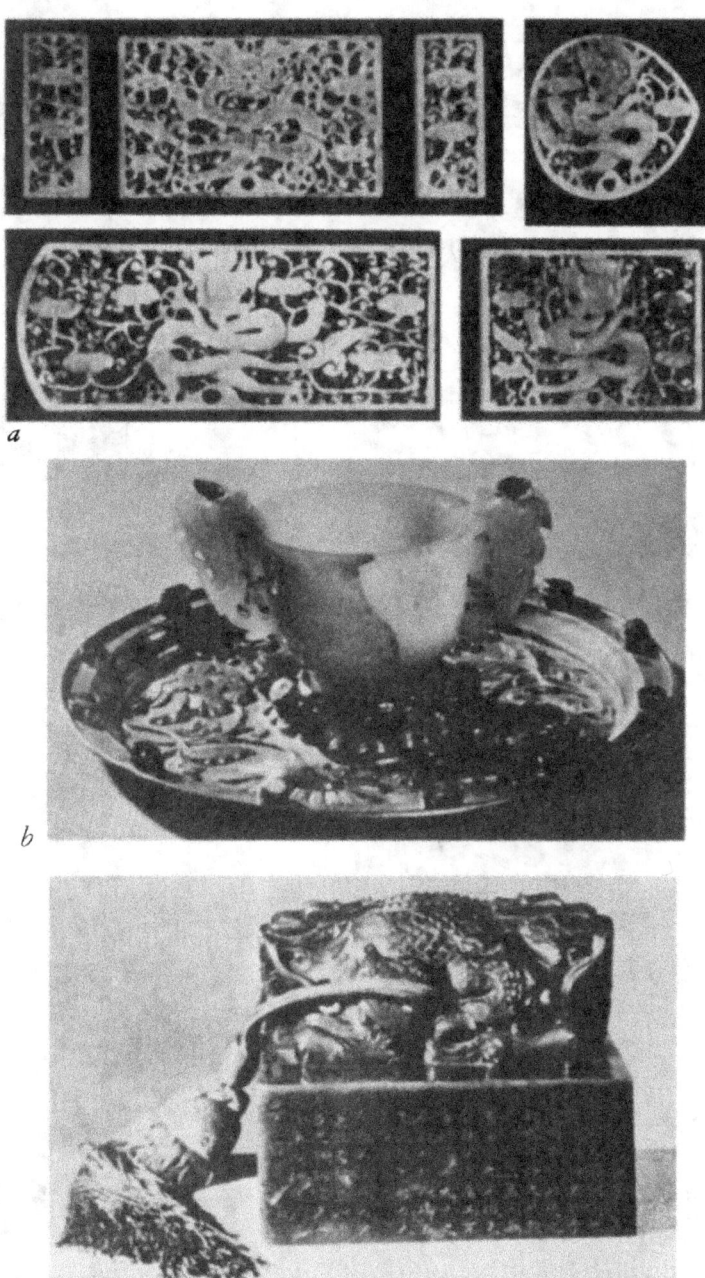

Plate XVIII — Ming and Ch'ing jade

(a.) A group of belt plaques with dragon designs in openwork. **4,** Pls. 7-12. (b.) Cup from Ting-lng (定陵), Peking. *Cambridge Exhibition of Archaeological Photographs from China,* 1974. No. 109. (c.) Square seal with inscriptions. **13,** Pl. 31.*a.*

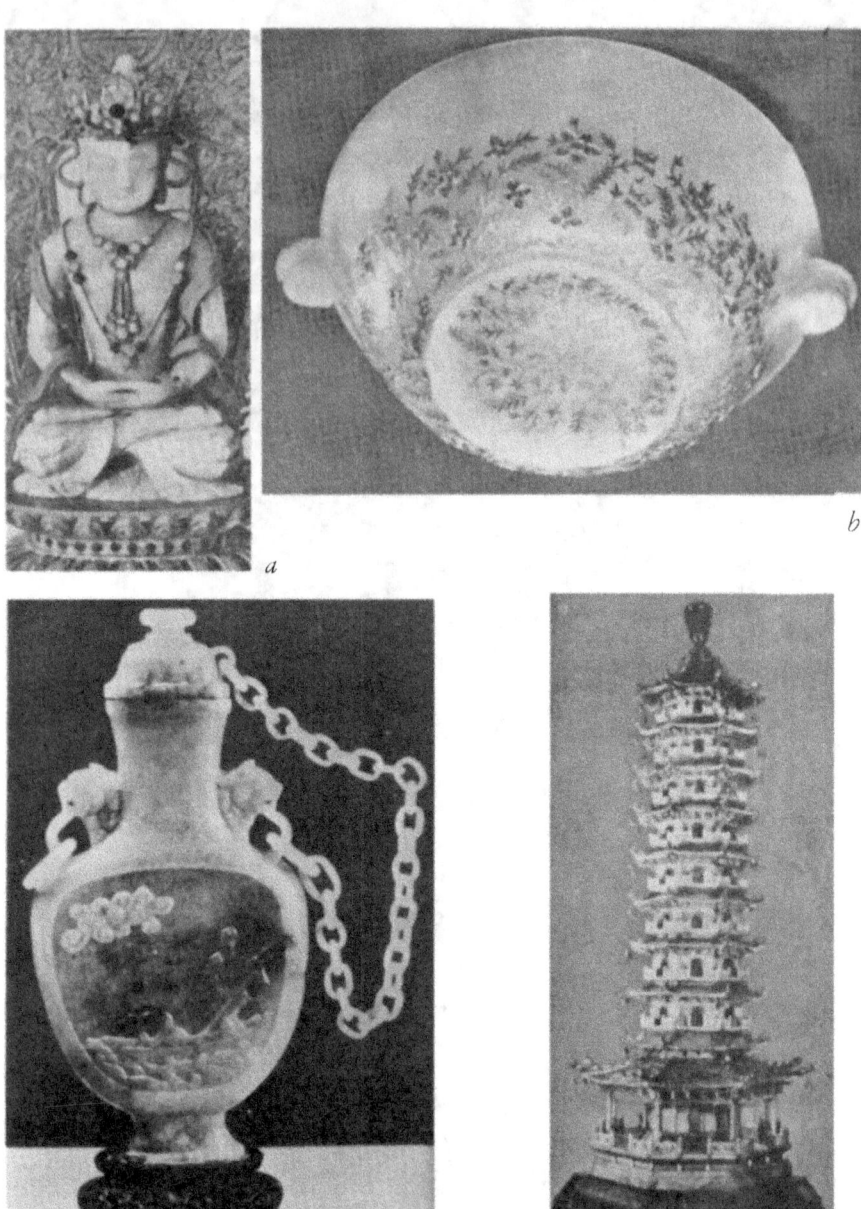

Plate XIX — Ch'ing jade

(a.) Seated Buddha with inlaid gilt mount. Queen Mary collection. **17,** Frontispiece.
(b.) Cup with inlaid gold and ruby design. **18,** No. 60. (c.) Vase with cover and chain.
17, Pl. 137. (d.) Pagoda. University Museum, Oregon, after *Life* magazine 57.5.27.

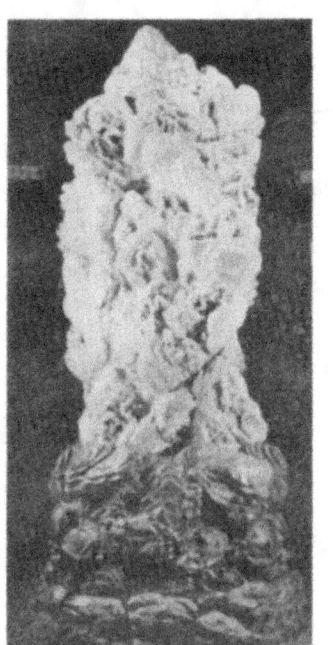
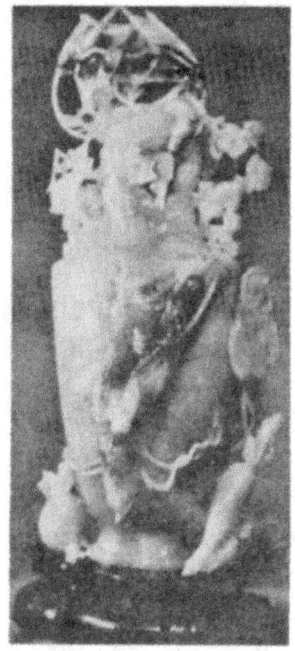

a   c

b

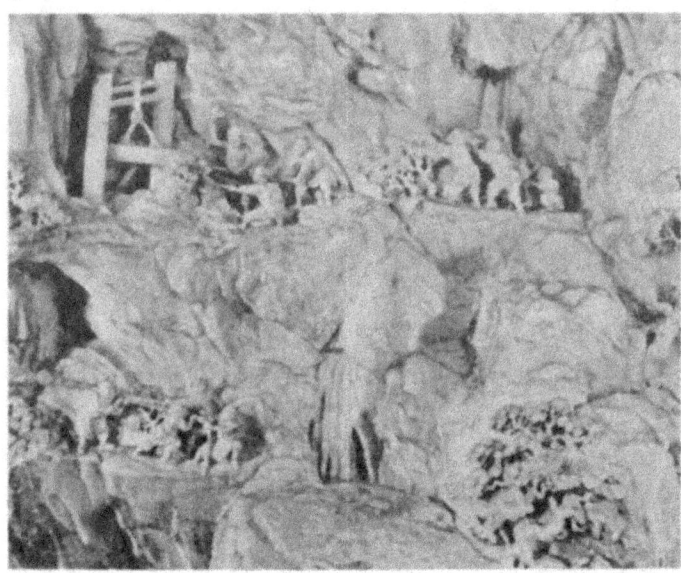

Plate XX — Ch'ing and Modern jade

(a.) Sceneries of Emperor Yu at work in flood control (大禹治水圖), dated 1788.
18, No. 66. *(b.)* Detail of *a*. *(c.)* Vase with insects and vegetables in high relief, multi-
coloured jade, carved in 1958. After *China Reconstructs,* 59.11.21.

中 國 玉 雕

（中文摘要）

作者：鄭德坤

　　玉器是中國文化特徵之一，其雕琢應用起源於史前時期。原人製造各種器具喜歡用硬度較高的岩石。最初對岩石的質料，並未加以分別。可是經過長久的利用及認識，發現有些岩石堅硬之外，還有鮮艷的顏色，細緻的質料，可以打磨出光滑可愛的器物。古人稱之爲玉。漢許愼《說文解字》說：『玉，石之美。』凡是漂亮的岩石都稱爲玉。新近考古發掘所得古代玉器，種類繁雜。顏色雖以綠和白佔大多數，但也有黃、黑或藍的色彩。硬度或高或低，比重也不一致。玉爲美石的通稱，自古就已開始了。

　　後代琢玉工業發展，技術進步，精選原料，才有軟玉和硬玉的分別。表面看來這兩種玉料很相像，可是質地却有重大的分別。軟玉是鈣化鎂矽，是透明的水晶體組成的。硬玉是鋁矽酸鈉，是屬於輝石體的礦石。軟玉是由纖維互相交組而成，而硬玉是微小晶體的結合，所以比較堅硬。加工雕琢之後，軟玉潤澤有如羊脂，俗稱羊脂玉；硬玉却比較透明，好的質地像玻璃，故又稱玻璃翠。

　　古代的玉器原是實用的器物。但是因爲質料細緻可愛，雕琢起來精美絕倫，遂成爲一班人士所欣賞的珍寶，或竟用玉爲禮器祭品。古人還用他來象徵各種的美德。《說文解字》說玉『有五德：潤澤以溫，仁之方也；鰓理有外，可以知中義之方；其聲舒揚，專以遠聞，智之方也；不撓而折，勇之方也；銳廉而不忮，潔之方也。』中國文化尚德的精神，可以玉爲代表。

　　古代玉石原料出於中土，應無可疑。但是產量零星有限，所以玉雕以小型的居多。卡和璞玉就是這種產品最精彩者之一。後代開發邊區，玉石原料才着漸充足，並廣泛應用。軟玉多數出自西域新疆，普通稱爲西玉或白玉。從西伯利亞貝加湖一帶輸入的顏色茶青，因名茱玉。硬玉是滇緬邊境的產品，鮮綠的最爲高貴，通稱爲翡翠，專供雕琢首飾之用。

　　中國雕玉工業，前後有六七千年的歷史。本文叙述雕琢技術

的演進之外，還介紹歷代若干標準作品，以供同好的參考如下：──

史前雕玉原與石器的打磨不分。原人雕琢技巧以劈擊，琢磨及鑽鋸為主。出品可分為兩類。器物包括各種工具，如斧、碎、鋤、鑿、刀、磺和尖形器之屬。飾物有璧、環、串珠及小動物等等（圖版一）。《說文解字》說：玉『象三玉之連，│其貫也。』串珠稱玉，由來已久矣。

商代玉雕工業已達到相當成熟的階段。出品除了工具和飾物外，還有各種祭玉和裝配零件。成品大小不一，線條的刊刻，浮雕的研磨，立體的雕塑，無不齊備。商代遺址及墓葬出土的玉器，數量很多，可見當時玉器的製造及應用的普遍。從一般器形的塑造及紋飾的雕琢可證明商代玉匠精通史前各種刊刻磨鋸的技巧外，還進而發明旋鉈，用旋轉的金屬輪盤，軸管及尖形器來攻解，琢磨及鑽研。他們所用的旋轉器大概是壓鑽，拉鑽及踏板鑽等等，設備雖極簡陋，但是雕玉技術顯然由打磨進入鑽研階段，使雕玉成為獨立的專業。這些簡單的工具就成為歷代雕玉工業的基本設備了。（圖版二──六）

周代玉雕因社會的需要更不斷的改進。初期的出品，承繼商的傳統，器形和技法和商器實無重大的分別。後來或因禮制的建立，祭玉便佔了重要的地位。新近出土整套佩玉，形形式式，雕琢都極精緻。許多祭玉如璧、璜、圭、璋等等，往往有細直的線紋，可見周代玉匠已知使用綫鋸。這是把金屬絲線，張掛為弓形器，用他來攻解玉璞，效率最高；同時刻劃直線更為便利。基本雕玉工具又增加了一種必須的利器，後代繼續不斷的應用。古來傳統的雕琢方法配合新的技巧，使周代雕玉有嶄新的進展。（圖版七──八）

周末戰國是中國玉雕全盛時代。當時各國大事擴張，為配合商業急激發展，工業技術也有顯著的改進。玉雕當然不是例外。新近出土戰國玉器充分表現玉器工業除了普通的工具祭器之外，還琢造各種的裝飾配件及日用器皿。他們精選攻玉細砂，並能利用高度堅硬的鑽石鑽。中國雕玉工具至此已告完備，技巧精湛，運用裕如。晚周燦爛的藝術可以戰國玉雕為代表。有的還進一步與金銀珠寶配合鑲嵌，開後代金銀珠寶首飾專業的先河。這種傳

統，一線相承，直至今日。（圖版八——九）

　　秦漢以下，中國玉雕繼續發展，從未中斷過。歷代古墓出土標本，種類繁夥，都可以證明玉匠經常能適應時尚，隨時應變，藝術作風跟着時代漫步進展。本文所舉漢代劍飾零件和立體雕塑（圖版十——十一），六朝的佛像動物（圖版十二）唐代的帶飾器皿（圖版十三）五代的玉册玉璽（圖版十四）宋代的杯碟玉花（圖版十五）元代的佩玉香爐（圖版十六）明代的器皿首飾（圖版十七——十八）等等都各具有其時代的特徵。清代以下，巨大的飾物器皿，尤爲時髦，作品無不巧奪神工，備集六七千年優良傳統的大成。（圖版十八——二十）中外時人愛玉，爭相玩賞，並不是偶然的。

Imperial Enamelled Porcelain of the Eighteenth Century — *Ching-tê chên or Peking?*

HUGH MOSS

It has often been said that the wares of the Ch'ing dynasty form a more difficult subject than those of the Ming. There is a lot to be said for that view, and I believe it is particularly true of the enamelled wares.

A study of the major collections formed during the first half of this century will often reveal relatively faultless selection in Ming and earlier wares combined with poor connoisseurship in the Ch'ing wares. It has been suggested that this may be due to relatively less interest over the years prompting less research, but this is clearly not the case; there is no shortage of works on later ceramics — they are just confusing.

Here we are concerned only with the Ch'ing enamelled porcelains which used the new palette of enamels introduced from Europe during the early years of the eighteenth century and we will confine ourselves to these.

With these wares there is a more fundamental reason for confusion; it is that, to this day, one essential fact has been overlooked in their study. The fact that there was more than one centre of enamelling, that these centres produced distinctively different wares, and most important of all, developed at different speeds.

This has in turn led major western scholars to dispute the authenticity of the group of wares marked *K'ang-hsi yü chih* (康熙御製), and thus remove from the source material the single most important group of wares — those that started the whole development of imperial painted enamels during the second decade of the eighteenth century — not only on porcelain but also on glass and metal.

I do not intend to go into the detailed evidence in favour of authenticating the *K'ang-hsi yü chih* group, because I don't believe it to be necessary — I hope their authenticity will become self apparent from this article. So, if we may, we will work from

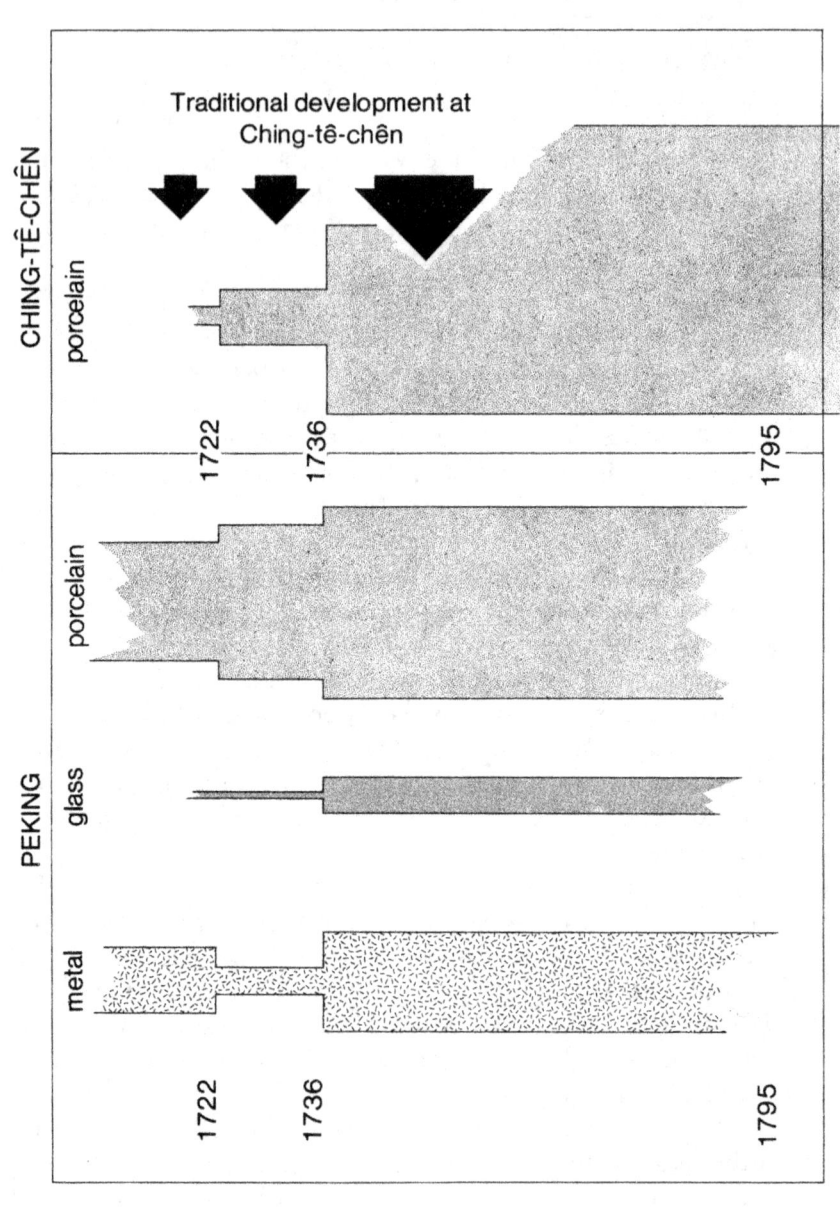

the premise that they are genuine, as marked, and if any doubt remains it can be discussed later.

To study the fine enamelled porcelains of the most important centre of enamelling, at Peking, it is necessary to look briefly at the allied crafts of enamelling on metal and on glass.

The K'ang-hsi emperor set up palace workshops in Peking for the production of various types of ware in the 1670s. He then continued to add to them as new crafts were introduced. We know that his attempts to actually make porcelain in Peking failed, and that he had to be content with enamelling it; we also know that he set-up, with European help, a palace glass works which was to supply the later glass enamellers with vessels.

These palace workshops developed the use of a new palette of enamels from Europe, painting with it on metal, glass and, as we shall see, porcelain. There is no shortage of evidence to show the K'ang-hsi emperor's keen interest in these imperial workshops or studios; he often visited them, and personally supervised their progress and development. It is very important to understand that there was close association between allied crafts within the palace, and throughout the eighteenth century the same artists in the same studio might have enamelled metal, porcelain or glass.

At some time during the second decade of the eighteenth century, a group of wares was developed in these palace workshops which consisted of painted enamels on metal, painted enamels on glass, and painted enamels on porcelain, and again I stress the importance of understanding that these wares were probably all decorated in the same studios by the same people. Nearly everything from this group is decorated with a floral design, mostly on a coloured ground, and they all bear the previously unknown mark *K'ang-hsi yü chih*, always in enamel, and in a variety of possible colours, including blue, ruby-red and black, or combinations of those colours. The substitution of the characters *yü chih*, which mean *imperially made*, for the more usual *nien chih*, which simply mean *made in the year of . . .*, suggest direct imperial patronage of the group.

From these wares developed the major part of imperial decorative enamelling on porcelain, glass and metal, for the rest of the Ch'ing dynasty — but more than that, the fusion of new ideas, new skills, and a new imperial taste which took place in Peking between about 1710 and 1722 created a decorative style that has lasted beyond the dynasty, and can be seen today, not least in Chinese restaurant crockery around the world.

The left hand side of the chart on p.90 illustrates the development of these Peking palace workshops. During this period, between about 1710 and 1720, Europeans at court were responsible for introducing the art of painting with enamels on metal, the art of enamelling on glass, and, of course, the new palette of enamels which was used with both these new crafts as well as on the porcelain wares also enamelled at the palace. This new palette included white, which allowed mixtures to form a variety of pastel shades previously unobtainable with the simpler traditional palette. It also included ruby enamel, which, when mixed with white, gave a rose-pink colour after which the palette was named '*famille rose*' by early French writers.

Using these new colours on metal, glass and porcelain, the Peking workshops produced the various wares of the *yü chih* group until the end of the K'ang-hsi reign in 1722. The metal wares are varied in form, because the metal bodies would have been made locally and were easy to order. The porcelain wares were less varied because of the relatively inconvenient distance of Ching-tê chên where they were made, and are nearly all bowls — although there are two vases and a single tripod incense-burner known. There is only one known piece of enamelled glass of the group, which judging by its decoration was probably made right at the end of the reign.

During the Yung-chêng period, from 1723 to 1735, the palace workshops concentrated on porcelain. Few enamelled metal wares were produced and that art progressed very little during the period; there is, once again, only a single piece of enamelled glass known, which is a snuff bottle in the Taiwan Palace Museum, and we may assume that the technical problems with enamelling on metal and glass, clearly unsolved by the end of the K'ang-hsi period, discouraged the Yung-chêng emperor's interest. The reason, however, is of no importance — the fact remains that the workshops during this period concentrated on porcelain, and in doing so, achieved a peak of technical brilliance sometimes equalled at a later date, but never bettered.

Under the reign of the Ch'ien-lung emperor from 1736 to 1795 this porcelain development continued but, unable to add anything in terms of technical control, the workshops extended the repertoire of forms and subject matter. Fortunately the Ch'ien-lung emperor was not as easily discouraged as his father and he developed the enamelled metal wares to a peak of perfection and, for the first time, produced a series of enamelled glass wares of consistently high quality — although throughout the century, glass enamellers never gained absolute technical control of their medium.

Imperial interest in the palace workshops appears to have died out towards the end of the century and was, by 1800, either virtually non-existent, or of such little importance as to appear so. The right hand side of the chart shows the parallel development with the new enamels at Ching-tê chên and we will return to that later.

Bearing in mind the importance of the close association between the three types of enamelled ware decorated in Peking we will now concentrate on the ceramics, and initially, those enamelled at Peking starting with those of the *K'ang-hsi yü chih* group.

This distinctive group of wares, with the possible exception of the Taiwan vase, is enamelled directly onto the biscuit, with no intervening glaze. This is often apparent in the faint lines of the potter's wheel which may show through the enamels. This method apparently gave the enameller greater control and we must remember that these were newly established workshops using unfamiliar materials and there is no reason why they should have been bound by the southern tradition of doing this sort of enamelling on a glaze. The white porcelain for Peking was sent up from Ching-tê chên with the interior and the foot glazed, but with the outer surface unglazed.

This gave the enamels of this group a distinctive appearance which is unlike any other group of wares made since, and although it is always difficult to describe shades of colour, or slight, though significant, differences in outward appearance, once seen, these enamels are not easily confused with others. There is a crisp and slightly undulating appearance to the heavily applied colours, and a distinctive opacity, not unlike thickly applied poster-colours.

On the single incense burner, the southern potters had no clear indication of where to glaze the foot for a mark, and so, left that too in the biscuit. The result is a blue enamel mark directly on the white of the porcelain. It can be seen that the mark has fired perfectly, whereas on the glaze, for a further fifty years or more, the Peking palace workshops were to have trouble correctly firing marks as we shall see later. The white lines forming a decorative border around the three feet are also left in white biscuit.

Another feature of these developing wares is that many of them show signs of inadequate control of the enamels. Technical control was still far from one hundred percent perfect, and several examples have poorer patches where the enamels are not as crisp or bright as they might be, or have misfired completely. Many of these bowls also have incised lines at their foot and rim, presumably intended to equate to the gilded rim on the painted enamel on metal wares and on the *cloisonné* wares from which they were derived. These lines, as might be expected of an experimental group, separated by perhaps as much as six months from its source of vessels at Ching-tê chên, were later either used or ignored. Again, not illogical for an experimental group such as this.

Having defined the group, placed it in Peking, and seen a little of its characteristics, let us trace its development. The floral motifs of these early Peking enamelled porcelains were initially formal, following closely the *cloisonné* types, that probably inspired them, although using the much wider range of coloured grounds now available, and sometimes incorporating formalised characters into the design, suitable, I believe, for an imperial birthday. Gradually these designs became freer and more realistic, and we begin to see the use of such motifs as the circular panel, where the circle is made up of part of the design. The formalised design is still apparent, however, and often re-appears throughout the dynasty, as we shall see. Decoration within a shaped panel is also introduced, and both designs were to become popular in the following reigns. Although formal in essence, the floral patterns were getting closer to the realism of the following period. With these wares it is easy to see the delight the enamellers were taking with their new found ability to shade, mix and wash large spreads of enamel successfully. There is a single bowl in the Taiwan Palace Museum which has a white ground, and is a link between the K'ang-hsi style and its development under the Yung-chêng emperor. Incidentally, the white ground on this example appears to be achieved not with glaze, but with white enamel and the concentric lines of the potter's tools can just be seen beneath it which is a feature of biscuit wares.

Yü chih type bowls were still made in Peking during the early part of the Yung-chêng period, but rarely, for, as we shall see, by that time their production had moved south to Ching-tê chên to make way for other developments at Peking. A rare early Yung-chêng bowl from Peking may still be found enamelled on the biscuit, but generally Yung-chêng palace wares are enamelled on a glaze. One example in the National Palace Museum, with its two coloured mark, is a hangover from the K'ang-hsi developmental period, which is unusual. The use of *nien chih* rather than *yü chih* also began on these bowls at this time. Progress with the new enamels advanced rapidly during the early Yung-chêng period, allowing proper control of the enamels on glaze, and the wares of Yung-chêng are technically the finest ever made in China — only equalled by the Ch'ien-lung workshops, but never bettered.

Coloured grounds were still frequently used and the painting was of superb quality. Subject matter was increasingly more realistic, and we see for the first time a combination of calligraphy with the subject. Technical problems were never completely overcome in the Peking workshops, and occasionally one of the finest pieces will have slight areas of misfiring. These slight, but continued problems of enamel maturity prompted another development. The Peking kilns found it difficult to consistently combine proper maturity of enamel on the body of a vessel with that under its foot, perhaps due to heat difficulties in the smaller kilns of Peking. And so wares were sent from Ching-tê chên which already bore underglaze blue marks. Many Peking palace porcelains have poorly fired marks. The most common fault during the Yung-chêng was pitting of the blue enamel of the mark. And during the Ch'ien-lung reign the mark often fired to an uneven grey-blue colour. This development meant that Peking enamelled porcelain from 1722 onwards appeared with any of a variety of marks, which deprives us of the simple rule of the K'ang-hsi period, that a raised enamel mark indicated Peking work, and underglaze blue, Ching-tê chên.

During the Yung-chêng period, the use of coloured grounds became less common as part of the principal decoration, and very effective designs on a white ground were developed. But the use of coloured areas, or coloured grounds remained in evidence throughout the century, often on the back of a dish, or later as a decorative border.

Forms were also expanded during the Yung-chêng period to include, occasionally, vases and other shapes such as the teapot. But these are the exception rather than the rule, and dishes and bowls of various shapes still formed the main production. Subject matter was still mostly floral, although landscapes, birds and insects appeared, and for the first time the use of a design in a single colour, such as blue, ruby or black, was introduced. Figure subjects are practically never seen on the Peking wares, whether on glass, metal or porcelain, from the K'ang-hsi and Yung-chêng periods, and European figure subjects never. This changed with the Ch'ien-lung emperor, who brought the vase and other forms fully into the repertoire and extended the subject matter widely to include many European figure designs.

With the Ch'ien-lung period, from 1736 to 1795, it is possible to find a rare northern *yü chih* type bowl, no longer on the biscuit, but a reasonably faithful continuation of the K'ang-hsi tradition. Often marks are misfired and a slightly uneven pale grey-blue tone is typical of many fine works of the period, because of which the practice of sending ready-marked pieces from Ching-tê chên was continued. The Ch'ien-lung workshops were unable to progress technically on the enamelled porcelain wares, as relative perfection had already been achieved, but they did extend the range of subjects and the range of forms considerably, and it is not unusual to find teapots, stem cups, and so forth, together with many shapes of vase not previously seen. Although there was no improvement technically over the Yung-chêng wares, neither was anything lost, and Ch'ien-lung wares continued to be brilliant in execution, if different in style. Although the reflection of his father's work was still very much in evidence there developed a distinctive style of decoration which was purely Ch'ien-lung, and owes much to the emperor's taste for European subjects.

A series can be shown which underlines the considerable European influence felt in the Palace workshops, and which brings us full circle in this brief survey of the Peking enamelled wares, as it can be shown to include a group of wares with distinctive European subjects which appear on porcelain, glass and metal.

The style is unlike any other, with the subjects, the figure drawing and the decorative borders, and a fuller study of the whole group shows beyond reasonable doubt that they were all produced in the same studios.

One more piece serves to establish this group firmly in Peking: there is a *cloisonné* ewer in the Taiwan Palace Museum which has panels of painted enamels of this group and with its combination of *cloisonné* and painted enamels must surely have been made at Peking.

Before we leave the Peking wares, let us just go back and briefly review the *yü chih* wares of the K'ang-hsi period, about which there has been so much controversy. It has been said that they are stylistically impossible for their supposed period, and here we are faced with the importance of the simple fact of more than one centre of enamelling. It would be quite true to say that they are stylistically out of context with Ching-tê chên, but not so of Peking, with its traditional craft of *cloisonné* enamelling.

In the formalised floral designs outlined on a coloured ground of the *cloisonné* wares, we surely have the stylistic origins of the *yü chih* group; indeed, the Ch'ing records show that the name used to describe these porcelains within the palace until the 1740s was *Porcelain body painted in cloisonné enamel*. It has also been said that compared to dateable southern wares — in particular armorial porcelain made for export to England prior to 1730 — the technical quality of the enamels on the *yü chih* group is too far advanced. Again, this is true of Ching-tê chên, but not of Peking, where use of the new enamels was initiated and developed probably ten years ahead of Ching-tê chên. In fact this second argument is an empty one, as it ignores the basic fact that one would expect an enormous difference between wares made for the Emperor, and those made for people considered to be foreign barbarians.

Now, let us move south to the parallel development at Ching-tê chên. Towards the end of the K'ang-hsi period, the southern potters began to make the bowls obviously popular in Peking. The idea was essentially the same, of a floral design outlined against a coloured group, and the mark was still *K'ang-hsi yü chih*, but executed in underglaze blue, which was the traditional method of the south. The enamels, however, were totally different; they either did not have, or could not yet control the new palette, and so they used the traditional, so-called *famille verte* colours to produce a similar effect. Iron-red was used as the coloured ground because it was opaque, and could be most easily controlled over a large area. There is only one type of southern bowl with the K'ang-hsi mark, and an almost identical bowl from the following reign suggests that it was made very late in the reign. The Yung-chêng example also has the *yü chih* mark and uses only traditional enamels. I believe we shall find that all the southern *yü chih* type bowls were made during the first few years of the reign, and it was during this period that the mark was changed from *yü chih* to *nien chih* and the use of the new enamels was tentatively adopted, although about half the known bowls of this southern group use only traditional enamels.

The popular flat bowl of the period falls into this category, but there is another example known where the new enamels are used in conjunction with the old and their lack of control clearly shows how far behind Peking Ching-tê chên was in their use. This hesitant and often clumsy use of the new palette in conjunction with the old is the pattern of this early Yung-chêng period Ching-tê chên production. The southern potters were clearly not as comfortable in their use of the new enamels as they might have been, and although control appears better on some, and probably the slightly later examples, than on others, it is still very much a case of struggling with the new enamels, in conjunction with the old. It is this southern discomfort with the enamels that has led people to doubt the Peking wares, but if we understand clearly the significance of the two centres, one considerably in advance technically of the other, the picture becomes quite clear, and perfectly logical.

Various underglaze blue marks were used during this early part of the Yung-chêng period, with either four or six characters, and *yü chih* or *nien chih*, sometimes enclosed either in circular or square panels. The use of *yü chih* was apparently not used again until 1916 as a mark on the base of a piece of porcelain. Several Ch'ien-lung and later examples which bear the mark have been seen by the author, but he has considered them all to be later forgeries.

Since we are concerned here with establishing a proper understanding of the different centres of enamelling, rather than in tracing their detailed development we will look only briefly at the Ching-tê chên development from the rest of the eighteenth century. The right hand side of the chart represents the southern wares. The very short period before 1722, and the early Yung-chêng period are the beginning of the Peking influence on southern wares. Following the manufacture of the group of bowls we have just discussed, traditional styles and types quickly became fused with the new Peking style, and within a few years the traditional *famille verte* palette had been virtually eclipsed. The new enamels were probably first controlled at Ching-tê chên during the second half of the Yung-chêng reign, and from then on there was a rapid fusion of old enamelled wares into new, and from that time a clear line of development can be traced to the present day. The influence of the Peking floral tradition is clearly seen from about 1723 onwards, and during the Ch'ien-lung period a series of wares was developed which clearly owed much to the *yü chih* tradition of Peking, and its fusion with the traditional Ching-tê chên wares became a purely Ch'ing decorative style. Traditional types were often fused with the new style, and help us to establish what is southern and what is northern enamelling.

The southern development included some interesting purely Ching-tê chên groups which can be easily identified and will, perhaps, be attributed to T'ang Ying, one of the better known superintendents of the potteries — an easier task once we have separated the Peking wares from the confusion which exists at the present. One such group is characterised by fine enamelling, landscape painting, with considerable use of tones of blue, and particularly by the method of enamelling trees, where the foliage is defined in a series of blobs, often of mixed pink and white enamels. The *yü chih* tradition of floral decoration on a coloured ground is never far from these wares, and appears often as a decorative border. This group often bears a poem and seals, sometimes with the emperor's name in them. It is tempting, but I stress premature, to attribute these to T'ang Ying, who was perhaps the most important official to influence the porcelains of Ching-tê chên during the Ch'ing dynasty period which concerns us.

Although we are far from a perfect understanding of Ch'ing enamelled wares, the author believes that if it is accepted that there was more than one centre of enamelling we are at least pointed again in the right direction. It then becomes clear that much of the finest enamelled porcelain was done at Peking during perhaps sixty or more years from about 1715. The superb quality of these wares could be explained simply by the direct imperial patronage, but it goes further. Because of this interest, which spanned three reigns, one basic difference developed — the northern enamellers were artists, and often top court artists and European painters, who were directed by imperial command to become enamellers; whereas, on the whole, the southern enamellers were craftsmen who developed some artistic talent. In this essential difference there is considerable significance.

In conclusion, I don't believe that any proper study can be made of Ch'ing wares enamelled with the new European enamels until the essential fact of different centres of enamelling is accepted, and until the *K'ang-hsi yü chih* wares are firmly re-instated, beyond any doubt, in their proper place — genuine as marked, and of fundamental importance to the development of Ch'ing enamelling on metal, glass and porcelain.

Note

It has proved impractical to illustrate the many slides which accompanied the above talk; however, the subject will be dealt with in my forthcoming book *An Introduction to Ch'ing Imperial Painted Enamels* which is illustrated with three hundred coloured photographs, many of which were part of this talk. The same work gives fully detailed source material for the conclusions reached above.

Hugh Moss, Hongkong, September 1975.

十八世紀御窯洋瓷——景德鎮或北京？

作者：Hugh Moss

常道清代陶器比明代更難了解，大致上此點頗爲中肯，我更相信以琺瑯瓷而言確是如此。從本世紀上半期所收集主要藏品來研究，就常發覺到明朝或早期的選品甚少瑕疵，而清朝選品則良莠互見。據說這可能是人們過去對此甚少興趣去研究，但事實並非如此，因爲關於後期陶瓷的著作並不缺乏，只不過衆議紛紜，有點混亂吧。現在我們只將清代採用十八世紀早期歐洲琺瑯釉製作的琺瑯瓷來討論。以這些瓷器而論，混亂的基本因素是我們的忽略了一個重要事項，這事實便是當時有着多過一所製造琺瑯瓷的場地，而這些場地各製造了顯著不同的器皿。更重要的地方是他們以不同的速度去發展。這因而引致大多數西方學者對繪有「康熙御製」器皿的眞僞發生爭辯，從而將這組重要瓷器資料删去。這組瓷製在雍正期間觸發起全部御製琺瑯瓷的發展，它的影響並不限於陶瓷而及於玻璃與金屬器皿。我不擬在此詳細引証這組康熙御製陶器的眞實性，因爲我不以爲這是必需的，但我希望這篇文字能給予充份的証據。是以，我們先假設這組瓷器的眞實，正如器上年欵所標明的，如或有疑問，稍後有作討論。

爲了研究這些精美琺瑯瓷的最重要生產地北京，我們必要簡短地兼顧到用玻璃或金屬的琺瑯製藝品。康熙皇在1670年間在北京宮中設立工場來製作各種陶瓷，並繼續製造新產品。他想在北京城內製瓷，未見成功，他只退而嘗試瓷器加工上琺瑯釉彩。我們亦知他曾利用歐洲方面的協助在城內建成一所製造玻璃器皿工場來生產後期作上洋彩的玻璃器皿。那些御用工場當時採用了歐洲的洋彩去製造金屬，玻璃及瓷器的彩繪製品。從許多証明中，康熙皇對這些工場懷有強烈的興趣，常常巡視及親自監督發展。我們要明瞭最重要的一點就是在這期間內，和整個十八世紀期中在御用工場中，那些技工同是製造着金屬，玻璃與瓷器上的繪琺瑯釉的工作。於十八世紀二十年代裏，那些內府工場曾製造了一批加繪洋彩的金屬，玻璃與瓷器的器皿。我想強調的便是這些器皿都是可能由同一批技工及在同一產地製造這一點。此批器皿幾

乎全部附有花卉圖案配以彩色底色，全用各種釉彩顏色如藍色、寶石紅色，黑色或其混合色彩去繪寫「康熙御製」這欵。從用「御製」來代替「年製」來看，那些都是皇帝親自監製的作品。清代彩繪瓷器、玻璃或銅器的製作都是從這組洋彩作品發展下來的。此外，自1710年至1722年間，那時北京正將新的御用欵式，新的技巧和新思想混合創造了一種圖案設計流傳了整個清代，它並影響到現時流行世界各地的中國陶瓷餐具。

　　左圖(一)顯示著當時北京內府御窰的發展。 1710 年至 1720 年間，朝中洋人經手介紹在金屬器皿上塗琺瑯釉的技法，及介紹玻璃與瓷器上塗琺瑯釉彩的新塗劑。這些新塗料包括了用白色顏料去混和其他色彩以產生各種前所未能獲得的各種粉彩顏色，這包括寶石紅琺瑯，這紅色跟白色混和之後，產生玫瑰紅色素。這一類的粉彩給早期法國作家改名爲 Famille rose 或稱頓彩。北京御瓷場採用了這種洋彩加繪於銅、玻璃或瓷上，便成「御製」產品，這類產品繼續出品直至康熙末年。那時金屬琺瑯器皿形狀不一，因爲此類金屬坯身則可能並且不難由當地配製。但瓷器形狀差異不大，因爲景德鎮與北京間距離頗遠交通不便。當時製品幾全屬碗形，雖則已知有二個瓶及一個三腳香爐的樣品。這批製品亦有一件琺瑯玻璃製品，從它圖案紋飾來判斷，那可能是康熙末期產品。

　　雍正時（1723年至1735年）內府御製場集中生產瓷器，很少製造琺瑯銅器，而技巧上在此期內進展甚微。正如上述已知的只有一件琺瑯玻璃製品，它是一個鼻烟壺，現藏於臺灣故宮博物館中。我們可以假設當時康熙年間仍未能解決的在金屬或玻璃塗上琺瑯的技術困難，却使雍正皇興趣銳減。其原因實不甚重要，事實就是當時只注重陶器製作，因而達到製作技巧高峯而爲稍後時間所僅能比擬的。

　　乾隆年間（1736年至1795年）洋瓷繼續發展，但在技術水平上或製欵形式上，並不能超越前期的成就。幸運地，乾隆皇並不像他的父皇那麼容易受挫折，他將洋瓷製作發展到極完美的境地，首次生產了好些優良品質的琺瑯玻璃製品，雖然在後來整個世紀中琺瑯玻璃技工們從未能將製造技巧完全控制得宜。

直到世紀末年或1800年左右，清廷對內府御塲的興趣似乎日漸衰微，甚至全部消失。

　　圖右顯示景德鎮同時所出產的新洋瓷製品，有關這類製品，稍後才作解說。

　　在討論過在北京上釉的三種互有密切關連的洋彩器皿後，我們繼續集中研討陶瓷，首先看看在北京上釉附有「康熙御製」的洋瓷。這批「康熙御製」器皿，除了那臺灣花瓶外，俱是直接上釉於坯上，沒有先加底釉的。這常可從轉陶製作時工具留下於坯身的幼線中見到。

　　這種技巧可令使用洋彩工人得到較佳的控制方法。我們應謹記那時工塲對新釉料運用並不純熟，而技工亦不用南方的洋瓷上釉的方法。當時景德鎮輸送往北京的白瓷只將內部及腳部上釉，外面是沒有上釉的。

　　這點使北京洋瓷顯著的與後期的製品不同，雖然我們難以描述釉彩的深淺，或其外表上微妙的異同，但若細心觀察，則不難發覺其特徵。從釉彩上，我們可以發現釉彩厚度，表面上些微不平滑，和它的明顯不透明釉色正像厚厚塗上了粉彩顏色一般。

　　在那三腳香爐上，那個南方製造技工上釉時並不知年欵該寫在爐腳上什麼地方，而將它塗於爐坯上。結果便是藍色洋彩年欵直接寫在白瓷上。我們可見該年欵經燒陶後仍很完整，但在釉上寫欵，在以後五十多年間，內府御窰對火候控制頗有困難，這點下文有述。三腳爐足部的白線圖案亦是同樣在白瓷上寫的。

　　此批洋磁另一特色就是許多都顯示著對琺瑯釉的使用未受控制。當時釉彩控制未能百份之百地完善；從幾件製品中發現有渾濁不清的地方，這由於釉彩沒有應有鮮明清脆的光澤，或許是火候欠佳的錯誤。很多碗邊和底部都有劃線，想是模仿金屬琺瑯製品上的金邊，或最原始琺瑯器的欵式。這些劃線有時在上釉時未被留意，這在試驗期間情有可原的。況且自景德鎮運出時，其中可能經過六個月的時間。

　　我們在討論這批洋磁之後，認定它是北京產品，並分析了它的特徵，現在試追尋其發展過程。最初這北京洋磁的花卉圖案是

拘謹的，是依着景泰藍的傳統，但是底色則比前較多，有時在圖形中加插如賀壽一般的中文字等。漸漸地此種圖飾變爲靈活，又變爲後來開光的紋飾，開光的地方屬紋飾的一部份。初期的花卉圖紋後來亦未盡消失而一直繼續使用。在特別形狀的開光內加繪亦漸受歡迎採用。雖然大致上是拘謹，花卉飾紋漸和後期的逼眞寫法相近。這些製品令到技工們喜悅，故能調製各種不同釉色，混合色素及成功地大幅度加繪洋彩等。在臺灣故宮博物館中現存一個白釉碗，乃是康熙和雍正期間的產品。可是這件製品的白釉看來並不是白色的磁釉而是採用白色洋彩。又碗底之下有製坯時遺下的重圈，可說是坯土上加洋彩的特徵。

雍正初年北京仍出產「御製」瓷碗，但數量甚少，因爲當時已由景德鎮担承了製造。北京當時着重出產其他品物。一個稀有於北京製成的雍正初期碗仍是在坯上加洋彩的。雖然一般的雍正御窰製品都是釉上加洋彩的，現存於國立故宮博物館中那件年欵有二色的只是康熙餘韻，實屬罕見。

在此期間開始，年欵上以「年製」代「御製」，同時用新洋彩技術猛進，對釉上加洋彩控制得宜。是以雍正產品是中國歷代技術上最好的，它只有乾隆製品可以比擬吧。

雍正洋瓷，底釉多是有色的，而釉繪質一流。繪畫逼眞生動，書法亦開始介入，北京工場從未獲得技術上完全控制，因而間有相當美好的製品有部份是燒壞的。這種輕微但經常發生的火候問題却引起另外一種發展。當時北京燒窰察覺很難處理將坯身上洋彩與碗底的洋彩釉同燒到剛好，那可能是由北京窰太小有了熱度控制的問題。但是那些在景德鎮燒的已有釉下青花年欵。許多北京御窰都有燒得不好的年欵，雍正製品常見的缺點是藍釉凹入。而乾隆產品的年欵常燒成不均勻的灰藍色。這種情況即是說自1722年以後，北京洋瓷出現了各式各樣的年欵。這和康熙年欵的簡易不同──凸起的洋瓷年欵代表北京產品而用青花藍的便是景德鎮的。

雍正時，用顏色底釉爲主的技法漸不普遍，而慢慢地時興用白底上加繪彩方法。可是用有色底釉或部份着色仍一直常用，多用於碟子後面或稍後期作器邊飾紋。那時期的形製亦有發展，有

時包括花瓶或茶壺等物。這些都並非主流，碗與碟仍為主要產品。飾紋仍以花卉為多，其他有山水及蟲鳥。單色釉的運用如用藍色，寶石紅色，黑色亦是首次出現。康雍時的北京製品從沒有人物圖繪的，不論是繪於玻璃、金屬器或瓷器上，亦從未試繪歐洲型人物的。至乾隆時，這風氣大變，有各式各樣的形製如花瓶等，塗繪的題材大為擴展，甚至把歐洲人士形像放在圖中。

從1736年至1795年乾隆朝代，間中有可能找到一隻珍貴的北方「御製」瓷碗，它不是坯上加釉而是因襲康熙年代式的產品。這樣製品常附有燒壞的年歟及少許不均勻的淺灰藍色素。因此仍然須要繼續由景德鎮將有歟的瓷坯送京。乾隆年代的工場不能將燒洋瓷技術發揚光大，因其已達到頗為完善境地。但乾隆時却從形狀與繪圖題材上發展起來。是以這時期的製品包括有茶壺，高杯等物及前所未見的各種花瓶樣式等。雖然乾隆製品未能盡得技術的進步，但仍能保持水準，而產品仍屬品質優美，歟型嶄異。乾隆製品因受歐洲作風影響而創有獨特乾隆風格，但仍保持有乃父時代的傳統。

從實物可見北京洋瓷是怎樣的深受歐洲風格影響，而在洋瓷發展中兜了一圈。這批實物包括在瓷器、玻璃、和金屬器等，均有顯明的歐洲人物主題的繪圖。這些製品的風格，在主題上，人物繪圖上，或邊緣飾紋等和別的不同。從這些專心研究就無可疑地知道它們都是全部由同一工場所造出來的。

還有一件器皿可証實這批確是北京的產品。臺灣故宮博物館有一景泰藍水壺，有着上述的洋彩繪畫，同時兼有琺瑯釉，可見是北京製品無疑。

最後，北京製品中還有點和康熙「御製」的問題有關的。這曾引起不少爭辯。有說那風格不可能那時候所能有的，這一點我們知道，事實上當時有多過一處的洋瓷工場。我們可以說那些是與乾隆製品風格上有差異，但和北京的相類，一樣承繼著琺瑯瓷的傳統技術。

洋瓷有色底釉上的拘謹花卉紋飾來看，可見「御製」瓷器風格上的淵源。事實上清代書籍說明1704年前內府的洋瓷就是繪琺瑯釉的瓷器。另說這批內府洋瓷跟當時有年份的南方洋瓷比較——特

別是和1730年前輸往英國的紋章瓷比較——「御製」洋瓷的技術水平是大大地超越的。在這方面，當然是指景德鎮製品而言，不是指北京洋瓷的。在北京這新琺瑯的使用較景德鎮早了十年。但是時間先後，徒是空言，因它忽略了一點事實——御用瓷怎樣與給「番鬼」用的輸外瓷器相提並論呢。

有關南方景德鎮方面同期發展，康熙末年南方陶工開始製造些在北京顯受歡迎的碗，那些製品仍用花卉飾紋繪於釉上，年欵照用「康熙御製」，但用南方傳統方法的釉下藍繪寫。琺瑯方面却斷然不同，因爲他們不熟練運用新洋彩，於是便採用傳統的燒硬彩方法進行。他們用礬紅作底釉，因它不透明緣故，且可以容易地控制大幅度的使用。南方製作碗中附有「康熙」欵的獨有一種，這和雍正所製的無異，是以可能是晚期產品。雍正洋瓷亦有「御製」欵，但只採用傳統的琺瑯釉。我認爲我們會覺得所有南方產品「御製」碗皆是雍正初期的產品。在此時間，年欵由「御製」改作「年製」，而釉料亦改用新洋彩，雖則這類南方製品約有過半數的碗只採用傳統上的琺瑯釉。

這期間內最受歡迎的淺碗是屬於這類製品，但有另一碗可資証明當時亦曾試將新舊洋彩並用，但控制不宜，可見景德鎮在用洋瓷方面是遠比不上北京的。這類非熟練性運用新舊洋彩製成的產品正是景德鎮雍正初年的特點。南方陶工顯然並不善用新洋彩。雖則或有較佳的製品——這多數是稍後的作品——但仍到處顯示出將新洋彩和舊釉齊用的困難。這就因爲南方技工之不熟練運用新洋彩緣故，却使人們懷疑到北京內府的製品，但若我們明瞭到那時二個製陶工場中心之差異，其中一個技術比另一個優勝，如此則疑問盡消，反覺合理非常。

雍正初年有各欵釉下藍年欵，有四個字的或六個字的，及「御製」或「年製」，或年欵在四方形或圓線內。至1916年止，碗底「御製」欵不曾再被採用。作者曾見過數件有「御製」欵的乾隆或稍後的製品，但均認爲全是後來僞造贋品。

因爲我們現在旨在了解兩地洋彩的使用，並非發展源流，故我們只簡略地一談景德鎮於十八世紀後半期的發展。圖(一)中右邊代表南方製品，雍正年初至1722年那一小段時間乃南方製品受北

京影響時代。瓷碗那時期開始，歷來的形製和風格漸和北京的混合，不數年間，舊法的硬彩釉幾全部斂迹。控制採用新洋彩可能是於雍正下半期在景德鎮始得成功，便繼續迅速地新舊釉並用，這樣的發展直至今天。北京花卉飾紋的影響由1723年起顯而易見，乾隆時，不少製品明顯地受到了北京「御製」傳統影響與昔日景德鎮製法混合而產生了單純清代風格。因為舊傳統式製品常與新法製品混合，故因而幫助了我們去鑑別南方產品與北方洋彩製品的差異。

南方洋瓷發展中，有些純是景德鎮作品，這些不難鑑別，或許認為是著名窰務監督唐英之作，在明確分辨北京洋彩之後，這種鑑別是輕而易舉的。此類製品特徵是優美的洋彩，山水繪畫，用多量青藍調，至於用洋彩繪樹，常以粉紅和白二色調和以堆砌粗點法繪寫尤其顯著。傳統式的「御製」有色釉上花卉飾紋，特別是邊緣飾繪，乃屬常見。此類作品認為是唐英所製，或許是操之過急，雖然他是清朝對景德鎮的陶瓷製作最具影響力官員。

雖然我們未能完全了解清代洋瓷，但作者相信如果我們確認那時曾有多過一所製洋彩瓷的工場，那麼我們就雖不中不遠的了。很明顯的，自1715年後的六十多年來，北京曾出產了現存大部份的精美洋瓷。那種品質優良的製作，顯然得力由於宮廷直接監管。但事情並不止於那樣，因為經三個朝代的監管，乃產生一種基本上的差異——北方製洋瓷的乃屬美術工作者，甚或宮廷御用畫家和歐籍畫家，後者是奉召參與製洋瓷工作。至於南方方面，大致上洋磁陶工是技工；他們的美術造詣是培養出來的。這方面的差異，是很重要的。

總而言之，洋彩的燒製是有不同的工場，有欵的「康熙御製」作品是無可置疑地確定了，琺瑯金屬品、琺瑯玻璃和琺瑯瓷的重要基本發展也澄清了，我們要把這些問題解決後才可以從事清代採用新洋彩的研究。

附註：拙作「清代御製洋瓷導論」(英文版)快將出版，內有彩色插圖三百，注釋詳畫，可補上文不足，並供參攷。

Ceramics in Chinese Painting

MICHAEL SULLIVAN

Our knowledge of early Chinese ceramics is based very largely upon what has survived and been revealed by excavation and tomb rubbing. But how representative are these pieces of the wares in use at any given time? We cannot assume that the Sung wares in our collections give an accurate impression of what would have been used in the home of an upper-class gentleman of the period. While our picture of T'ang ceramics is still dominated by the lead-glazed three-colour wares, thought typical of T'ang taste, these were made largely, if not exclusively, for burial: they are not shown, to my knowledge, in any T'ang painting and may not have been used in the home at all.

The literature is not very much help, for it is small in quantity and hard to interpret, as readers of the fourteenth-century connoisseurs' compendium *Ko-ku yao-lun* know to their cost. Eighteenth-century books such as the *Ching-tê chên t'ao-lu* and the *T'ao-ya*, while probably reliable on Ming and Ch'ing wares, consist, for the rest, of collectors' lore and dealers' rule-of-thumb methods of identification which do not stand up to critical examination. Moreover, they sometimes refer to wares which it is now impossible to identify.

The most certain results, of course, are coming from the systematic excavation of kiln sites that has been in progress since 1949. But there are other possible sources of information, one of which is painting. A large number of paintings from the tenth century onwards show ceramics, chiefly in interior scenes, standing on the scholar's desk, or beside the collector or connoisseur in a more formal portrait. The limitations of this method of studying Chinese ceramics are obvious. Many of the paintings which are claimed to be of Sung date, for example, are later copies, pastiches, or outright fakes, and if taken as authentic could lead us far astray. Sometimes, moreover, the ceramics are depicted with great care, sometimes so carelessly that one wonders what particular ware, if any, the painter had in mind. Some paintings are revealed as later works by their style, or by the very ceramics they depict. But just as there are paintings in which the ceramics tell us something about the painting itself, so there are paintings from which we can learn something about early ceramics. Well-known works which might be usefully studied from this point of view would include the following:

Yüan Kao (tenth century): Fairies in a Garden (Handscroll, Palace Museum, Peking). One of the attendants is drawing a gauze cover over the table on which are nine winecups on cup-stands which suggest Yüeh ware. Beside them is a metal ewer such as would be used for heating the wine over a charcoal brazier (Fig. 1).

Attributed to Ku Hung-chung (tenth century): The Night Entertainment of Han Hsi-tsai (Handscroll, Palace Museum, Peking). A scroll depicting the extravagant entertainments of a minister to the Southern T'ang emperor Li Yü. A variety of porcelain vessels is depicted on the table in the detail shown (Fig. 2), including wine-pots standing in deep foliated bowls of hot water of a type familiar in the *ch'ing-pai* ware of the Sung Dynasty. Moreover, the style of the landscapes painted on screens and the panels of bed-couches in this scroll is that of the late Northern Sung or Southern Sung. So this painting in itself cannot be taken as proof that this type of wine-pot existed before the Sung, although it is highly probable. As yet, there is no evidence that it goes back to the T'ang, however.

Anon: The Palace Concert (National Palace Museum, Taipei). A mis-named work generally attributed to the T'ang Dynasty, but possibly of Southern T'ang date, and possibly, like the Night Revels, depicting not a concert but the dissipation of the court ladies, who are shown in undignified attitudes, with flushed faces and bleary, sad eyes. On the table is a variety of vessels which include what appear to be lacquer *yü-hsiang* (winged cups) of traditional design, jade cups, and bowls of what is most probably Yüeh ware (Fig. 3).

Yüan Kao (X century): *Fairies in a Garden*. Detail of a handscroll on silk. Detail of a handscroll on silk. Ku-kung Collection, Peking.

When we come to the Sung Dynasty, the material for study is much more abundant, if no less controversial:

Attributed to Ch'en Chü-chung (Northern Sung): Lady Wen-chi's Return to China (National Palace Museum, Taipei). This rather touching painting shows a servant pouring a farewell cup of wine from a phoenix-head ewer, a type familiar in the ceramics of North China from the T'ang Dynasty onwards. Ch'en Chü-chung was a court painter at the end of the Northern Sung

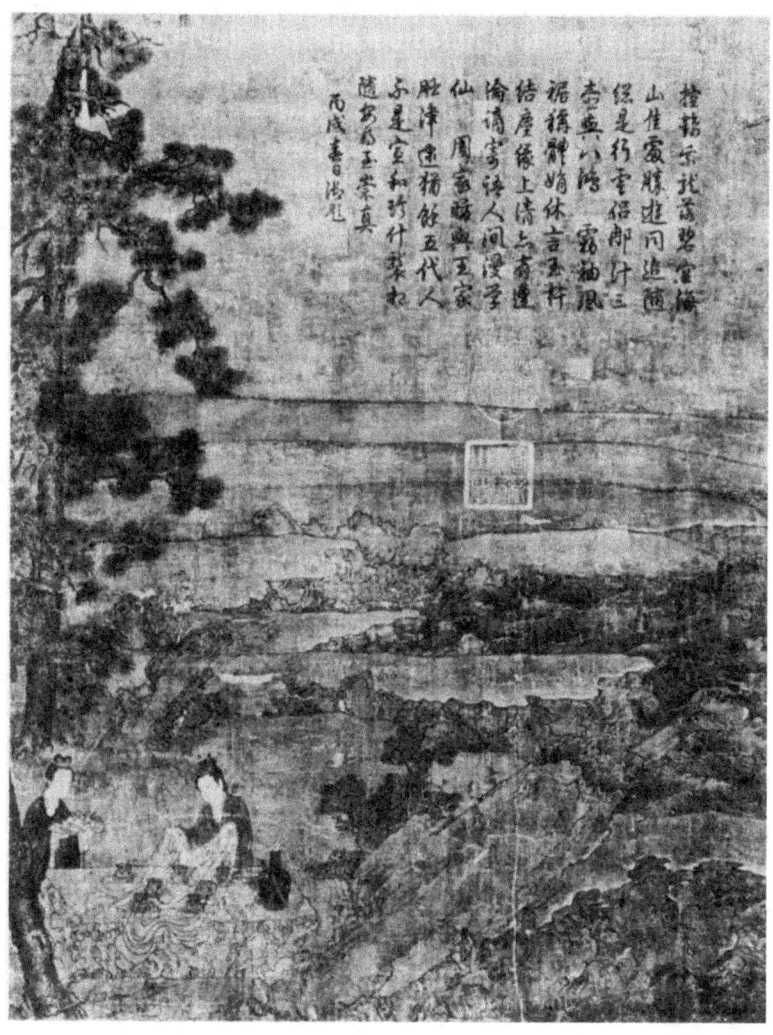

Ku Hung-chung (X century): *The Night Entertainment of Han Hsi-tsai*. Detail of a handscroll on silk. Ku-kung Collection, Peking.

---

period, and would have taken great care over such details as dress and utensils. While the attribution is plausible, the painting could as well be by a court painter of the Liao Dynasty, or even a careful copy of the Chin or Yüan.

Among Northern Sung paintings an obvious choice is The Literary Gathering, a hanging scroll in the National Palace Museum, Taipei, attributed to the Emperor Hui-tsung (r. 1101–1125), but more probably the work of one of the painters of the Imperial Academy. A group of scholars is sitting round a table on which the utensils are clearly depicted (Fig. 4); they include bowls of what might be Northern *kuan* or some other form of high-class celadon, cups on cup-stands that might be Ting (Fig. 3). In the foreground the servants are heating the wine; metal ewers rest on the coals; others, perhaps of porcelain, stand on the table. One servant holds a large dish of a decorated white ware, which once led a prominent authority to suggest that this detail was proof that blue-and-white was already being made at the end of Northern Sung. However, this is more likely to be a form of Ting-yao, which was still the official courtly ware at the beginning of Hui-tsung's reign. It has also been suggested that the dish is a kind of Tz'u-chou ware. While this is remotely possible, it seems unlikely that even the finest Tz'u-chou wares reached the Northern Sung court, while in the Sung paintings I have examined (by no means exhaustively) I have found no other piece that looks remotely like Tz'u-chou.

Southern Sung album leaves and fans often give an intimate glimpse of the life of the court and of the gentry class, in which details of architecture, furniture and utensils are drawn with care, not yet conventionalised to the degree that we find in the professional painting of the Yüan Dynasty and later. In the Palace Museum Collection, Taipei, works attributed to Southern Sung court painters such as Ma Kung-hsien, Chao Po-chü, Li Sung and Liu Sung-nien show a variety of what appear to be celadons and white porcelain, the latter presumably chiefly *ch'ing-pai* and the wares from Chi-chou. However, the ceramics themselves,

112

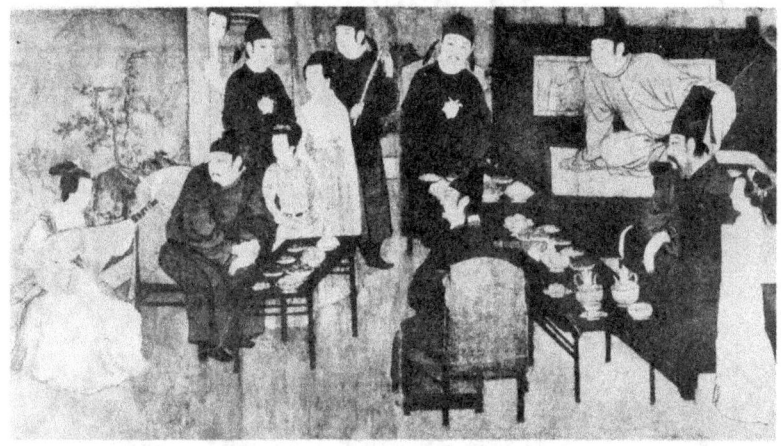

quite apart from the other features, sometimes betray the late date of the painting. The scroll of the Eighteen Scholars attributed to the twelfth-century artist Liu Sung-nien (National Palace Museum, Taipei), shows a gentleman warming on a brazier a bowl of typical fourteenth or fifteenth century shape, an obvious anachronism.

The artist may take trouble to get his details right in one painting and be careless of them in another. The fifteenth-century professional painter Ch'iu Ying's Spring Morning in the Han Palace (National Palace Museum, Taipei) shows ladies of the court amusing themselves in a variety of ways. The picture is full of intimate detail, but nowhere has Ch'iu Ying attempted to suggest, by the architecture, furniture, dress or accessories, that his idealised picture is that of the court life of fifteen hundred years earlier. The ceramics depicted are such as might be found in the court or in the house of a wealthy man of his own time. When we turn to his painting of the Chin-ku-yüan (in the Chiōn-in, Kyōto), however, we find that in several ways he has suggested the atmosphere of the Golden Valley Garden in Nanking, in which the famous third-century millionaire Shih Ch'ung had enjoyed life with his scholarly friends and with his concubine Green Pearl. The arrangement of the scholars round the table is reminiscent of the ladies in the Palace Concert; the exaggerated reverse perspective is archaic, while on the table are stem-dishes

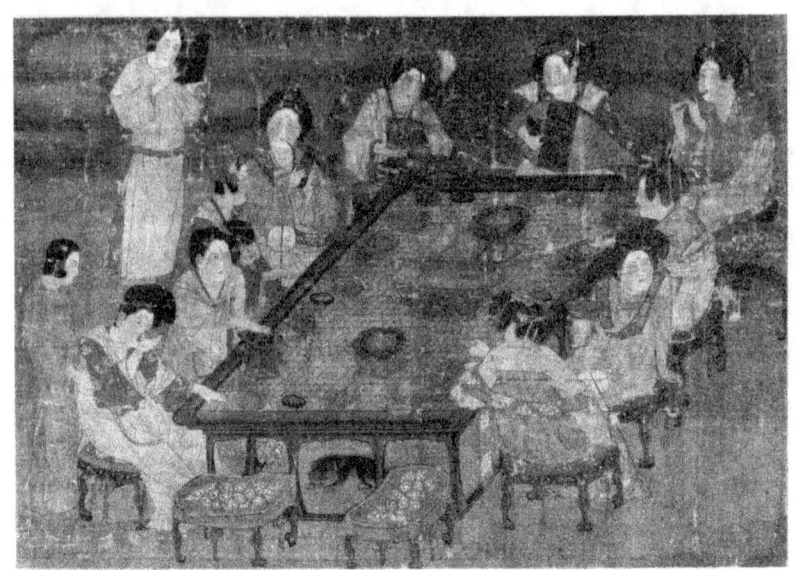

Anon. (X century): *The Palace Concert*. Hanging scroll on silk. National Palace Museum, Taipei.

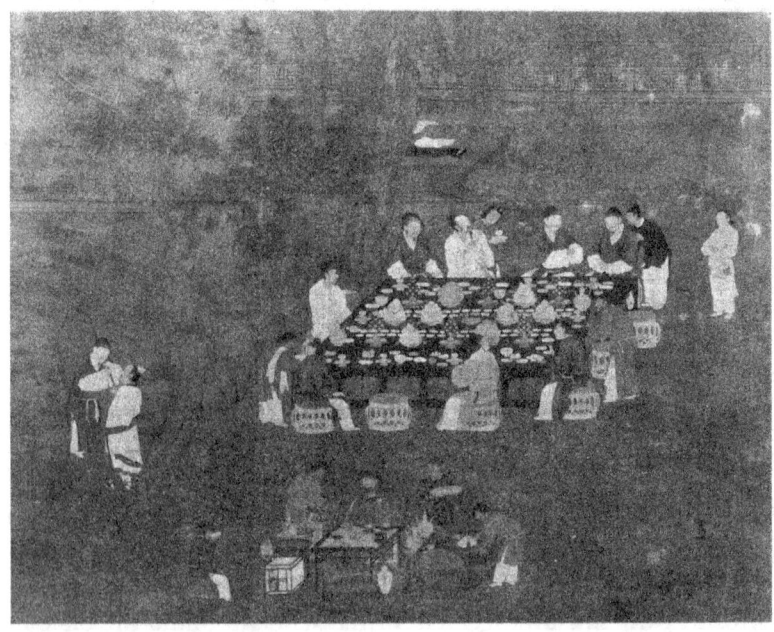

Attributed to Sung Hui-tsung (r. 1101-1125): *A Literary Gathering*. Detail of a hanging scroll on silk. National Palace Museum, Taipei.

of a type that was popular in the sixth century and T'ang but of which I know of no examples of later date than the tenth century. Such details suggest that Ch'iu Ying may have been copying, or reworking, a much older composition that is now lost.

From Ming times onwards, painters sometimes attempted in a somewhat free-and-easy fashion to suggest an air of antiquity in their figure-painting by such accessories as the ceramics or bronzes. Ch'en Hung-shou's handscroll, for example, Episodes in the Life of T'ao Ch'ien (Honolulu Academy of Arts) shows the fourth-century poet in several poses in a garden. In the detail illustrated here (Fig. 5) he sits on a plantain leaf with a rock behind him on which stand two porcelain vases and a heavily-crackled covered jar which suggests Southern *kuan* ware. Whether the artist knew that Southern *kuan*, and porcelain imitations of antique bronze vessels such as the *tsun* on the left, were not made in T'ao Ch'ien's time we will never know, and in any case it is not really important. What is interesting is that he evokes antiquity by putting in types of Sung ware that were themselves inspired by the antique, and that is enough for his purpose.

If we examine a large number of paintings we encounter representations of vessels of which no known counterparts seem to have survived into our own day. In some cases they may be the

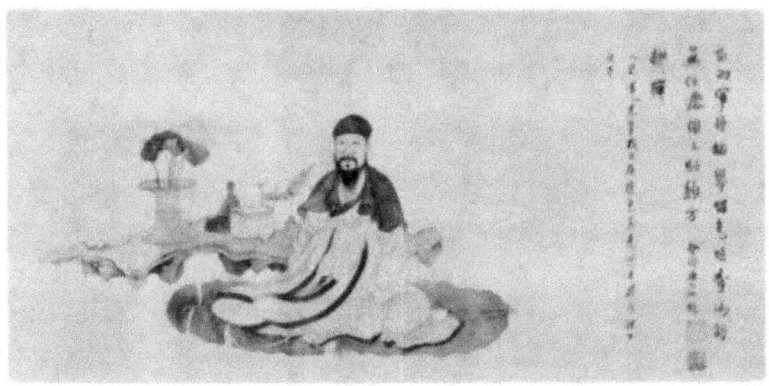

Ch'en Hung-shou (1599–1652): *Scenes from the life of T'ao Yüan-ming*. Detail of a handscroll on silk. Charles A. Drenowatz Collection, Zürich.

product of the artist's fancy; in others they may indeed represent wares which once existed, and are referred to in the literature, such as *ch'ai* ware and Tung ware, but which cannot now be identified. Metal ewers figure in a number of paintings. Very few of these have survived, for they were evidently not considered worth the collectors' attention. They must have been widely used, however, particularly for heating water or wine directly on the charcoal fire.

Some later paintings show a gentleman surrounded by his art treasures. Among the most informative are two by the Jesuit painter Lang Shih-ning (Giuseppe Castiglione, 1688–1766), depicting the Emperor Ch'ien-lung, the one in his garden, the other an interior scene. Here the drawing is so careful that we can clearly identify the antique bronzes, and the ceramics in antique shapes. One of these paintings suggests, however, that not all Ch'ien-lung's treasures were antiques. Among the vessels standing on the table in the latter picture is a blue-and-white vase that is typically Ch'ien-lung in its shape and decoration, and must have been a very new piece when the painting was executed.

Even more clearly identifiable among Lang Shih-ning's works for his imperial patron are the pieces in the two well-known hanging scrolls of flowers, arranged in vases, that have their exact counterparts in the Percival David Foundation: the one a Southern *kuan* bottle, the other a small square blue-and-white vase of Hsüan-te date (Fig. 5). Since much of the David Collection came from the Palace itself, it is just possible that these are the very pieces Lang Shih-ning depicted.

A thorough study of all available material, which would include not only scroll, fan, and album paintings, but wall-paintings at Tunhuang and in tombs, would certainly reveal a great deal more than I have suggested. It would be an extremely laborious task, out of proportion to the solid information it would yield, while it would be complicated by the problems of connoisseurship and authenticity that I have mentioned. Such a study should not, perhaps, be pushed too far. But even a

---

Lang Shih-ning (Giuseppe Castiglione, 1688-1766): *The Vase of Flowers.* Hanging scroll on silk. National Palace Museum, Taipei.

preliminary excursion into this territory suggests that, if the material is handled with caution, there is something to be learned about Chinese ceramics from the study of the paintings, and about paintings from an examination of the ceramics depicted in them, and that in the process we may gain some new insights into the history of Chinese taste and attitudes to antiquity.

(A summary of a lecture given to the Oriental Ceramic Society of Hongkong on September 5, 1975)

中國畫中的瓷器

主講：Michael Sullivan
（1975年9月5日在香港東方陶瓷學會）

我們對中國早期陶器的認識，主要來自現存的古物、拓本及從發掘所得的資料。但這些古物或圖像是否當時器皿的眞實形製呢？舉例說，我們不能假設我們收藏的宋瓷確實是宋朝士大夫日常用的器皿。又我們對唐代陶瓷的認識多以最能代表唐代風格的唐代鉛釉三彩陶器爲主，可是這類陶器大部份或許是全部是供陪葬之用的。據我所知，唐三彩從未見諸唐代繪畫，或許從不是家庭用器。

從典籍來引證中國古代陶器難會有什麼成就。因有關陶瓷的文獻甚少，況且詮譯不易。這一點，凡曾細讀十四世紀古物專著「格古要論」的，當知斯言不謬。至於十八世紀的書籍，如「景德鎮陶錄」及「陶雅」等，明清陶瓷部份仍或可靠，其他部份只是藏家傳說及古玩商的鑑別指南，多是經不起嚴格的對証，其中論及某些陶瓷，是現在無法鑑別的。

一九四九年以來，中國考古學者從事有計劃地發掘窰址，這方面所得的資料，當然最爲可靠。此外，從繪畫或其他方面亦可獲有關的資料。十世紀以來，很多國畫在寫書齋案頭上，或在收藏家或鑑賞家人像旁多繪有陶瓷。顯然，從繪畫中研究中國陶磁是有局限性的。例如，許多所謂宋畫，可能只是後人做作，複製或贋品，一不審愼，便會引起錯誤、以訛傳訛。至於畫中的陶器，有時是刻意描繪，有時却是粗枝大葉，只得輪廓，不知所指。但是，有時從畫中的風格或畫中的陶器，我們可推定該畫是後人作品。是以，正如我們可從畫中的陶器而認識那畫，同樣我們亦可從畫而認識陶器的。下列各畫，可作爲這方面的引証：

「仙女圖」（十世紀，手卷，北京故宮博物館藏）一僕役以紗蓋桌，桌上放置有座酒杯九隻，似爲越窰。旁炭爐上有作煮酒用之金屬瓶(圖一)。

「韓熙載夜宴圖」（十世紀顧閎中作。手卷，北京故宮博物館藏）——是描寫南唐後主李煜重臣韓熙載家中盛筵夜宴情況。桌

上置各種瓷器(圖二)，有一盛酒壺的深碗，形狀和常見的宋代青白瓷相像。還有榻屏上之景物頗近北宋末或南宋格調，是以我們頗難斷定畫中之酒壺在宋時已有，更難証實其為唐朝之物。

「宮樂圖」(作者：佚名。臺北國立故宮博物院藏)—— 一般認為唐人手筆，但可能是南唐作品。此畫標題英文譯作音樂之樂，似屬不確，所繪的正如夜宴圖一般，並非宮廷奏樂塲面，因畫中女郎緋腮胭目，意態並不莊重，似為宮中婦女狂歡作樂之景。卓上有器皿多種，有類似古樸漆製之「羽觴」、玉盃及可能是越窰的瓷碗。

至于宋朝繪畫、可供參考的資料較為豐富，但亦有不少問題存在。

據說是北宋陳居中所作的「文姬歸漢圖」（現存臺北國立故宮博物院）。這幅非常動人的名畫，描繪一僕人用鳳首瓶注酒杯中，這瓶是唐朝以來華北瓷器中所常見的。陳居中是北宋末期的宮廷畫家，對畫中人服飾及器皿等，當會絲毫不苟。是以這幅畫說是陳居中所作，亦無不可，但說是遼代宮廷畫家所作，甚至是金元時仿擬之作，亦有可能的。

北宋名畫，首推「文會圖」，（現在臺北國立故宮博物院），據說是宋徽宗（在位時期由公元1101至1125年）所作，但更可能是出自畫院名家手筆。圖中是一羣學者圍坐方桌（圖四），桌上器皿包括北宋官窰碗或其他精美青瓷，和一些可能是定窰的瓷杯（圖三）。桌前一僕人焙酒，金屬酒瓶在炭爐上，桌上還有些器皿可能是瓷器。另一僕人持一繪花的白瓷大碟。一位著名權威人士曾認為這大碟是北宋末期青花的實証。但這大碟極可能是定窰。徽宗執政初期定窰是宮廷御用瓷器。或說該碟是磁州產品，這頗難置信，因為磁州窰器無論是怎樣精緻，亦難作北宋宮廷御用瓷器，且據本人涉覽所及，宋徽宗的瓷器絕無與磁州窰器相近的。

南宋册頁和扇畫上的畫，經常可以反映出宮廷及士大夫生活情況，其中建築、傢具、器皿等，均見刻劃入微，但仍未算流於元朝以來一般呆板的因循抄襲。臺北國立故宮博物院藏畫中，從南宋宮廷畫家如馬公顯、趙伯駒、李嵩、及劉松年的作品中所繪的磁器，形狀多像青瓷和白瓷，白瓷多為青白或吉州窰。畫中其

他特色暫不置論，只從這些瓷器，亦可見那些畫實屬較晚工作。現存臺北國立故宮博物院的卷軸「十八學士」，據說是十三世紀畫家劉松年所作，該畫火盆上有十四世紀或十五世紀時典型的瓷碗，這顯然在年代上有錯誤。

同一畫家在某幅畫中，為求將一切細節刻劃入微而會費煞苦心，但在繪另一幅畫時，亦會粗心大意，掛一漏萬的。十五世紀畫師仇英的作品「漢宮春曉圖」（現在故宮博物院），刻劃宮廷婦女享樂情景，畫中個人瑣事，表露無遺，但仇英在這畫中，並未試圖從建築、傢具、服飾等反映出比當時早一千五百年的實況。而所繪陶瓷的形狀是當時宮廷或富豪家中均可見到的。但是，我們翻閱他的「金谷園圖」（現存日本京都），却發現他從各方面表達南京金谷園的氣氛。金谷園及十四世紀著名鉅富石崇和寵妾綠珠與友享樂之地。畫中人繞桌而坐，使人聯想「宮樂圖」中婦女圍坐的情景。畫中那誇張的反透視畫法是遠古的，但桌上高碟的形式却是六世紀及唐朝所盛行的。據本人所知，在十世紀以後，那種高碟從未之見。凡此種種，可見這幅畫可能是仇英擬模，或添潤一幅較早時期的作品（而該作品現在已失傳的）。

自明朝以還，畫家有時有意無意中，在人物畫裡加襯陶器和銅器，以示古樸，就以陳洪綬寫「陶潛隱居」之軸為例（現在火奴魯魯美術研究院），圖中可見晉朝詩人在園中各態，圖五是他坐蕉葉上，後有一石，石上有二瓷瓶及一滿冰裂紋的有蓋罐，想是南宋官窰，陳洪綬是否明知晉時應該沒有南宋官窰和在左邊的倣銅尊的瓷器呢？這點我們無法證明，且亦屬無關重要。值得注意的只是陳能借用重於倣古的宋瓷以示高古之風。

當小心檢閱多幅古畫後，會覺察有些陶瓷竟是現今所無，這些陶瓷或許是畫家的創新，或是據古時形狀繪畫的，這些陶瓷雖已不存，但經典有載，例如柴窰、東窰等，此外金屬瓶在畫中亦屢見，可見這瓶是當時常用于炭爐上作煖酒水之用，但這物流傳現世不多，顯然地這瓶究竟不是藏家搜購之物。

比較近期的作品中，人像旁每畫有他珍藏的古董。最好的例子是郎世寧（耶穌會會士，生於公元 1688 年，終於 1766 年），他寫乾隆在園中和內院的兩幅作品。由於該兩畫精細繪寫，畫

中陶器極為清晰，是做古器皿。但其中一個青花花瓶算是例外，它的形狀和紋飾都非早期，而是典型乾隆之物，是當時新出的產品。郎世寧的畫，清晰詳細，各種陶器，極易分辨。其中最易鑑別的是兩幀著名的花卉，畫中兩個花瓶跟倫敦郭大維所載的雷同，一是南宋官窰，另一是宣德青花小方瓶(圖五)，郭氏藏品大部份來自清宮的，因此郎世寧所繪的很可能直是當時在宮中所陳列的。

　　據現有的資料作徹底詳盡的研究 —— 這包括卷軸、扇面及册頁，甚至敦煌及墓穴壁畫等——便會發覺更多這一類的問題。這當然是一項艱苦的工作，所付出的努力會遠遠超過所獲得資料的代價。還有，各種上面提及的鑑定及考證問題，將會更為繁複。其實，這方面的研究該是有限度的。可是，話說回來，雖是普通涉獵，如果是審慎處理，亦可從中國繪畫，獲得關於中國陶磁的知識；同時，從畫中的陶瓷亦可得到較多關于該畫的情況。就在這互證過程中，就中國歷來對古物的志趣和態度，定會獲得相當的啓發。

HONORARY MEMBERS

Sir John Addis, K.C.M.G.
Dr Rayson Huang

Dr Li Choh Ming, K.B.E.
(Hon.)

RESIDENTIAL MEMBERS (*As at 31st October 1975*)

Alleyne, Mrs E.L.
Alleyne, Mr S.E.
Andrau, Miss Nicole
Armstrong, Mr G.C.
Armstrong, Mrs M.
Arsan, Mrs Karin
Au, Mr Bak Ling
Babington, Mr H.H.L.
Barden, Mr S.A.
Barrow, Mr John F.
Barrow, Mrs Mary R.
Bernau, Mr K.J.
Bernau, Mrs Marjorie
Birley, Mrs Mona A.
Birnbaum, Mrs Pamela Q.
Bloch, Mr George
Bonsall, Mr Geoffrey W.
Bordwell, Mr John H.
Bordwell, Mrs M.S.
Borgeest, Mr G.U.S.
Braga, Mr Paul
Brahamsha, Mrs Maria
Brake, Mr Brian
Broomhead, Mrs J.P.
Cameron, Mr Nigel
Capell, Mr G.W.
Carpenter, Mr G.P.T

Carter, Mr R.H.
Chan, Mrs Mary Lou
Cheung, Mr Sing Hoi
Chiu, Mrs S.C.
Chow, Mrs Patti
Chu, Mr Philip
Chuang, Mr Quincy
Chung, Mr Wah Man
Cockell, Miss J.V.
Coffey, Mrs Mary
Crampton, Mr Richard Barry
Crowe, Mr D.C.
Davidson, Miss Eileen
Diamond, Mr A.I.
Diamond, Mrs I.R.
D'Oliveira, Mr E.C.N.
Donald, Mrs Hope
Downer, Mrs Christine
Edmunds, Mrs Joan H.
Edwards, Mr Michael
Errington, The Viscount
Evans, Mrs Lucille
Feldman, Mr Sam I.
Fleming, Miss Paula
Foldes, Mr L.
Foldes, Mrs P.C.
Fong, Mr Wing-Foon, Bucky

Forsyth, Mr A.H.
Forsyth, Mr James
Francis, Mrs Nancy T.
Fry, Mr R.A.
Fung, Mr Kenneth H.C.
Fung, Mrs Leatrice
Fung, Mr S.L.
Fung, Mrs Sidney S.K.
George, Mr R.H.
George, Mrs R.H.
Gibb, Mr Hugh
Gleeson, Dr Patrick William
Go, Miss Lydia
Goldney, Miss C.M.
Graham, Mr Andrew
Grant, Professor Charles John
Grieve, Mr J.H.
Grieve, Mrs Suzanne-Louise
Haworth, Mrs Susan C.
Heatherington, Mrs Elizabeth
Henwood, Mrs Rosalind
Ho, Mr Eric Peter
Ho, Mrs Grace
Hodgson, Mrs Monica O.
Hodgson, Mr R.A.R.
Hodgson, Mrs Kirsty
Hodson, Mr John C.
Howe, Mrs Mamie
Hownam-Meek, Mrs E.A.P.
Hu, Dr Shih-Chang
Hung, Mrs Audrey
Hutcheon, Mrs Beatrice
Hutson, Mr P.E.
Hutson, Mrs P.E.
Hyui, Mr Peter
Inglis, Mrs Rosemary A.
Ip, Mr Che
Ip, Mr Vincent
Ip, Dr Yee
Irik, Mr W.
Ismail, Mr Aladin
Izard, Mr William Godfrey

Jones-Parry, Mr Rupert
Kehoe, Mr Thomas J.
Kehoe, Mrs T.J.
Kelly, Mrs Philippa
Kennedy, Mr C.G.W.
Kennedy, Mrs G.G.W.
Kerbs, Mr Larry
Kilburn, Mr R.S.
King, Mr Dunt
King, Mr G.J.H.
Kinoshita, Mr James H.
Kinoshita, Mrs J.
Kirkwood, Mrs Jean
Kohl, Mr David G.
Kunizuka, Mr Kazunoki
Kwan, Mr S.M., Simon
Kwan, Dr S.Y.
Lack, Mrs Rowena
Lai, Mr T.C.
Lam, Dr Veronica
Lau, Dr Michael
Lau, Mr Ming Sai
Lau, Mrs Poh Chit
Learmonth, Mrs Louise M.
Lee, Mr Charm Fun
Lee, Mr J.S.
Lee, Mrs Terese W.F.
Leonard, Mr Justice P.F.X.
Leonard, Mrs P.
Li, Mr Raymond
Liu, Mr Kenneth
Lloyd, Mr Richard L.
Lo, Mr Kam-Kau, James
Lo, Mr K.S.
Lo, Mrs Robert K.L.
Lo, Mr Sai Keung, Louis
Lofts, Professor Brian
Loo, Mrs Jean
Low, Mr C.C.
Lu, Mr Li
Lung, Mrs Christabel
Ma, Professor Meng

Macaulay, Mr I.
Macintosh, Mr Duncan John
  Hutton
Macintosh, Mrs Somsri
Mallory-Browne, Mr G.E.
Mao, Dr Barbara
Mao, Dr Wen-Chee, Philip
Marion, Mrs Barbara
Markbreiter, Mr Stephen
Matthews, Mr Peter W.
McElney, Mr B.S.
Mendenhall, Mr George A.
McCarlie, Mr J.
McCarlie, Mrs P.M.
Miller, Mrs E.D.
Miller, Mr Robert Fenwick
Mills-Owens, Mr Richard J.E.H.
Mohan, Mrs Bagwanti
Moran, Mr John Dominic
Moss, Mr Hugh
Munro, Mr John S.
Ng, Mr Kai Yuen
Nye, Miss P.
Oliver, Mrs Frances
Orlandi, Mr Alessandro
Ozouf, Mr Peter Emile
Pain, Mr John Hugh
Palin, Mr Michael Gordon
Piccus, Mr Robert P.
Piccus, Mrs Alice Y.
Pridham, Mrs P.M.
Radez, Mr Richard E.
Radez, Mrs Bonny Siu Sin
Redding, Dr S.G.
Reynolds, Mr Jack
Roberts, Mrs M.B.
Robinson, Mrs Joanne
Robinson, Mr James G.
Rowan, Mrs Roy
Saunders, Mrs Irene
Sherman, Mrs Laura H.

Shiu, Mrs Vera T.
Siu, Miss Anna Victoria
Siu, Mr Tsun-Tak
Smith, Miss Toni
Stempel, Mr A.
Stempel, Mrs A.
Szeto, Mrs Angela D.
Talamo, Mr C.R.
Talamo, Mrs Laine
Tam, Mr Laurence C.S.
Tan, Miss Beverley
Thompson, Mr Peter
Thompson, Mrs P.
Ti, Mr Po Shing, Paul
Tingle, Miss Julia
Todd, Professor David
Tseng, Mrs Chung Wai-Yee
Tso, Mr Chi Hung
Tso, Mrs Priscilla
Tso, Dr Shiu Chiu
Tuyet, Mrs Nguyet
University of Hong Kong Library
Wang, Mr Richard
Warner, Mr John
Whitelegge, Mr D.S.
Whitelegge, Mrs D.S.
Wilkinson, Miss Ann M.
Williamson, Mr Peter
Wong, Mr Edwin
Wong, Dr John
Wong, Mr Kai-Ka
Wong, Mrs Ling Shang, Joy
Wong, Mr Peng-Cheong
Woo, Mr James
Yang, Mr Justice
Yip, Dr Shing Yiu
Yuen, Mr Chi-Chew
Yuen, Mr N.M.
Zecha, Mrs Bebe
Zimmern, Mrs Doris

NON-RESIDENTIAL MEMBERS *(As at 31st October 1975)*

Allen, Mr E.
Australia
Ang, Mr Kwang Ming, John
Singapore
Chan, Mr D.L., David
Singapore
Colinet, Madame Paul
New Hebrides
Cook, Mr G.S.
Singapore
Cullings, Mrs B.
England
De Koenigswarter, Baron Patrick
Philippines
Hall, Mr R.A.
England
Hartwig, Ms J.L.
W. Australia
Herridge, Mr R.I.C.
Korea
Hickley, Mr F.
Singapore
Hickley, Mrs P.F. I.
Singapore
Hon, Mr Heng Lem
Malaysia
Jarvis, Mrs M.
New Zealand
Johnson, Mr Richard S.
Thailand
Khong, Mr Siang San
Malaysia

Lim, Mr Beng Haw
Malaysia
Missbach, Mr G.E.
U.S.A.
Munro, Mr J.S.
Australia
Misugi, Mr Takatoshi
Japan
Myrtle, Mr John Hepburn
Australia
Oline, Mrs B.J.
Japan
Rea, Mr James L.
Philippines
Rochelle-Thomas, Mr Alfred P.
U.S.A.
Roginski, Miss Donna Jean
Hong Kong, normally in
Philippines
Rooney, Mr James P.
Thailand
Shapazian, Mr Robert Michael
U.S.A.
Sorsby, Dr William S.
U.S.A.
Valenstein, Mrs Suzanne
U.S.A.
Volk, Mr S.J.
Philippines
Wolters, Mr Fritz
Israel

126

The Oriental Ceramic Society of Hong Kong
Bulletins 1 and 2

First published 1975-76
Reprinted Orchid Press, Bangkok 2018

ISBN 978-974-524-205-0